THE LATIN AMERICAN
MILITARY INSTITUTION

THE LATIN AMERICAN MILITARY INSTITUTION

EDITOR: Robert Wesson

CO-AUTHORS: Gene E. Bigler (Venezuela)
David V. Fleischer (Brazil)
Anthony W. Gray, Jr. (Argentina and Colombia,
Chaps. 1–5)
Richard L. Millett (Guatemala)
David Scott Palmer (Peru)
Steve C. Ropp (Panama)
Paul E. Sigmund (Chile)
Stephen J. Wager (Mexico)
Robert Wesson (Argentina and Colombia, Chaps. 6–7)

THE LATIN AMERICAN MILITARY INSTITUTION

**Edited by
Robert Wesson**

*Published with the support
of the Hoover Institution
Stanford University
Stanford, California*

PRAEGER SPECIAL STUDIES • PRAEGER SCIENTIFIC

New York   •   Westport, Connecticut   •   London

Library of Congress Cataloging-in-Publication Data
Main entry under title:

The Latin American military institution.

"Published with the support of the Hoover
Institution."
  Includes index.
  1. Latin America – Armed Forces – Addresses, essays,
lectures. 2. Sociology, Military – Latin America –
Addresses, essays, lectures. I. Wesson, Robert G.
UA602.3.L37   1986   306'.27'098   85-28301
ISBN 0-275-92084-4 (alk. paper)

Library of Congress Catalog Card Number: 85-28301
ISBN: 0-275-92084-4

First published in 1986

Praeger Publishers, 521 Fifth Avenue, New York, NY 10175
A division of Greenwood Press, Inc.

Printed in the United States of America

The paper used in this book complies with the Permanent
Paper Standard issued by the National Information Standards
Organization (Z39.48-1984).

10 9 8 7 6 5 4 3 2 1

PREFACE

The political activities of various Latin American armed forces have been abundantly treated, but very little has been written concerning the forces themselves beyond what is to be found in standard reference works. It is the purpose of the present volume to fill this void at least partially by presenting information on the ordinary soldiers and noncommissioned officers, the origins and training of officers, career patterns, foreign influences, relations between service branches, ideology and doctrines, and the political role of the armed forces.

It seemed excessive to try to cover the armed forces of all Latin American states, so nine were selected. Brazil, Chile, and Argentina were obvious choices because of their size and the political role of their military establishments. The Mexican military is also significant and has potential political importance. The armed forces of Venezuela and Colombia are of special interest because of their positions in South America's more stable democracies. Those of Peru are noteworthy not only because of the considerable importance of that country but also because of their extraordinary effort to carry out a social revolution from 1968–75. Guatemala seemed to require attention as the most populous country of Central America, which has been dominated by the military from 1954–1985. Panama, finally, offers the picture of an army emerging from a strictly police force, which has been politically dominant for many years. We have omitted Cuba because its forces represent more Marxist-Leninist than Latin American patterns. Uruguay is interesting, but it is a very small country decidedly under the shadow of Brazil and, in part, Argentina. Because of the civil war and the impact of the American presence, El Salvador seemed difficult to treat properly. Likewise Ecuador, Bolivia, Paraguay, Honduras, and Nicaragua hardly seemed to justify expansion of the present volume.

The format of this book is unconventional in that the contributions of the several experts are not chapters but sections of chapters. The task of the editor was mostly to cut and paste, making minimal additions or changes for purposes of coordination and putting a brief introduction at the beginning of each chapter. The specialists on Mexico, Guatemala, Panama, Venezuela, Colombia, Peru, Brazil,

Chile, and Argentina were asked to deal with a series of questions, and their responses form the respective country sections of the respective topical chapters (except that the editor did the sections on Argentina and Colombia in Chapters 6 and 7). The writers with official positions (Bigler, Gray, and Wager) do not, of course, speak in any way for their respective agencies. The editor is responsible for the Preface, Introduction, introductory sections of chapters, and Conclusion.

This project presupposes, of course, that there is such a thing as the "Latin American Military Institution" and that the armed forces of the various countries are sufficiently alike to be usefully considered together. This seems true. They all come out of fairly similar cultural environments. Despite all the differences of geography, economic level and development, racial and ethnic composition, Iberian background, and historical experience, Latin America is something of a unity. The language is essentially the same from Tijuana, Mexico to Santiago, Chile; mores and psychology are a good deal alike; and Latin Americans can feel fairly well at home in countries far from their own. The various Latin American armies, in other words, come out of societies for the most part more similar in modes and values to one another than to nations of other regions.

The armed forces of the various countries also tend to resemble one another because of shared and mutual influences. Since World War II, the chief model has been the United States, and thousands of officers have undergone advanced training in the United States or at U.S. facilities in Panama. Latin American armies also look to one another, or especially those of the smaller countries look to those of the larger countries. This influence is both informal, as they observe the ways of their counterparts, and formal, as officers go to military institutions and schools in other countries and serve as attaches abroad. Latin Americans have some feeling of regional solidarity, despite many quarrels, and it is far easier for them to adopt practices of a fellow Latin American service than an Asian service. To what extent the parallels are real and more important than the differences, however, the reader may judge from this book.

CONTENTS

Preface   v

Introduction   ix

Chapter 1   The Ranks   1

Chapter 2   The Officers: Origins and Training   19

Chapter 3   The Officers: Career Patterns   49

Chapter 4   Foreign Influences   71

Chapter 5   Interservice Relations   104

Chapter 6   Ideology and Doctrine   125

Chapter 7   Political Role   157

Conclusion   213

Index   225

About the Editors and Contributors   235

INTRODUCTION

The armed forces are probably the most important and certainly the strongest single locus of power in Latin America. Mexico is the only country in which armed force has not intervened directly in government since 1945, and there has been some talk of possible military intervention in Mexico. Only in Costa Rica can it be said that the military is not at least in the background of politics. In the two firmest democracies of South America, Venezuela and Colombia, the generals are very much on the scene. Particularly in Venezuela, with its long history of military rule, rumors of a possible coup are recurrent, and it is doubtful that constitutional government could survive a severe crisis. Military-backed dictators rule three Latin American countries, Chile, Paraguay, and Haiti; and in the two Marxist-Leninist states, Cuba and Nicaragua, the rather militarized armed forces have close links with the government. In a majority of Latin American countries (Argentina, Bolivia, Brazil, Dominican Republic, Ecuador, El Salvador, Guatemala, Honduras, Panama, Peru, and Uruguay), the military leadership has withdrawn from government. But in no case have the generals surrendered the capacity to intervene if they should judge it necessary.

In all regions of the world except the industrialized West, the armed forces represent at least a potential political force. In the Marxist-Leninist countries, armies and generals play a major role. In South Asia, the Near East, and Africa, military regimes are familiar, potent if not dominant almost everywhere except in India and Sri Lanka. Military rule comes naturally to the Third World. Political parties are commonly weak, corrupt, and personalistic; trade unions are narrow and unrepresentative; the press is feeble and venal; business organizations are seldom capable of looking beyond their immediate interests; democratic institutions, constitutions, and legality in general are shallow. The military remains not only the possessor of force but the most coherent sector and, in the view of some, the body most expressive of the nation and possibly an effective modernizer. The military may have an advantage in education, also. Training probably has more to do with career progress in the armed forces than in any other major profession. From the raw recruits upward, rank is attained to a large extent by the completion of courses, giving more or less academic or technical qualifications; and professional competence up to the rank of general is testified not by a single certification, as in the case of a physician, but a graded series of qualifications, obtaining which helps to keep soldiers occupied.

Professionalization of the Latin American military is fairly recent, however. The early Latin American armies were irregular bands of soldiers loyal to leaders who could reward them with the spoils of power. Only in the last decades of the nineteenth century did armies become more regularized, with some form of conscription. First the larger and wealthier countries, then the smaller and poorer established training schools, especially for officers and generally with foreign aid and guidance. Shared education developed not only competence but also confidence and integrating traditions. The importance of schools and schooling has generally tended to grow to this day.

It was widely assumed that the professionalization of the armed forces, proceeding steadily through the period of the world wars, would lead them to retreat from political activity. There has, indeed been an overall long-term tendency in Latin America toward civilian government, but the pendulum has swung irregularly. Up to 1930, the tide was toward civilian, more or less democratic, government. This was reversed by the great depression and the rise of fascism, an ideology with considerable potential appeal to bearers of arms. The victory of the United States and the antifascist alliance in World War II brought the overthrow of many dictatorships and a democratic tide. This lasted through the 1950s. But tensions grew after the Cuban Revolution (January 1959), which was followed by a blood purge, unexampled in Latin American history, of the defeated army. The Brazilian military takeover of 1964 gave impetus to a movement toward military government, which ultimately swept over all countries of South America except Colombia and Venezuela. From 1978 the tide has reversed, and the military have withdrawn partially or fully from the governments of a majority of Latin American countries, a withdrawal brought about partly by the wearing out of the popularity or capacities of military regimes but also moved by U.S. policy in favor of human rights and democracy and by grievous economic conditions.

Latin America has thus seemed in recent years to be leading the Third World away from military government. Nonetheless, this has been something of a Latin American specialty. Only a minority of the 20 Latin American countries have had more than a single generation of civilian government in this century. This minority includes Brazil, Chile, Colombia, Costa Rica, Mexico, Panama, and Uruguay. There has commonly been an oscillation over the decades between military and civilian rule, as in Peru and Ecuador. Some countries, such as El Salvador and Guatemala, have been under military rulership continually for long periods, about 50 years in the case of El Salvador.

Military political power in Latin America is also distinguished by its corporate tendencies. The essence of military rule has commonly been personal, the leadership of a leader whom the forces accept as boss and support, much as Napoleon commanded the French army and made himself emperor of France. Dictatorship of this kind has been common in Latin America in the past, and it continues to exist in Paraguay and Haiti. However, power may be exercised more by the military as a corporate body, or by the corps of high officers, which is capable of elevating one of its number to the presidency or deposing him. This has been most strikingly the case of Argentina, where many presidents have been made and unmade by consultations among the generals and admirals. In countries where a military coup is conceivable, the fear is generally not that an individual will conceive overwhelming ambitions and organize a coup for the benefit of himself and his intimates but rather that the officers as a body will become discontented and resolve that change is in order. The ability of the armed forces leadership to act more or less as a corporate group, with its internal rules and understandings, requires a great deal of esprit de corps and primary loyalty to the military or one of its sectors. This esprit de corps is based on training and specialization. One result is that armed forces have been able, or have thought themselves able, to carry on the leadership of the state, even perhaps to staff the upper echelons largely from their own personnel, as they did in Peru from 1968 to 1975.

The historical prevalence and higher development of military politics in Latin America may be attributed in some degree to the Iberian, especially Spanish, tradition. More than any other European nation, Spain had a military birth, as it took shape in the centuries-long Reconquest of the peninsula from the Moors. The national consciousness was shaped by this secular preoccupation; the respected professions were soldier and priest. The conquest and appropriation of the New World were practically a continuation of the anti-Moorish crusade, and rule by conquistadors set its stamp on the Spanish colonies.

Probably equally important was the manner in which the new states of Spanish America were born. There was hardly any local self-government to organize the struggle for independence early in this century, in contrast to the British colonies, which had effectively autonomous governments capable of declaring independence and organizing the fight for it. The Spanish colonies' fight for freedom had to be carried on by armies, at first very crudely organized, without civilian control of any kind. In victory, the leading generals almost automatically became the new rulers. Military government was consequently built into Spanish America. Although republican government was an aspiration, the reality was military power. The republican ideal took hold only gradually and irregularly after mid-nineteenth century. It has usually been on the upswing since then, most remarkably in the last decade; but it is still far from displacing the tradition of military politics.

It is clearly wrong, however, to attribute overwhelming importance to the heritage of previous centuries. Nations change their political cultures under pressure, sometimes rather rapidly. For example, the quite democratic Japan of today came out of the fanatical emperor-worshipping military dictatorship of a mere 40 years ago. The tradition of military power has seemed to have receded or to have nearly disappeared in various Latin American countries, especially in Uruguay and Chile before 1973, only to resurge powerfully in difficult times.

It is also significant that Brazil came to military-dominated politics like Spanish America, although its heritage was quite different. Portugal was less involved in the Reconquest and never became a military-autocratic state like Spain. The acquisition of Brazil was more a settlement and less a conquest than that of Spanish America. And independence came pacifically, the former colonial government simply assuming sovereignty in the void caused by Napoleon's occupation of Portugal. For the first 40 years of its independent existence, until the war with Paraguay, Brazil had exceptionally small and uninfluential armed forces. Yet after the army overthrew the emperor in 1889, it played a political role similar to that of its counterparts in various Spanish American countries. It supported the Vargas dictatorship, 1930–45, and then overturned it. The army injected itself repeatedly into the politics of the republic from 1946–64 and governed effectively from 1964–85.

If Latin America has seemed more inclined to military power than other areas of the Third World, it may be mostly because Latin America became independent over a century earlier than most of the Afro-Asian world. The Latin American military institution has had a much longer time to mature and develop in a situation where, as noted earlier, armies are the strongest potential force in otherwise weakly structured societies. So far as Latin America is genuinely moving away from military politics, the basic cause must be the maturation and modernization of the societies of the region, which as a whole is by far the least poor and most industrialized of the Third World.

1

The Ranks

Despite their power, Latin American armed forces have not (except perhaps in Marxist-Leninist states) militarized their societies. They are generally a small percentage, well under 1% of the population. Excluding paramilitary organizations, recent figures are 123,000 or 0.17% of Mexico's 72 million; 34,000 or 0.5% of Guatemala's 7.2 million; 11,000 or 0.57% of Panama's 1.9 million; 73,000 or 0.25% of Colombia's 27.5 million; 135,000 or 0.74% of Peru's 18.3 million; 322,000 or 0.25% of Brazil's 125 million; 97,000 or 0.86% of Chile's 11.3 million; and 180,000 or 0.64% (in 1984) of Argentina's 28 million. Of these numbers, the overwhelming majority are the enlisted ranks, volunteers or conscripts, usually serving for a short period of a year or so. These are the men who should convert officers' orders into actions, and doubts as to their docility has at times caused commanders to hesitate.

For the most part, because Latin American societies are economically unequal and socially elitist, the ranks are almost exclusively of lower-class origin; only in Argentina and to some extent in Chile is it seriously attempted to apply conscription to all classes. Recruits are usually a mixture of conscripts and volunteers, volunteering being encouraged by prospects of being caught up involuntarily.

The prestige of the ordinary soldier is not high, but the military has a priority call on resources. Consequently, military service offers opportunities for advancement for poor boys, literacy for the illiterate, and more or less technical training. Even in Guatemala, military service may raise an Indian to the *ladino* category. The enlisted ranks

1

are divided, of course, into ordinary personnel and noncommissioned officers (corporals, sergeants, and technical specialists), the latter being ordinarily permanent. Training and reenlistment are the way to noncommissioned officer status and a military career. The noncommissioned officers (NCOs) are numerous, deal directly with the soldiers, and may at times carry political weight. But it is seldom possible for NCOs to leap the abyss separating them from the commissioned officer class, and there is in most armies a large social difference.

MEXICO

The regular Mexican armed forces are volunteer. The basic enlisted recruit must have successfully completed primary education, possess Mexican citizenship by birth, and not have a criminal record. Educational requirements vary, depending on the specialty for which the recruit has applied. Both males and females can join the armed forces, but only males can apply for the service academies.

Recruitment takes place in the military zones and separate battalion/regiment installations. The initial tour is normally three years. Those who sign up for an additional three years will usually attain the rank of sergeant. The recruit can remain close to home at least during his first tour of duty.

The National Military Service Program is another source of recruits. It requires all males to register in January of the year of their eighteenth birthday for training with active duty units for 38 Saturdays or Sundays of that year. Only a small fraction of the eligible males (selected by lottery) participate in this weekly training. Some conscripts serving with active duty units on weekends become aware of vacancies within their units and enlist for these positions.

The regional composition of the enlisted personnel corresponds roughly to the disposition of military units, since recruiting takes place at the local level. Most recruits come from the Federal District and the central states of Mexico. They are almost exclusively from the lower class, many having indigent backgrounds. They view military service as a means both of employment and upward social mobility. The armed forces provide literacy training to all service members. Upon completion of their training, soldiers possess the equivalent of a primary school education. Although base pay for recruits tends to be modest at best, its monetary value surpasses both the national rural and urban minimum wages. In addition, fringe benefits for enlisted personnel may exceed 50% of their base pay, including free food, housing, and uniforms. Moreover, a good percentage work second jobs after duty hours to supplement their military pay. The steady improvement in military life over the past two decades has helped to attract a growing number of youths with peasant or urban lower-class backgrounds. An advantage for the military is that a growing number of recruits remain in the armed forces until voluntary retirement after 20 years of service.

After an enlisted soldier has spent some time in basic training at his post, he may have the opportunity to attend one of a number of schools or courses which offer specialized training in various administrative and logistical specialties, such as the tactical and technical aspects of radio communications, fingerprinting, office administrative procedures, the organization of unit archives, foreign languages (English, French, and German), and aerial photography.

Most training for NCOs takes place on the job. An NCO school was established in 1948 to train potential high-ranking NCOs in infantry, cavalry, and artillery tactics and doctrine. Each year, the national military academy (*Heróico Colegio Militar*) enrolls a small number of first sergeants, who have graduated from the NCO school and have demonstrated exceptional leadership ability, into an officer preparatory course.[1]

NCO relations with both enlisted and officer personnel are quite formal. There is no fraternization between the ranks. Whereas the NCO is often referred to as the backbone of the army in the United States, such is not the case in Mexico, in part because of the larger number of officers in relation to NCOs and enlisted personnel. Mexican officers do not rely as heavily on the NCOs as U.S. officers do; and, given the personalistic nature of relations within the armed forces, they are normally reluctant to delegate much responsibility to their subordinates.

GUATEMALA

Throughout its history, the Guatemalan army has relied upon the forced conscription of lower-class youth, mostly of the depressed Indian half of the population. Under the Guatemalan constitution, all male citizens are liable for military service, but this has never been applied to the middle or upper classes and is infrequently applied to ladinos, who include persons of Indian blood who have adopted the Spanish language and European culture and dress. A complex series of exemptions and deferments relieves better-off Guatemalans of service obligations, and only about 5% of the yearly class are inducted. The selection of youths for service gives the military commissioners considerable power and opportunities for self-aggrandizement. It can also produce anger and in recent years has reportedly led to violent attacks on commissioners.[2] Combined with the needs of the military for additional recruits due to recent expansion, this has led to increasingly arbitrary methods of conscription. Buses are stopped, and youths who do not have evidence of prior military service may be dragooned on the spot.

Such tactics contribute to low morale, frequent desertions, and widespread efforts to avoid military service. They also provide numerous recruits under the legal draft age of 18. Forcible recruitment has led to clashes with the Indian population and conflict with the church and has reportedly caused some youths to join the guerrillas.[3]

The term of compulsory military service has varied from 18 months to 3 years. Recruits usually spend their first few months at one of three basic training centers. There they are taught basic military skills and discipline, often with considerable brutality. A high percentage of the conscripts are illiterate, and many do not even speak Spanish. Considerable time is spent in teaching rudimentary Spanish and basic literacy. Literacy training is supposed to continue when the recruits are assigned to their units, but this is usually sporadic at best. Literate recruits may qualify for technical training and a chance for noncommissioned status, but the bulk of the conscripts are sent directly to local garrisons or to combat units. There is some effort to select the most promising for the elite units, the parachute and special forces (Kaibiles) battalions.

Some conscripts are taken for the marines, but the navy is filled with volunteers, most of whom have previously completed service as marines. The air force relies on volunteers for its small enlisted component, and they must be literate. Most of its enlisted men get some form of technical-mechanical training, a scarce opportunity in Guatemala. They have a much better chance at NCO status and do not have to serve a fixed term. Finally, the ranks of the Mobile Military Police (PMA) are open only to those who have completed a full term of service in the army and who volunteer to transfer to the PMA.

Except for the air force and the PMA, only a small percentage of soldiers reenlist. Recruits traditionally serve either near their own home areas or in the major cities, but there have been reports in recent years of deliberate efforts to send Indians to areas where their native language is not spoken.

NCOs can be divided into two distinct categories, the *técnicos*, such as the air force mechanics, who possess a special skill, and line NCOs, who have chosen to reenlist and who stay with garrison or combat units. It is usually impossible to be promoted to corporal in a line unit during an individual's first tour of duty, promotion being used as a reenlistment incentive. Virtually no specialized training is given to the regular NCO. For some, basic training is the last formal training.

The great majority of NCOs are ladinos. This is virtually inevitable, since, in Guatemalan society, the Indian is identified more on a linguistic or cultural basis than on the basis of racial ancestry. A career NCO must speak Spanish, live a basically ladino lifestyle, and in most meaningful ways abandon his Indian identity. Thus an individual who might have been classified as an Indian when conscripted would be likely to be identified as a ladino after several years in the military.

The line NCO has virtually no chance to become an officer or in any way to penetrate into the ruling class. Only limited authority is given to most NCOs; and many tasks that in the United States would be performed by senior NCOs are, in the Guatemalan army, given to junior commissioned officers. For line NCOs, promotions are slow and pay and benefits limited. Like commissioned officers they can retire at 20 years, but most prefer to retire with full pay after 30 years. This contributes to a certain degree of stagnation at higher NCO ranks.

A unique feature of the Guatemalan military system is the chain of five Adolfo V. Hall schools scattered throughout the nation. These are junior military academies which offer education to ladino youths, including many from poor families. Students enter after six years of primary education and stay for from two to six additional years. Most live at the schools. Some are as young as 11 or 12 years old. Those who finish two years at an Adolfo V. Hall school may become NCOs and some do. After four years they are eligible for entry into the *Politécnica*. A minority who stay the full six years receive reserve commissions as second lieutenants in the army and in a few cases enter active service, but they are always second-class citizens in the officer corps.

PANAMA

Panama's conscription law has never been activated because of the lack of a serious external or internal security threat. In practice, service in the Defense Forces (called the National Guard before 1983) is voluntary, and there have always been a large number of potential recruits, most of whom make a lifelong career of military service.

Recruits must have six years of education. After some preliminary training, they are sent, depending on whether their assignment is to police or military duty, to either the Police Training Academy or the Center for Military Instruction, both in Panama City. The Police Training Academy was established in 1956 to offer systematic police instruction. The Center for Military Instruction was founded in 1974 to furnish military training for the new light infantry companies. In 1980, the National Guard further expanded its training programs to include courses offered in the military zones and field units, a move intended to take advantage of the training skills and abilities of personnel temporarily stationed outside Panama City. This allowed the Guard to cut its training costs and still offer advanced courses on an ad hoc basis.[4]

The political component of enlisted personnel training became pronounced after 1974, when General Omar Torrijos established a National School for Political Capacitation (ESCANAP), which regularly brought together officers and enlisted men with civilians from various sectors to discuss national problems. This degree of politicization or indoctrination of the enlisted ranks is unusual in Latin American armies. The line between enlisted personnel and officers has never been as clearly drawn in Panama as in other Latin American countries, probably because of the Defense Forces' traditional police functions. Although the officer corps has come to be increasingly dominated by military academy graduates granted direct commissions, as late as 1975 six of the top 22 officers had come up through the ranks.

Many enlisted personnel were recruited from urban slums when the organization was primarily performing police functions (1930–60). Today, there are approximately 6,600 in police units and 2,000 in light infantry companies. Infantry troops seem to be more heavily recruited from the countryside. Probable reasons for this difference include the fact that infantry troops are paid less than police and that General Torrijos recruited infantry personnel from areas loyal to him personally, such as Veraguas Province.

VENEZUELA

During most of the *caudillo* period (1830–98) Venezuelan soldiers, recruited by local leaders for indefinite periods, had very little training and often received no pay other than booty. Most militiamen came from the humblest ranks of society, and divisions of a quasi-racial nature existed well into the nineteenth century. A regular army and a conscription system were established in 1899, and some basic training was given in a regularized military organization with the collaboration of loyal Andean officers.[5]

There was little change over the next 40 years. Conscription was restricted to the illiterate, rural sector of the population. The main occupation for soldiers through the 1930s was as forced labor on the extensive agricultural properties of General Juan Vicente Gómez, dictator from 1908 to 1936. After Gómez's death the quality and quantity of military training gradually improved.[6]

With the coming of democracy in the late 1950s, there began a set of major changes with respect to recruitment, origins, and training of soldiers. In little more than a decade, the composition of the army ranks reversed from nearly 80% with rural backgrounds to about the same proportion coming from cities. However, 80–90% continued to be of low socioeconomic status, despite the fact that the basic educational level improved greatly. Illiteracy declined from over 50% in the early 1950s to 15–20% in the 1960s and 1970s and only 6% in 1979. But 72% of the ranks recently had only two years of secondary school or less, and only about 1% had completed secondary school or had some higher education.[7]

In 1978 a new law on military service was passed to create a more equitable pattern of military participation, but it has yet to achieve its goals. Although there are a few more conscripts of middle-class origin, evasion is still easy for the upper half of society. Other changes in the law include a reduction of obligatory service from 24 to 18 months and fairer operation of the lottery. There has been an increase in voluntary enlistments, and efforts have been made to improve treatment of new recruits. The quality of training and educational opportunities for the ranks have improved enormously. Mandatory military service is now clearly an educational/occupational boon for the socially marginal classes.[8]

Military instruction occupies a very large part of the 18 months of a mandatory enlistment period. The first 6 months are taken up with primarily military training. The next 12 months may be largely devoted to vocational education in addition to unit operations. These training programs mostly involve internship and apprentice-type experiences—12 weeks in the case of the petroleum industry program—and the results are extremely positive in terms of both troop and eventual employer satisfaction.

Despite the success in providing basic educational training and the increasing number of voluntary enlistments, the Venezuelan armed forces still have great difficulty in keeping men in the ranks beyond their obligatory 18-month service period. Pay, perquisites, and the potential for additional training are just not very attractive. The Venezuelan equivalent of an NCO is a *sub-oficial profesional de carrera* or professional career under-officer (SOPC), who has volunteered after a regular tour of duty. The rankings in the army begin with third technical sergeant and rise through six ranks to master technical supervisor. Pay is fairly good, especially in the higher ranks.

Many of the duties typically performed by NCOs in European armies were carried out by officers in the Venezuelan army well into the 1950s, when the Venezuelan armed forces were greatly overofficered. Long service in ranks as low as captain or major—44 years were permitted until 1958—also created a system in which long-service, intermediate-ranking officers were performing duties akin to those of more senior NCOs in Europe and the United States.[9]

The Army Service School in Maracay was recently restructured as the Army Technical School, where the two-year basic course for SOPCs is provided. The Maracay school graduates as many as 75 third technical sergeants per year, but this still compares poorly to the 80–150 second lieutenants graduating from the military academy. The continuing difficulty in incorporating sufficient mid-level technical manpower directly into the armed forces through the noncommissioned ranks has been compensated for to a great degree by the use of civilian employees of the Ministry of Defense. They now number over 17,000, or close to one-quarter of the number on active duty in the four services.

The navy and National Guard seem to have done better than the army in meeting their needs, which are also relatively higher, for NCOs. Basic pay systems in all the services are the same, but the navy and National Guard have been more innovative—women were first allowed to become National Guard noncommissioned officers in the early 1970s, and nearly 20% of naval academy cadets are now women—and have developed more special-duty remuneration programs and benefits.

Relations between enlisted men, SOPCs, and officers are very difficult to observe and rarely mentioned in reports and studies. The few observations that have been made indicate that relations are fairly formal, specialized, and reflective of considerable social distance. Less formality and social distance is evident between NCOs and the ranks, but a high degree of subordination and the limitation of interaction to task communications is evident. Indeed, it would seem that there may be a pattern of closer bonding between officers and the ranks than between the ranks and their NCOs, who are at times somewhat distant from unit esprit de corps.

COLOMBIA

The Colombian armed forces are among the smallest in Latin America in relation to the total population. Although the constitution requires that all Colombians serve in the military whenever there is a need to defend the country or its institutions, only 16,000 to 20,000 of the 150,000 Colombian boys who attain the age of 18 annually are drafted. Nearly all conscripts come from the lower classes, a large majority being of peasant origin. A minority of secondary school graduates are also drafted, but they have easier conditions and usually remain in the city.

Conscripts are chosen by lottery in each municipality. Exemptions are provided for students, members of religious orders, those with medical problems or economic hardships, and so forth. Males between 16 and 50 are eligible to volunteer for the army or navy. The minimum age for the army is 19, 16 for the navy.

The period of service is two years, or one year for secondary school graduates. The first year is occupied in basic military training and, in the case of illiterates, basic language education and elementary career training. Some receive technical training, especially in electronics. It is widely felt that the term of service is insufficient to produce fully experienced soldiers, particularly in counterinsurgency operations. Military service can also be done in the police force. Discharged conscripts remain in the reserve until age 45.

Candidates for career NCO status are selected from volunteers in each class near the end of their term of service and are screened by a board of officers. They are required to pass a course of academic and practical military subjects before being appointed NCOs. As in most Latin American military, there is a wide gap between officers and enlisted personnel. Many of the functions normally performed by NCOs in the United States are performed by officers in the Colombian military; there is fear of granting too much authority to the NCOs.

There are several excellent schools for enlisted personnel. The navy has a technical school complex in Barranquilla. The Army Lancero or Ranger School at Melgar provides high quality training for officers and enlisted personnel destined for the elite special forces branch.

There has been concern over the class origins of the majority of the soldiers and their potential resentment at discrimination and the frequently harsh conditions to which they are subjected. It has also been feared that many of them might have ties with the guerrillas or leftist insurgents whom the army is chiefly occupied in combatting. For this reason an effort was made in the latter 1970s to reduce the peasant percentage of conscripts, draw in more city boys, and extend conscription to middle-class, more or less educated youth.[10] The composition of the forces was not fundamentally changed, however.

PERU

The army has about 75,000 men in uniform, 59,000 conscripts and 16,000 volunteers. The vast majority of conscripts are in the army, though a few are to be found in the 20,500-strong navy or the 40,000-person air force. About 177,000 males are eligible for conscription each year, with selection accomplished by lottery, but exemptions are regularly granted. Indians from the *sierra*, often recruited through rural roundups on market days, have comprised the majority of conscripts. The period of duty is two years. Women must also register, but they are not drafted. A small number volunteer and serve in noncombatant positions in each service.[11]

During the past 25 years, some attention has been paid to literacy and vocational training. The army has long had a reputation in Peru for having the best vocational training schools in the country. The army claims it teaches literacy and gives citizenship training to 6,000 illiterates a year. "The military provides one of the major points of contact between Andean society and Peruvian coastal society."[12] Military service is an important integrating institution for lower-class citizens of traditional rural villages.[13]

Before World War II there were some opportunities for enlisted men to rise through the ranks to become officers, but since the 1940s men have had to graduate from military academies to qualify to become officers. In the Peruvian armed forces the traditional ratio of officers to NCOs and enlisted personnel is approximately 1:10. When the army had 33,000 men in 1965, there were 3,500 officers; the navy, with 7,100 in 1965, had 650 officers.[14]

Volunteers are needed by all three services for technician positions at NCO levels. These positions are relatively well-paid compared to civilian jobs, and most persons occupying them make a military career. Under the Peruvian Center for Military Instruction (CIMP), the army has several branch schools for NCOs and enlisted personnel, including infantry, artillery, armor, engineer, signal, ordnance, medical, veterinary, and paratroop. The Navy Technical and Training Center offers courses for both officers and enlisted men in electronics, engineering, and other specialized subjects. There is also an Air Force Technical Training School for enlisted specialists and NCOs, who take quite lengthy courses.

A substantial number of NCOs and technicians receive specialized training offered abroad or by foreign military missions. Between 1970 and 1975, for example, 311 NCOs received training at the School of the Americas.[15]

The American Popular Revolutionary Alliance party (APRA) made considerable efforts during the 1930s and 1940s to recruit militants from among the NCOs and junior officers. There were at least seven unsuccessful APRA-led rebellions from among such elements within the military between 1933 and 1948.

BRAZIL

The Brazilian armed forces, although small in proportion to the total population, are the largest and among the best organized of Latin America. They currently number 279,000; 185,000 in the army, 45,000 in the air force, and 43,000 in the navy. This total had been held constant since 1974, when the 1955 quota of 257,000 was increased.[16] Legislation adopted in late 1983 would increase this total to 394,500 by 1993; 296,000 in the army, 54,500 in the air force, and 44,000 in the navy.

Brazilian men must register for the draft upon reaching age 17 and are eligible to serve at age 18. Of the 1.5 million youths registered each year, some 75% are deferred for various reasons.[17] Upper- and middle-class families find ways of excluding their sons from conscription; the ranks are drawn from lower- and lower-middle-class backgrounds. A substantial portion of recruits, recently over one-third of the total, are volunteers.

Youths have two possibilities for military training: one year of regular enlistment at a nearby army garrison, or a 6-month part-time course conducted in their hometown. The latter is designed to permit completion of high school and is conducted during off hours and on weekends by resident sergeants. Youths in this program are given rudimentary military instruction and physical training, plus target practice and small-arms-maintenance training. The army attempts to provide recruits with viable professions upon their completion of the 12-month period of regular enlistment.

In 1985 the army is expanding its contingent of more professionalized troops who will receive more constant training with modern weapons for 18 months. About 30,000 men will be maintained in this category.

Most regular enlisted men serve at garrisons near their hometowns. This enhances close local/regional ties, reduces emotional problems of adaptation to army life, and saves money because of frequent home leave. The local/regional ties of enlisted men and NCOs also may be politically disadvantageous. In 1961, when the nation was on the brink of civil war, the Third Army of Southern Brazil sided with then Vice-President João Goulart (a native of Rio Grande do Sul) as the constitutional successor following President Jânio Quadros's resignation. When the military junta ordered garrisons from the Third Army to march on Pôrto Alegre, nothing happened.

The 65,900 NCOs in Brazil's army represent 36% of its total. The 31,700 sergeants are by far the most important, both as middle-level technicians and command linkages between officers and ranks. Following successful completion of the basic one year of enlistment, the most qualified and interested recruits are selected for promotion to corporal. The commission of sergeant is tied to successful completion of the one-year course at the Sergeants' School. Recruitment to this course is both from corporals as well as directly from civilian life, candidates from both routes taking a competitive examination. Only a small minority of candidates are accepted. Within the Third Army, 95% of career corporals and 75% of the sergeants were locally born, as contrasted to 100% of enlisted men and 55% of commissioned officers.[18] There is no promotion to the officer corps in times of peace.

Vertical relations within the army hierarchy have changed considerably over the past 60 years. In the 1920s junior officers had more direct contact with the troops and the NCOs' role was reduced. The lieutenants (*tenentes*) had the support of the ranks in a semi-traditional patron-client relationship and were able to muster their support against senior officers (considered closely tied to the rural political oligarchy of the time). This relationship was important during the 1930 revolution and gave the tenentes disproportionate power during the Vargas provisional government of 1930–34.

By the early 1960s, the professionalization of the sergeants and the new technical duties of the junior officers had progressed to the point that the former had assumed many of the latter's traditional relationships with the ranks. Following the NCOs' critical role in preventing a coup against Vice-president Goulart's inauguration in 1961, the new government actively sought their support, through contacts with labor and political leaders and by providing better housing and other benefits.

However, the raised educational and professional status of the sergeants did not produce similar advances in social or political status. While officers were allowed to vote, run for elected public office, and hold appointive civilian positions, NCOs and enlisted men were prohibited from voting by the constitution (until 1985) and barred from candidacy for elective office.

When the Supreme Court ruled that two deputy-sergeants elected to Congress in 1962 could not serve, the NCOs in Brasilia took control of the city and took hostage one of the Supreme Court's judges, the president of the Congress, and many senior officers.[19] Although the revolt was crushed in 12 hours, it became a key point in galvanizing support for the coup in 1964, even among Goulart advocates. The NCOs' movement and its political linkage with the militant trade union movement had threatened the officers' image of the armed forces as being "above class conflict," an important element of the pre-1964 concept of the army as the "moderating power." The day after the Brasilia revolt, General Humberto Castelo Branco, having become chief of army general staff, began coordinating the anti-Goulart conspiracy.

In 1964, Goulart appeared to be inciting NCOs to become activists in the reformist struggle. After granting amnesty to officers and ranks involved in a naval mutiny in Rio, the president assured the sergeants that legislation to accommodate their just demands was already going before Congress.[20] On March 31, after watching the televised speech, the commander of the Fourth Military Region, General Mourão Filho, marched on Rio. When the coup erupted, the army had control of the ranks and the NCOs (except in Rio Grande do Sul), and the movement was a quick success. Since 1964, senior officers have carefully observed the performance and relationships of NCOs with the ranks and civil society.

CHILE

The Chilean army consists of six combat divisions and one brigade, totalling about 58,000 men, of whom about one-third are regulars and two-thirds are draftees. The 2-year period of service in 1983 was reduced to 15 months. The navy numbers 18,000 and the air force 12,000, while there are 27,000 members of the national police (*carabineros*), of whom about 10,000 are ready to be mobilized for military purposes.

Enlisted men have tended to come from the lower classes, both because it is an attractive career for a young person from a poor background and because Chile's compulsory military service law has tended to be applied on a class basis. After a certain number of postponements for educational reasons, a student is exempted from service, and it has also been possible to fulfill the draft requirement through short-term training programs during university vacations. The Pinochet government has attempted to upgrade the quality of draftees, since it is felt that more qualified enlisted men are needed to fill many of the technical positions in the military service. In the early 1980s, therefore, educational deferments were not to be granted on the generalized basis used in the past. The navy and air force do not rely on the draft to the same degree as the army, but enlisted men in both services are partly conscripts.

Relations between commissioned officers and NCOs are formal and influenced by the differences in education and social background of the two groups. In the more technical branches there is more contact between the two levels on a functional rather than hierarchical basis. While there has been little evidence of dissension in the ranks, there was some fear during the Allende period that the Left would attempt to arouse the lower ranks against their officers, and one of the justifications given for the 1973 coup was that an effort was being made to incite navy enlisted men with the public support of a Socialist senator.

All three services have schools for NCOs, which may be entered from secondary school or later. The NCOs tend to come from middle- and lower-middle-class backgrounds. Entrance requirements for the two-year course to be a career NCO are less strict than for the officers' school but still require two years of secondary school. The NCOs, like the commissioned officers, tend to come from the urban areas of Santiago, Valparaíso, and Concepción.

Like the commissioned officers, the NCOs attend prescribed courses and are advanced on the basis of their merit, as well as on the basis of seniority. They also benefit from a generous retirement system after 30 years.

In all three services it is possible for an NCO to apply for training to receive a commission. If he is accepted, he takes a two-year course and receives a commission that has an upper promotion limit below the upper command levels, which are open only to graduates of the four-year program of the *Escuela Militar* or its navy and air force equivalents.

ARGENTINA

Until the late nineteenth century there was no unified military, the ranks being formed of lower-class men, often of doubtful character, dragooned into service. It was not until 1882 that training facilities for enlisted personnel were established, and conscription was established, on German inspiration, in 1901. Strong German influence from 1899–1940 had a significant effect on the training and discipline of the enlisted personnel. Particularly during the early part of this century, the military served as a melting pot for the nations and included a very large immigrant population.[21]

The bulk of the forces are made up from conscription. All males must register for service upon reaching their eighteenth birthday. It is estimated that at least 40% of the 200,000 males who have reached 20 each year are called. Personnel are selected by lottery. Service is normally for 12 months in the army and 14 months in the navy. Individuals between 17 and 30 may enlist for periods not to exceed five years if their conscript number has not yet been called. It is estimated that the army is composed of 25% volunteers, whereas the navy and air force are made up of 50% volunteers. Although exemptions for service are granted for education and economic reasons, conscription cuts across all classes of society, a trait unique among the Latin American countries (except Cuba).

Training is reportedly thorough and continues throughout the year's military service. Training is in two tracks, minimum essential skills for conscripts and more advanced skills for the career NCOs. A major portion of the training for conscripts is accomplished by the units to which they are assigned. Conscription takes place once a year, so that each year's conscripts leave the service at the same time. After the Falklands/Malvinas War considerable criticism was leveled at the fact that the bulk of the Argentine soldiers were little more than raw recruits and ill prepared for the conflict.

Professional NCOs comprise 25% of the army and 50% of the navy and air force. The military has long given upward mobility to the lower classes. Military life is arduous, but the military has enjoyed prestige and has always been concerned for the welfare and comfort of its members. Quarters for NCOs and other facilities on Argentine military bases are quite good, including excellent family quarters. Career NCOs can retire after 10 years service on one-third pay and on 90% of base pay after 25 years. Training afforded to career NCOs is quite good. In addition to training at Argentine facilities, the Argentine military has taken advantage of training provided at the military schools in Panama (and in the United States until the cutoff of security assistance). Relations between officers and NCOs are similar to those of most Latin American countries, with sharp class differences between officers, NCOs, and the ranks and no possibility of crossing the barrier between enlisted and commissioned personnel.

There has been little friction between the officer corps and NCOs in the recent decades. In the past, however, several efforts were made by political leaders to secure support of the lower ranks by promising various benefits, including the possibility of rising to officership. In particular, Juan Domingo Perón, during the latter part of his rule (1952–55), cultivated the NCOs to check the officers who were becoming restive. The former conspired against anti-Peronist superiors, especially in the navy; and the 1956 insurrection to restore Perón was largely supported by NCOs.

NOTES

1. Jesús de León Toral et al., *El ejército Mexicano* (Mexico City: Secretaría de la Defensa Nacional, 1979), pp. 518–20.

2. Amnesty International, *Guatemala: A Government Program of Political Murder* (London: Amnesty International, 1981), p. 20.

3. Shelton H. Davis and Julie Hodson, *Witness to Political Violence in Guatemala* (Boston: Oxfam America, 1982), p. 30.

4. Richard F. Nyrop, ed., *Panama: A Country Study* (Washington, D.C.: U.S. Government Printing Office, 1981), p. 193.

5. Historical accounts by Venezuelans or in Spanish include Angel Ziems, *El Gomecismo y la formación del ejército nacional* (Caracas: Editorial del Ateneo de Caracas, 1979); Jacinto Pérez Arcay, *La guerra federal* (Caracas: Oficina Central de Informaciones, 1974); Robert Paul Matthews, *Violencia rural en Venezuela, 1840–58* (Caracas: Monte Avila Editores, 1977); and many others. See John V. Lombardi, "The Patterns of Venezuela's Past," in *Venezuela: The Democratic Experience*, eds. John D. Martz and David Myers (New York: Praeger, 1977).

6. Rosario Febres de Briceno, *El servicio militar obligatorio en Venezuela* (Caracas: Instituto de Estudios Advanzados de Defense Nacional [IAEDN], Curso III, tesis, 1974) and Cnel. Alfonzo Romero Romero, *La nueva ley de conscripción y alistamiento militar* (Caracas: IAEDN, Curso X, tesis, 1981). Much of this section depends on these two works and interviews conducted in Caracas during the summers of 1983 and 1984.

7. Cnel. Carlos A. Gallanti C., *La movilidad social promovida por el sistema educativo militar* (Caracas: IAEDN, Curso XII, tesis, 1983).

8. Cnel. José Antero Núñez, *Imagen del servicio militar en la población venezolana* (Caracas: IAEDN, Curso IX, tesis, 1980).

9. Besides interviews and works cited earlier, this section draws heavily on Cnel. A. Guerrero Gómez, *Desarrollo de un modelo como solución a la crisis de*

oficiales subalternos en el Ejército (Caracas: IAEDN, Curso IX, tesis, 1980) and Cnel. Bernardo Alfonso Leal Puche, *Problemas de administración de personal de las Fuerzas Armadas* (Caracas: IAEDN, Curso II, tesis, 1973).

10. Gustavo Gallón Girardo, *La república de las armas* (Bogotá: Centro de Investigación y Educación Popular, 1981), p. 79.

11. *Defense and Foreign Affairs Handbook*, 1983 ed. (Washington, D.C.: Copley and Associates, 1983), p. 502; *Lambert's Worldwide Directory of Defense Authorities*, 1984 ed. (Washington, D.C.: Lambert Publications, 1983), p. 423; American University, Foreign Area Studies, *Peru: A Country Study* (Washington, D.C.: U.S. Government Printing Office, 1981), pp. 212, 222; and John Keegan, *World Armies*, 2d ed. (Detroit, Mich.: Gale Research Company, 1982), pp. 561–68.

12. Henry F. Dobyns and Paul L. Doughty, *Peru: A Cultural History* (New York: Oxford University Press, 1976), p. 210, 236–37; Luigi Einaudi and Alfred C. Stepan, *Latin American Institutional Development: Changing Military Perspectives in Peru and Brazil* (Santa Monica: Rand Corporation, April 1971, R–586–DOS), p. 52.

13. David Scott Palmer, "Adult Socialization and Rural Political Development: The Influence of Military Service on Peasant Conscript in Peru." Unpublished paper.

14. Lyle N. McAlister, "Peru" in *The Military in Latin American Sociopolitical Evolution: Four Case Studies*, ed. Lyle N. McAlister, Anthony P. Maingot, and Robert A. Potash (Washington, D.C.: Center for Research in Social Systems, 1970), p. 26.

15. North American Congress on Latin America (NACLA), "U.S. Training Programs for Foreign Military Personnel: The Pentagon's Proteges," *Latin America and Empire Report* 10 (January 1976): 24–31. Data are taken from U.S. government sources.

16. *Estado de São Paulo*, August 7, 1983, p. 6.

17. Alfred C. Stepan, *The Military in Politics: Changing Patterns in Brazil* (Princeton: Princeton University Press, 1971), p. 159.

18. Stepan, *The Military in Politics*, p. 14. Data are from 1967.

19. Stepan, *The Military in Politics*, pp. 159–63.

20. Peter Flynn, *Brazil: A Political Analysis* (Boulder, Colo.: Westview Press, 1979), p. 292.

21. *Area Handbook for Argentina* (Washington, D.C.: U.S. Government Printing Office, 1974), pp. 329–32.

2

The Officers:
Origins and Training

The bulk of the forces consists of the enlisted ranks, but officers are by definition those who lead, and in particular those who take part in politics. Hence our main concern is with them, how they are selected and from which social classes. It is assumed that political attitudes are to some extent determined by class or social origins; and the affiliation of officers and their families in the community certainly affects their political and economic philosophy, their willingness to intervene politically, and the causes for which they are prepared to intervene.

Latin American armed forces are rather similar in regard to the origins of officers. Most come from the middle or lower-middle classes, few from the affluent sectors, and few from the poorer strata. The reasons are simple. Young aristocrats are not eager to spend years in rigorous schools alongside their social inferiors and then to climb slowly up a career ladder when they can with much less effort enter a business or professional career, if not simply enjoy the ease and status of an hacienda owner. This applies more to the army than to the less plebeian and more technologically oriented navy and air force. On the other side, poor boys can seldom obtain the modicum of education necessary to enter the military educational system, if indeed their families can afford for them to be nonearners for many years. But for youths of the middle or lower-middle strata, the military career may be an inviting road to prestige, relative affluence, and possibly political power. A corollary is that sons of military men are likely to find the military attractive, the NCO's child probably aspiring to officer status. A large percentage of officers have military relatives, and there seems to be some tendency for Latin American forces to become ingrown, especially as technical specialization becomes increasingly important.

If the officer corps is predominantly middle-class in background, the effects of such composition on philosophy and politics are unclear. However, it is clear that the influence of the military in politics has been overwhelmingly conservative, although liberal-reformist tendencies have existed in most military establishments. One army made a strong effort to carry out a virtually revolutionary program, namely, in Peru, 1968-75. Reasons for this conservative inclination are considered in the last chapter of this book.

Perhaps more than being reformist or conservative, the armed forces are disposed to look to their own interests. It is a highly self-regarding profession, whose members, like members of a religious order, are strongly socialized to their discipline. This is above all the result of extensive training programs—the Latin American officer spends a larger part of his career going to school at some level than perhaps any other professional in the world, and more of his career advancement (at least up to a quite high level) depends on his academic performance than does that of any other occupation.

Training schools are thus a central part of the Latin American military institution, the more so perhaps as there have been few wars (although there has been considerable counterinsurgency action) and consequently little learning by experience. Training and more training has been the way to keep the officers reasonably busy and supposedly raise the effectiveness of the forces. The beginnings of military professionalism came with the establishment of academies in the last part of the nineteenth century and the first part of the twentieth. Since then schools have proliferated—general academies, technical institutions for special qualifications, and command schools for higher ranks. Especially interesting are the higher war colleges set up by most countries to teach not only strictly military tactics and strategy but also broader matters of national problems and purposes, thereby qualifying generals for positions of national political leadership, possibly both in reality and in their own minds.

MEXICO

To be eligible for one of the nation's military academies, an individual must be male, a Mexican citizen by birth, single, between the ages of 16 and 21 at enrollment, and have successfully completed secondary school or equivalent training. The candidate must pay a fee (equivalent to approximately $40 U.S.) and present evidence of language and mathematical competence. He is then subjected to a series of physical, psychological, and aptitude tests. The three principal military academies are the Heroic Military College (army), the Naval College, and the Military College of Aviation. Approximately 90% of all officers are products of these schools. A few officers either obtain a direct commission or come from a select group of NCOs who attend a special course at one of the academies.[1]

With regard to geographical and socioeconomic origins of Mexican officers, information is scarce. The Mexican government considers it to be a sensitive subject, not to be publicized, and there is some doubt that the respective defense ministries have actually compiled extensive information of this type. In any case, a survey taken in the early 1960s shows that over a ten-year period, cadets enrolled in the Heroic Military College came from the following areas:[2] Federal District, 38%; Central Zone (11 states), 33%; South Pacific Zone (4 states), 11%; Gulf Zone (5 states), 8%; Northern Zone (7 states), 7%; North Pacific Zone (3 states), 3%. There is no reason to believe that these percentages have changed greatly since the 1960s. The vast majority of cadets must be still recruited from the Federal District and Central states.

The fact that the proportion of cadets from the Federal District is almost double its percentage of the national population is a reflection of the superior secondary education available there. In addition, the physical presence and visibility of the ultramodern army academy in Mexico City (the naval academy is in Vera Cruz) has some influence. Moreover, entrance examinations are administered in the Federal District, and applicants from outlying states have to meet travel and lodging expenses.

Most officers come from families in the middle and lower-middle classes. About 10–15% are recruited from lower-class families, while less than 5% are drawn from the upper class. Social mobility is a major consideration for the middle class and some of the urban working class, and the military profession is a good way to an improved financial and social position. For the lower strata of the middle class, it provides a fully subsidized university-level education, job security upon graduation, and opportunities for regular career advancement.

Throughout the 1960s and the early 1970s, the expanding Mexican economy provided a wider range of alternative employment for the middle levels of the middle class. It also furnished greater educational opportunities for children of lower-class background. As a result, in recent years a greater number of cadets have been drawn from the lower strata of the middle class and the urban working class.

Cadets from military families comprise about 20% of the total. However, the number of those who have extended family members (uncles, cousins, and so on) serving in the armed forces or formerly affiliated with them is about double that percentage. Social mobility is also evident. A father or uncle who held the rank of sergeant more often than not sees his son or nephew become a cadet.[3]

Many cadets marry a woman from a military family after they graduate. This is quite significant when one considers the personalistic nature of the Mexican armed forces as well as their small size. Unlike the situation in the United States, where such a relationship would have insignificant consequences on an officer's career, the Mexican officer's family relationships can have a major bearing on his career, especially if his relative is a senior officer.

The Mexican officer spends a substantial portion of his career attending military schools. The current military education system has its roots in the late 1920s. In the aftermath of the 1910 Revolution, General Joaquín Amaro, minister of war under President Plutarco Elías Calles, revolutionized the antiquated military education system. He completely revised the curriculum of the Heroic Military College, which had been founded in 1823, seeking to form competent and well-disciplined officers obedient to the civil authority.[4]

The Heroic Military College, founded in 1823, is located on the southern fringes of the Federal District. The present facility was opened in 1976 and has the capacity to train 3,000 cadets. Present enrollment is only about half capacity. It offers a regular four-year curriculum and a special one-year curriculum for exceptional NCOs. The curriculum includes military subjects, liberal arts, and physical education. For the first year, all students take a common program. Thereafter, each cadet enters a special branch (infantry, artillery, cavalry, combat engineer, administration, or quartermaster) and for the remaining three years follows a special curriculum designed for the specific specialty. Branch selection is normally based on projected requirements, student aptitude, and personal preference.[5]

Other officer formation schools include the Military Communications School (*Escuela Militar de Transmisiones*), which has been in operation since 1925 for the purpose of training army and air force communications officers; the War Materiel School (*Escuela Militar de Materiales de Guerra*), established in 1946, which trains cadets to be army and air force ordnance officers; and the Military Nursing School (*Escuela Militar de Enfermeras*), founded in 1938.

As part of the military educational reforms initiated by General Amaro in the late 1920s and 1930s, the Center of Branch Application and Enhancement (*Centro de Aplicación y Perfeccionamiento para Oficiales de las Armas*) was created in 1932 to provide post-graduate military education to lieutenants and second captains. This center furnished intermediate military training at least three years after commissioning but prior to attendance at the Superior War College (*Escuela Superior de Guerra*), the next highest echelon of military training. Two schools now form this second tier of military education, the Military School of Application in Infantry, Artillery, Engineers, and Support Services and the Military School of Application in Cavalry (*Escuela Militar de Caballería Hermengildo Galeana*). Attendance at one of these schools is mandatory for all officers in those respective branches, and in recent years, these courses have become a prerequisite for attendance at the Superior War College. The air force and the navy provide comparable advanced and specialized training for their commissioned officers also.

Until recently, the most prestigious school in the highest echelon of military education was the Superior War College (Escuela Superior de Guerra). It was founded in 1932 by General Amaro to train officers, generally those with five to ten years in service, in command and staff procedures as well as advanced tactical and strategic doctrine. There is a battery of tests for admission. The school offers a three-year curriculum which includes military tactics, administration, logistics, geopolitics, psychological warfare, unconventional warfare, general strategy, international law, and other related subjects, plus electives such as military history, sociology, and English. The course is roughly equivalent to the United States Command and General Staff Course at Fort Leavenworth. It prepares its students to serve as battalion and regimental commanders and staff officers on military zone staffs and the army general staff. The navy has an equivalent school in Vera Cruz. The air force staff college is co-located with the Superior War College, but the air force course lasts only two years. Completion of the three-year program is recognized by the National Autonomous University of Mexico.

Graduates of the Superior War College are identified as *diplomados de estado mayor* (DEM), which translates into general staff officer. Being a DEM has considerable prestige and financial advantages. An officer in any of the three services receives an extra stipend equal to 10–25% of his monthly salary, depending on his rank, for the remainder of his active service. Perhaps more important, his potential for advancement is much improved. Without a diploma from the Superior War College, the highest rank an officer can hope to attain is lieutenant colonel. Graduates are practically guaranteed the rank of colonel, and many eventually become generals.

A recent and significant addition to the superior studies system is the *Colegio de Defensa* or National War College. This school, inaugurated in September 1981, has replaced the Superior War College as the most prestigious school in the military education system. Graduation from a superior staff college is prerequisite for admission. A key component of the armed forces' modernization program, it was created to provide training in the formulation of national defense strategy, force development, international affairs, and economic and social studies to a select group of senior colonels, generals, and admirals from the three services.[6] "At the highest level of strategic thinking . . . Mexican elites have, for the first time in modern history, begun to think through the formulation of an overarching national security policy."[7]

The other two schools in the superior studies category are the Military Medical College (*Escuela Médico Militar*) and the Military Engineering School (*Escuela Militar de Ingenieros*). The former, founded in 1916, graduates approximately 50 military doctors a year. The latter, in operation since 1960, is an institution with academic and professional prestige at which officers study construction, chemical, electrical, mechanical, and communications engineering.

All army and air force military schools are controlled by the Army and Air Force University, created on January 1, 1976, which is a headquarters for coordinating the instruction and operations of all the schools to lend continuity, uniformity, and congruence to the doctrine and ideology of the military education programs. The secretariat of the navy exercises comparable control over the naval military education program.

GUATEMALA

The major source of Guatemalan officers is the national military academy, the *Escuela Politécnica.* Every year between 400 and 500 young Guatemalan males apply for admission, and between 100 and 150 are admitted. Requirements are Guatemalan citizenship, age between 16 and 22, completion of nine years of elementary and secondary education, and ability to pass a rigorous physical examination. Character references (which provide a check on political reliability) are also important.

The requirements effectively exclude the Indian half of the population and give special opportunity to those of middle-class background. The Adolfo V. Hall system (see Chapter 1), however, insures the presence of a fair number of cadets of somewhat lower-class background. In recent years sons of officers have increasingly entered the Politécnica. The location of the Adolfo V. Hall schools throughout the nation also gives the class a somewhat wider geographic distribution than might otherwise be expected. There are a few officers who are not Politécnica graduates. Some specialists, such as physicians, may get direct commissions. Another small group has graduated from some other nation's military academy, most likely in Central America, although at least one West Point graduate is currently an active duty colonel.

The Politécnica course lasts four years. There is a high attrition rate during the first year. Most of those who leave do so because they are unable to accept the discipline, at times verging on brutality, which characterizes their first year. Academic failure is much less common, and most of those who survive the first year graduate; about 40% of those admitted do so. Facilities are quite good since the school moved to new quarters outside of Guatemala City in the late 1970s. After two years of study, an internal selection process separates those destined for service branches, such as quartermaster corps, and those destined for combat arms, including engineers and air force.

The former group are thus effectively removed from the road to power. Top graduates get their choice of branches, the engineers, infantry, and air force having the most prestige. Class rank, established at graduation, remains a factor in establishing precedence and assignment throughout much of an officer's career.

There are special ties among members of the same graduating class (*promoción*). Class loyalties are highly important and success for one member (such as rising to chief of staff, minister of defense, or president) benefits the promoción as a whole. These ties can obscure political or class differences. There is a widely believed story that in the 1960s one of the officers who had founded and was then leading a guerrilla group returned to a reunion party of his promoción and, despite the fact that the other class members were fighting against him, was accepted and allowed to depart freely.[8]

Another bond established at the Politécnica is known as *centenario*. Each cadet is given a number and a special bond is established between those whose numbers have the same last two digits. This is especially true while the cadets are in the Politécnica; but the two officers, usually two or three years apart, may continue a close relationship throughout their careers.

Officer education continues after the Politécnica with both intermediate and advanced officer courses. The intermediate course was formally established in 1945 as the *Escuela Militar de Aplicación General Manuel Arzu*. This program encompasses both basic and advanced courses. Since 1973 the basic course has been required for promotion to captain and the advanced course for promotion to major.[9]

In 1970, the army established the Center for Military Studies (CEM) to provide additional advanced studies for officers. The heart of the CEM was the Guatemalan Command and General Staff College. Previously Guatemalan officers had received such training only in other countries. Several other courses, including a Course of Higher Military Studies, were projected for the CEM, demonstrating a desire on the part of the military for both further education and less dependence on foreign studies. Attendance at the Command and General Staff College was made a requirement for promotion to lieutenant colonel. For a time, the CEM seemed to be providing a center for discussion of a broad range of national problems as well as giving advanced military instruction. But during the turmoil of the Lucas years it lost favor with the military high command, and the increased level of conflict with the guerrillas made it difficult to release officers for a full year's instruction. By 1980 the CEM was closed, but it was reopened in 1984.

Under these circumstances, foreign instruction remains important for Guatemalan officers. Between 1966 and 1976, 39 officers attended U.S. service schools at the command and general staff level in the United States, and another 20 attended the course offered at the School of the Americas in Panama. In addition, 5 officers went to El Salvador, 2 to Mexico, 3 to Peru, 2 to Colombia, 6 to Italy, 2 to Germany, and 1 to France. The dispute over Belize insured that none attended British or other Commonwealth schools. After 1977, attendance at U.S. schools was suspended, but it was resumed in 1983–84 with one officer at the Army Command and Staff College and another at the Air Force Command and Staff College. Guatemalan officers also participate in the Inter-American Defense College at Fort McNair and attend lower-level military schools such as the Advanced Officer Course at Fort Benning and the Squadron Officer School at Maxwell Air Force Base. The number of Guatemalan officers enrolled in U.S. service schools declined in 1984–85, probably more because of fiscal difficulties than suspicion of U.S. influence.

PANAMA

Prior to the 1950s, the officer corps was quite small and composed of cronies of the politicians in power at the moment. There were only a handful of academy-trained officers, the most influential being the commander, José Antonio Remón, who had been schooled in Mexico. However, this pattern changed rapidly when the police force was converted into a National Guard in 1953. Within the context of a Cold War redefinition of the functions of the guard, scholarships became available, particularly to attend Central American military academies. These scholarships attracted members of the urban and rural middle class, such as Omar Torrijos. By 1959, 35 of the 192 officers in the guard had received academy training.[10]

This first group of professionally trained officers was "deprofessionalized" upon entering the guard. The guard in the 1950s was still basically a police organization with a few narrowly defined paramilitary functions. Officers who had been trained in infantry, artillery, or cavalry branches were made street cops. Just as Remón had experienced a sense of status deprivation when he entered the guard that led him later to upgrade the institution, the first generation of academy-trained officers remolded the institution in its own image when it came to power in 1968. Many of the organizational changes made by Omar Torrijos as commander of the guard (creation of air force, navy, and infantry companies) reflected this vision.

The Cold War generation of officers was recruited from the middle class and largely trained in Central American military academies, particularly those of Nicaragua and El Salvador. When Omar Torrijos came to power in 1968, officer training shifted dramatically from Central America to South America, where the most prestigious military academies were located. The Peruvian academy was particularly appealing as a source of training due to the ideological impact of the Peruvian Revolution of 1968. It is clear that most of the officers entering the Defense Forces today are trained in South American academies, although we do not have exact figures.[11]

Many officers are still promoted from the ranks, particularly those associated with police units. In 1979, 315 of 700 officers had received academy training.[12] Officers promoted from the ranks represent an important link of the Defense Forces to their police past and a bond with the urban masses, since many police enlisted men are recruited from the urban slums.

Although cadets emerge from Latin American academies as branch specialists, they are soon cross-trained in the Defense Forces. While General Torrijos was commander (1968–81), there was a deliberate and concerted effort made to move officer personnel between various types of assignments and units. An officer trained in artillery might have as his first assignment the command of an urban traffic detachment. Although probably serving to create esprit de corps and unity within the guard, this policy had the effect of discouraging the more professional foreign-trained cadets from choosing a military career. Numerous Panamanians have graduated from West Point, but apparently none have served in the armed forces.

VENEZUELA[13]

The last *caudillos* and first praetorians, Generals Cipriano Castro and Juan Vicente Gómez, chose their officers from among their local cronies and relatives, from just-graduated high school students of their region, and from the traditional leaders of paramilitary gangs who joined their cause. These officers received little or no formal training, many were semi-literate, and advancement was based entirely on loyalty and field performance. However, in 1910 the Military Academy was reestablished, in 1912 a Naval Academy was opened, and the School for Military Aviation was inaugurated in 1920. Thus by the mid-1920s the officer corps was becoming professional. (The National Guard, which was started in the 1940s, did not have a separate academy until the 1960s.)

The biggest obstacle to changing recruitment patterns was the Andean origin of Castro and Gómez and their reliance on personal, familial, and regional loyalty. Nearly all the cadets in the first class of the School for Military Aviation in 1920 were either Andeans or sons of Gómez loyalists, and after Gómez's death the presidency and armed forces command passed to fellow Andeans López Contreras and Medina Angarita. Thus the period from 1898 to 1945 is known as the Andean hegemony. (After the three-year hiatus of rule by *Acción Democrática*, another Andean officer, Marcos Pérez Jiménez, ruled until 1958.)

At the turn of the century the Andean region had just over one-fifth of the Venezuelan population, but throughout the period of Andean hegemony this region provided over half of all officers and between 70 and 80% of those who reached flag rank. However, the increasing professionalization of the military and quasi-democratization of society under General López and Medina, along with further changes under civilian democracy after 1958, rapidly reduced Andean predominance. By the late 1960s and early 1970s only about one-third of the individuals promoted to general were of Andean origin. The proportion of high-ranking Andeans seems to have declined still further in the last decade, and the regional origins of military cadets for the service academies now reflect statistically minor imbalances.[14]

The level of prior education required and the competition for admission to the Venezuelan service academies have increased steadily over the years, as has the level of training the academies have provided. Prior to 1936, only primary education and connections were needed. From 1936 to 1950, one year of secondary school was required, and some open competition for admission occurred. From 1950 to about 1970, there was at times considerable competition for admission (as many as ten qualified candidates per place at times of high prestige and low guerrilla activity), and at least three years of secondary school were required. All of the service schools have required high school graduation for entering cadets since the early 1970s. Concomitantly, the educational level of the military academies has risen from basic high school subjects, such as drill, ceremony, and military engineering, to college-level scientific, engineering, management, and even liberal arts instruction. In 1974 the service academies were recognized as university colleges, and their graduates since then have been granted licentiate (baccalaureate) degrees in military (or naval, air force, and so on) arts and sciences.

The increase in the number of applicants has not, however, always provided adequate numbers of sufficiently qualified cadets, especially in the mid- and late-1970s, when many other excellent educational opportunities were available to Venezuelan youth because of the abundance of petrodollars. Thus there has been considerable variation in student intake and class sizes. With the economic crisis of the last few years, the entry classes are stabilizing at about the desired level of 250 students. The proportion graduating is usually near 50%, far higher than the 10% rate common in Venezuela and other Latin American civilian universities.

The almost exclusive reliance on the military academies as a source for Venezuelan officers—only about 0.75% come from the ranks and about 0.25% from lateral entry—is often seen as a major weakness of the Venezuelan officer corps.[15] However, such dependence on the academies contributes to homogeneity in backgrounds and formal education. Although now racially and regionally heterogenous, most officers seem to be of middle-class to lower-middle-class origin (largely white-collar and self-employed occupations), with few from peasant, slum, or country-club background.

A recent study showed that over 70% of a sample of civilian employees were recruited to work for the Ministry of Defense because of personal (including familial) contact with officers. Institutional loyalty is also involved, just as in the tendency for some families to send their children to certain schools. It seems rare to find a Venezuelan officer who does not have one or more brothers, cousins, uncles, grandfathers, or godparents who were officers, too.

Officers may spend as much as half their active duty in various schools and courses, either as students, instructors, or training program administrators, although 15 to 20% of active duty time is more common. The typical pattern of training for an army officer after four years of military school and commissioning is as follows:

1. A basic arms or branch course of about 6 months is taken as a second lieutenant.
2. An intermediate arms or branch course of about 5 months, emphasizing small unit and tactical leadership, must be passed for promotion to captain.
3. An advanced arms or branch school of 7–10 months' duration is usually also completed as a captain.
4. An additional course of 3–6 months in either tactical command and administration or in auxiliary and command staff functions is required for promotion to major.
5. As a major or lieutenant colonel an officer may compete for entry into the 18–month command and staff college course at the Advanced Army School.
6. At the same rank an officer may also or alternatively take—by competitive admission—the year-long joint command staff course.
7. As a lieutenant colonel but more often as a full colonel an officer may be invited to take the year-long course of the war college–the *Instituto de Estudios Avanzados de Defense Nacional* (IAEDN).

Thus an officer with 25 years' service and at earliest eligibility for promotion to brigadier general will probably have spent 5 or more years in these general courses.

The patterns of the navy, air force, and National Guard, or *Fuerzas Armadas de Cooperación* (FAC), are very similar to those of the army. In the navy and air force and in communications and engineering in the army, however, there is often more extended training with respect to new or complicated weapons systems and technical equipment and duties. On the other hand, naval officers may be a little more likely to omit command and staff courses without impeding their careers. In the army, the high rate of turnover in the ranks and the lower proportion of NCOs probably requires a typical army officer to spend a greater proportion of his time in instruction than do his counterparts in the other services.

The elaborate, high quality system of life-long education for officers outlined above is of recent origin. Basic arms and services schools developed multiple levels of training 15–30 years ago. Command staff and tactical training tended to diverge and become more specialized about 15–20 years ago. IAEDN was founded only in 1971. Specialized or advanced—called post-graduate in the navy and FAC—

programs in logistics, communications, electronics, and so on are less than 10 years old.

At one time service academy curricula were dominated by narrow military subjects. The basic scientific-technical orientation in the early 1970s has now given way to a broader humanistic-scientific-creative orientation under the Andrés Bello Plan. Under this program, physical, moral, civic, leadership, critical, and other abilities and attitudes are developed along with mathematics, engineering, and military skills. An effort is also underway to reduce the rigidity of discipline and the sense of isolation or remoteness from civil society that have often accompanied military academy training. In this respect the FAC (National Guard) Academy has led the way. Similarly, an effort to increase the retention rates for the academies—sometimes as low as 30%—is beginning to shift the attention of military leaders to pre-admission programs, popular images of the armed forces, recreational activities, and so on. Another important reform still under way in the military academies relates to the admission of women. The navy began admitting women in 1978 and the air force followed the next year, but the army and FAC are still studying their policies. Women perform some specialized roles, especially as surgeons, through assimilation to the officer corps of all the branches, but they do not yet have normal career paths in any branch. Still, women are making professional progress in the military, as they are throughout Venezuelan society.

Although the military academies have granted college degrees for only a decade, the Venezuelan armed forces have encouraged their officers to acquire university training since the late 1950s. By the late 1960s officers were increasingly pursuing advanced degrees in management and technical and scientific fields, although leaves of absence and special financial assistance were rarely granted for this purpose. During the period from 1960 to 1974, a total of about 270 first university degrees were completed by active duty officers, and while this would indicate that only about 5% of the officers on duty had achieved degrees by 1974, it is still a noteworthy number for Venezuela at the time.

The creation in the late 1970s of graduate-level programs through the Polytechnic University Institute of the Armed Forces (IUPFAN) is almost on a par with the development of graduate studies in Venezuela's national universities.[16] Over 700 individuals, including some civilians, were already studying full-time in IUPFAN programs in

1983–84. It is now estimated that there are nearly as many officers with advanced degrees as there were with first degrees just over a decade ago.

COLOMBIA

Officers are prepared at the service academies, the Military Academy in Bogota, the Naval Academy in Cartagena, and the Air Force Academy in Cali. Candidates for the academies must be Colombian by birth, have a minimum of two years of secondary school, and be between the ages of 18 and 20. Candidates must pass a physical examination and comprehensive examinations in mathematics, geography, physics, history, and Spanish. Only individuals with highly specialized skills, such as doctors and lawyers, can earn a commission without attending the service academies.

Due to the educational entrance requirements, the lower classes are largely excluded from the service academies. Because of the general lack of a military tradition and the generally antimilitary sentiments of the elite, youth of the upper classes do not usually choose military careers. Therefore, the great majority of the officers come from the middle classes. Surveys have shown that the majority of parents of officer candidates are merchants, white-collar workers, small farmers, or military, from all parts of Colombia. Urban and rural backgrounds are equally represented, but a large number come from the center of the country. The socialization process at the academies tries to eliminate class consciousness. In a deviation from the common Latin American practice, only a small fraction of officers—5% in 1972—came from military families.[17]

The Military Academy was established in 1907 as part of the modernization and professionalization program of President Rafael Reyes after the civil war (the Thousand Day War), in which the army performed quite poorly. Depending on prior schooling, the course of instruction at the academy is two, three, or four years. Ordinarily only one-third of the cadets entering the Military Academy graduate. Cadets may choose between economics, engineering, or international law as specialization.

Schooling continues throughout an officer's career. Courses at the Rangers School (*Escuela de Lanceros*), which General Gustavo Rojas Pinilla established in 1955 for antisubversive training, are required for promotion to first lieutenant. A 40-week course in a particular branch is necessary for promotion to captain. Later in the career, a one-year course at the Command and General Staff College is needed for promotion to lieutenant colonel. Completion of the course at the Superior War College is necessary for promotion to higher grades and for general staff duty.

The Superior War College offers a 45-week course for colonels and captains as a prerequisite for promotion to general and admiral. Its objective is to teach the formulation of national security policy and to analyze subjects of general national and international interest. The Superior War College does not occupy a position of importance comparable to Brazil's *Escola Superior de Guerra* or Peru's *Centro de Altos Estudios Militares.* The college also has a 14-week Military Operations and Strategy Course designed to equip lieutenant colonels and commanders to participate in planning for regular and irregular warfare. A 45-week course for majors and lieutenant commanders is a requirement for promotion to lieutenant colonel and commander. It is designed to train for general staff duty and for joint operations. A 16-week Military Information Course is designed for majors and lieutenant commanders with professional degrees who are technical specialists and who do not attend the General Staff Course. Finally, the War College offers a 23-week National Defense Information Course for representatives from government agencies and civilian organizations. This course is designed to indoctrinate in the mission, organization, and function of the military forces, as well as in national policy.

The Colombian Naval Academy was established around the time of World War II. The Naval Academy trains officers for the navy, the merchant marine, and the marine corps. The course of instruction is usually four years, and the entrance requirements are similar to those of the Military Academy. Of the time spent at the Naval Academy, nearly a year is spent at sea in the sail-training ship, *Gloria*, during which time seamanship skills receive great emphasis. The navy has its own command and staff college, but naval officers attend the War College and Superior War College with officers from the other services.

Aviation has a tradition in Colombia dating back to the early part of the century. The leading airline, *Avianca*, was founded in 1919. Military aviation also got an early start with the aid of European missions. In the 1930s there was established an informal U.S.

military aviation mission, which is still in Colombia. Requirements for the Air Force Academy are similar to those of the Military and Naval Academies, with a great concentration on technical subjects.

To supplement regular officers' training, courses were established in 1977 that qualify professionals not subject to conscription for appointment as lieutenant or captain in the reserve. Some hundreds have participated yearly, strengthening bonds of the armed forces with civilian society.[18]

PERU

Each military service academy accepts applicants on the basis of their performance in competitive examinations and their physical and general health. The army, alone among the three services, imposes a regional distribution requirement as well, on the basis of the department in which the fifth year of secondary school is taken (with 20% of vacancies allotted to northern departments; 50% to north-central, including Lima and Callao; 25% to south-central and south; and the remaining 5% to the eastern and northern jungle departments).[19] Despite this regional distribution requirement, 56% of those attaining the rank of general in the army between 1955 and 1965 were born in the *sierra* or *selva*.[20] A sample of army officers from the mid-1960s indicated that "the pattern of [army officer] recruitment was scattered and nationally representative, except that there were disproportionately more officers from rural districts and small and medium-sized provincial communities than from large urban areas."[21] Of the group of army, navy, and air force officers in one or another of the Velasco cabinets, 23% of those from the navy, 31% of those from the army, and 64% of those from the air force were of immigrant origin. All figures are well above the proportion of immigrant population in Peru.[22]

Most military men are considered, and generally consider themselves, as belonging to the middle class. Of 52 army officers for whom data were collected in the mid-1960s, 47 entered the military academy from public high schools, in a country in which upper-class and upper-middle-class parents usually send their sons to private secondary schools.[23] While the military secondary schools established between 1943 and 1962 did not attract as large numbers of candidates for the military academies as originally anticipated (only about 10%

of the graduates of the three-year program), they also failed to attract many sons of upper social strata families.[24] An examination of the backgrounds of those army officers who held cabinet positions during the General Juan Velasco Alvarado administration (1968–75) and who most identified with the progressive *velasquista* line shows that many were the sons of provincial middle-class families of modest means, in some cases on the borderline of poverty. The cabinet-level army officers between 1968 and 1975 who were not identified with the more progressive sectors of the Peruvian military government of those years were "more solidly anchored in . . . middle and upper class society" (6 of 26 had upper-class backgrounds and 10 were born in Lima).[25]

A large proportion of army officers are related to other officers. Of 461 promoted to colonel or above between 1961 and 1971, at least 272, or 59%, had relatives graduating between 1931 and 1962.[26] This tends to instill and perpetuate a more military than class-based world view and value system, especially when combined with the extensive training that accompanies a military officer through his career. The educational prerequisites and height requirement, in turn, distance the military from large sectors of Peruvian society, particularly the large Indian minority.

Information on the navy and air force officer corps backgrounds is not as complete but suggests a substantially greater proportion from both urban and upper- or upper-middle-class backgrounds. Up to 90% of naval officers come from urban areas and particularly from greater Lima, including many of upper-class origin. Youths who have received their primary and secondary education in naval preparatory schools have had a distinct advantage in the entrance examinations, and they have been almost exclusively the sons of naval officers or of their close relatives or friends.[27] Somewhat larger numbers of lower-middle- or lower-class youths are beginning to enter the Naval Academy, but they tend to serve in the technical and specialized branches of the service and rarely reach top rank.

While all class backgrounds are represented in the air force officer corps, its smaller size, more recent origin, and greater selectivity due to the physical and technical requirements have tended to weight its class distribution toward the upper-middle and upper end of the spectrum. As of the mid-1960s, about 40% of active air force officers were from the Lima area, 15% from Iquitos, and the balance from the remaining provinces.[28] Of those navy and air force officers who were members of General Velasco's cabinets between 1968 and 1975 whose class backgrounds can be ascertained, all came from the upper class.[29] All of the officers most involved in the preparation and carrying out of the 1968 coup which overthrew elected President Fernando Belaunde Terry were from the army; the navy and air force were brought in only in the final stages to symbolize armed forces unity.

A special feature of Peruvian politics served historically to keep the politically dominant army from identifying as much with the middle class as its origins might have suggested. This feature was the presence of the American Popular Revolutionary Alliance (APRA) party and the military's alienation from it, an alienation that both strengthened the corporate or institutional aspects of the military and contributed for many years, between 1932 and 1962, to the upper class's ability to influence the military's behavior. Until 1968 the military did not offer political programs that presented an alternative to those of the upper class.[30] The process of developing an orientation designed to benefit the middle and popular sectors of Peru came about slowly, primarily by means of training and experiences within the military itself.

Since World War II, the Peruvian military has placed a great deal of emphasis on the need for and the importance of education and training. An officer of the Peruvian army spends an average of 30% of his active career in school.[31] This includes four years in the Military Academy, or five if a preparatory year or the extra year required of prospective engineers is included; two courses in Specialization School totalling one and one-half years; two years in the War Academy; one or two years in Intelligence School or training abroad; and a year in the Center for Higher Military Studies (CAEM). Other special courses of up to six or nine months in duration may also be included. Most of these courses are required for promotion to higher grades and to general officer. The War Academy (*Escuela Superior de Guerra*) is particularly competitive, with some 500 applications for the 90 places each year. While a would-be candidate can apply up to four times, it is estimated that only 30–50% of all applicants are eventually admitted. CAEM invites about 40 students a year to attend its ten-month National Defense course; the 1951–71 distribution, which is typical of recent years, included 47% from the army, 9% from the navy, 8% from the air force, 7% from the police forces, and 30% from the civilian population, for a total of 483.[32] Of the army officers promoted to general between 1965 and 1971, 80% had attended the National Defense Course at CAEM (in comparison with 46% of comparable navy promotions and 33% of comparable air force promotions).[33]

Of army division (two-star) generals on active duty between 1940 and 1965, 80% graduated from the top 25% of their classes at the Military Academy, as did 54% of the brigadier (one-star) generals.[34] Although the directors of the War Academy determine final class rank, so that the highest ranking student academically is not always first in his class, and although examples can be cited of personalistic and particularistic criteria in making promotions, the importance of education and performance in determining successful advancement in the armed forces cannot be gainsaid. Emphasis on professional training and education in the promotion process has made the members of the military among the most merit-oriented within the state bureaucracy, if not all Peruvian society.[35] The importance attached to training is also indicated by the fact that 49% of army general officers between 1940 and 1965 had received foreign training[36] and that 13 of the first 19 cabinet ministers of the 1968 military government were graduates of CAEM.

Most students of the Peruvian military and its role in recent Peruvian politics attach considerable importance to its training in general and to CAEM in particular, both of which were instrumental in forging a new definition of national security that revolves around national development and a new confidence in the military's capacity to deal with key concerns in terms of policy formulation and implementation. Beginning in the late 1950s and early 1960s, CAEM started to deal with these concerns in a systematic way, especially in its year-long National Defense Course. This course dealt with general principles, national reality, national potential, national objectives, national strategy, and case studies, and it contributed to a heightened concern for the defense of national sovereignty in order to increase Peru's autonomy vis-a-vis the outside world, particularly the United States. A second component of the defense of national security was "to insure an order conducive to 'national well-being', that is, the well-being of all Peruvians, not just the dominant social classes." There was also a concern for "morality, discipline, and patriotism, and a dislike for civilian politicians,"[37] even though this contradicted the military's need to play politics.

Increased training in turn contributed to increased self-confidence. The military institution of Peru is organizationally developed and professional by Latin American standards. The self-confidence derived from higher educational and bureaucratic standards has strengthened military pressures for policies to produce greater economic development. "[This] new variety of military professionalism . . . is focused on the nexus of internal security and national development, . . . unlimited in scope and . . . by its very nature [it] is inherently political."[38]

BRAZIL

Prior to the 1939 transfer of the Army Military Academy (AMAN) to Agulhas Negras near Rio de Janeiro, the Military School of Realengo, located in the city of Rio de Janeiro, provided the basic two-year officer preparation course. The school, which was founded in 1811, commissioned its graduates as second lieutenants. The AMAN was enlarged to provide a full four-year course. Currently, the navy has its equivalent at the Naval School in Rio de Janeiro, and the Air Force Academy is located in Pirassununga, São Paulo.

Candidates for the competitive examinations for entry into the three military academies come from three types of secondary schools: regular civilian high schools, military high schools, and special cadet training schools. The latter are specialized by the three branches: air cadets in Barbacena, Minas Gerais; army cadets in Campinas, São Paulo; and navy cadets in Angra dos Reis, Rio de Janeiro. Admission to the cadet schools is also by competitive examination and is open to those who have completed eight years of primary education. No tuition is charged and room and board are free.

Military schools (*colegios militares*), located in most state capitals, accept students from the fifth grade level. Tuition is free to sons of military officers, which is a considerable perquisite as well as a major contribution to inbreeding in officer recruitment. Sons of civilians pay tuition. The new government in 1985, however, reportedly planned to phase out these schools.

Stepan found that in 1939, 62% of students entering the AMAN were graduates of civilian high schools, but by the 1962–66 period this figure had dropped to only 8%. This trend of "decivilianization" of the army means that approximately 90% of the 1960s generation of officers entered the military academic system at the age of 12.[39] A further sign of the inbreeding of the Brazilian army is that the proportion of sons of military at AMAN increased from 21% of all cadets admitted in 1941–43 to 35% in 1962–66. In 1966, a new AMAN recruitment policy was adopted to counteract this trend, whereby the top three male graduates from any accredited high school were eligible for AMAN without taking the entrance examination.

Comparing class entrants of 1941–43 and 1962–66, Stepan found that sons of the upper class decreased from 20% to 6%; those of the middle class remained nearly constant at 76–78%, while the lower-class share grew from 4% to 16%.

During the earlier period, a military career was still an attractive option for sons of the upper class, and those from the lower class had fewer opportunities to complete a quality secondary education. By the mid-1960s, however, upper-class youths with top quality secondary educations were finding more attractive career alternatives in the private sector. With better educational opportunities, nutrition, and so on, but with more restricted civilian career opportunities (via a university education), lower-class entrants had quadrupled by 1966.[40]

Due to the economic recession which began in the mid-1970s, the number of civilian candidates has increased dramatically. From 1950 to 1965, there were fewer than 2 applicants for every place in the academy.[41] But in 1981, 5,200 civilian candidates applied for the 40 places reserved for them, while the remaining 310 places in the entering class were reserved for graduates of the military and cadet preparation schools.[42] This represents a marked reversal; in 1967 and 1968, following the 1966 aggressive civilianization campaign, almost half of the cadets had gone to civilian schools.[43] The trend may, of course, be reversed if the military preparatory schools are phased out.

Because of a large concentration of military families in Rio de Janeiro (First Army headquarters, federal military bureaucracies, plus many retired officers), Stepan found that Rio de Janeiro with only 4% of the national population accounted for 42% of the 557 cadets entering AMAN in 1964–66.[44] Rio Grande do Sul, with its long regional military tradition and the Third Army garrisoned on Brazil's southern frontier, had 14% of the cadets, double its 7% of national population. Minas Gerais had the third largest contingent of cadets (10%), but with its 14% of national population it was underrepresented. The impoverished northeast region, with 31% of Brazil's population, furnished 14% of the cadets.

After graduating from AMAN, a lieutenant must serve about ten years before advancing to captain. To attain this rank, he must pass a one-year course at the Junior Officers' Training School (EsAO), which was founded in 1919 following World War I and is located at the Vila Militar in Rio de Janeiro. In 1977, the EsAO graduated 274 captains: 222 from the navy, 30 from the marine corps, and 22 foreigners. The average age of students is 34.[45] The air force has its junior officers' school at the Cumbica Air Base in São Paulo, and the navy has its school in Rio de Janeiro.

To be eligible for promotion to general or appointment to the general staff, officers must pass the three-year Command and General Staff School (ECEME) located at the Praia Vermelha in Rio de Janeiro. The air force and navy have general staff schools located at the Galeo Air Base and in Rio de Janeiro, respectively. Admission to these schools is difficult; only about 25% of the applicants pass the ECEME examination each year.[46]

The final training school in the armed forces is the Superior War College (ESG), located in Rio de Janeiro. Founded in 1949, only two years after the United States National War College, the ESG was supported by the U.S. military mission and was staffed initially by officers who had served in the Brazilian Expeditionary Force (FEB) in Italy during World War II. Its organizer, General Cordeiro de Farias, argued that Brazil as a developing nation should not divide its War College, as did the United States (Industrial College of the Armed Forces and the United States National War College); for example, national security was not separated from economic, social, and political development.

Currently, about two-thirds of ESG's students are civilians, and women have been admitted since 1973. After 30 years of activities, ESG had graduated 2,365 students (1,334 civilians and 18 women).[47]

The army also operates an accredited engineering school in Rio de Janeiro, the Institute of Military Engineering (IME). Its basic sequence of two years is considered equivalent to the AMAN course. Thus officers need take only the final three-year sequence to acquire the B.S. in military engineering. IME offers an M.S. program in mechanical engineering for both officers and civilians. Officers may also complete the one-year course at the National Information School (ENI) within the National Information Services (SNI) in Brasilia. Incorporating courses similar to those of the Army Ministry and the ESG, the ENI received its first class of 40 students in 1972.[48]

Because of a chronic shortage of highly specialized officers, the navy recently opened direct officer recruitment to university graduates in specific technical areas, mainly engineering, medicine, and computer sciences. Selection is by competitive examination, and after successful completion of a short orientation training program, recruits become commissioned officers. However, such officers are not eligible for promotion to admiral.

CHILE

The officer corps of the army was originally drawn from the land-holding families that dominated Chilean politics in the nineteenth century. After access to officership became based on merit rather than family connections as a result of the reform of military training following the War of the Pacific (1879–83), the top leadership of the army tended increasingly to come from middle-class backgrounds, although the navy still was viewed as more upper-class. In recent years, as the military has moved into influential positions, it has become somewhat more acceptable for those from upper- and upper-middle-class backgrounds to enter the officer corps, but it is rare to find the names of Chile's elite families among the top military leadership.

With few exceptions, discussed in Chapter 1, army, navy, and air force officers are graduates of the service military academies. In the case of the army, this is the *Escuela Militar*, entrance to which is based on competitive examination as well as on interviews and psychological and physical examinations. The examinations are taken during the second year of secondary school, and the first two years of the Escuela Militar are roughly equivalent to the last two years of secondary school. Standard secondary school subjects are taught, as well as military and physical training. In addition, throughout the four-year program there are courses in professional ethics, emphasizing patriotism, honesty, and national values. At the end of the second year, most students take the standardized Academic Aptitude Test (PAA), and military school cadets achieve high standing nationally. During the next two years, there is more emphasis on strictly military subjects and on the exercise of command. About 200 cadets enter in each class, but not all receive commissions, the number of which depends on the needs of the service. The combination of educational and physical prerequisites and the requirement of the payment of a small monthly tuition charge as well as a financial deposit tends to limit the socioeconomic background of the entrants to the upper-middle sectors of Chilean society. The application form requires detailed information about all family relatives and a number of references who have known the applicant for at least ten years. A substantial percentage of the cadets come from military families.

Following graduation, cadets who receive their commissions spend one or two years commanding troops. They then take advanced courses, depending on their areas of specialization. As captains they will choose between careers as line and staff officers or as technical specialists, and a competitive selection process chooses those who are to study at the War Academy (three years) or the Polytechnic Academy (four years). Officers slated for higher command posts later attend the National Academy of Political and Strategic Studies (ANEPE), which includes officers from the three services as well as civilians from various ministries—mainly Finance, Foreign Affairs, and the Controller-General.

The navy also admits cadets to the *Escuela Naval* after the second year of secondary school. The course places greater emphasis on physics and mathematics, but increasing attention has been paid to the humanities and social sciences in recent years. Admission is also selective, with only about 20% of applicants admitted. As in the case of the army, families with a naval tradition were well represented in the school. After graduation, if they receive commissions, the new officers spend six months on a sailing vessel, the *Esmeralda*, which serves as a training ship. They then spend two years on board ship, often on a small ship in the southern areas with considerable command responsibility. This is followed by a one-year course as a regular officer or two years of specialized engineering or technical training. After further command or technical experience, they return to the Naval War Academy at Playa Ancha for a one-year course, the first half of which is devoted to the study of strategy and tactics and the second half of which is given to social sciences and statistics. Those who are successful in their studies and in a competitive examination take an additional year in a command and staff school. As in the case of the army, further advancement involves attendance at the National Academy of Political and Strategic Studies.

Those interested in careers as air force officers apply to the *Escuela de Aviación Capitán Avalos.* Applicants must be in the third year of secondary school, and the physical and psychological screening is very rigorous. About 120 are in each entering class of the school, which is located at El Bosque, south of Santiago. After a four-year course that emphasizes technical subjects but also includes flight experience with training planes, those who are selected for pilot training take flight training in the north of Chile and then join combat or transport units. Those who are assigned to engineering, technical, or financial specialties attend the Aerial Polytechnic Academy, where they take courses varying in length from one to four years. After experience with an aviation unit, all officers of the grade of captain take a four-month course at the Air War Academy, and those promoted to squadron commander return for a two-year general staff course. There are also specialized courses in flight-related fields, and some officers take university courses that are relevant to their fields. The most promising officers are sent to the National Academy of Political and Strategic Studies before receiving senior command posts.

The officers of the national police (*carabineros*) come from somewhat lower strata than the other services. Founded in 1927 by President Carlos Ibáñez, who combined the local police, the fiscal police, and the military police that served primarily in the mining and border areas, the carabineros were under the control of the Ministry of the Interior until 1974, when they were formally integrated into the Ministry of Defense. Because of their lower-class extraction and close links to the people, the Allende government expected them to support it in the event of a military coup. They failed to do so, but they only joined the 1973 conspiracy at the last moment and after a change in the top command. However, they have been loyal to Augusto Pinochet throughout his tenure of office and have not hesitated to use force to repress antigovernment protests. As in the other services, advancement depends on performance in service schools and in command and staff positions.

ARGENTINA

The majority of Argentine military officers are from the urban middle class. About 10% in the army are from the upper classes, a greater percentage in the navy and air force. For a regular line officer (as opposed to a technical specialist), the only path to commissioning is through one of the service academies. Men between 16 and 21 may apply for the service academies. Applicants must have completed a minimum of four years of secondary school, and selection is based upon a competitive examination. There are provisions for application to the academies by noncommissioned officers up to age 28. Additionally each service maintains a one-year preparatory course for youths between the ages of 15 and 20 to prepare for the entrance examinations. Academy training is rigorous, and only top graduates are chosen for command and administration posts. The academies graduate about 200 students annually. The Military and Air Force Academies have a four-year course with a curriculum leading to a bachelor's degree. The Naval Academy five-year course includes a one-year cruise in the sail training ship *Libertad*.[49]

The curricula are designed to promote character, honor, and pride appropriate for an officer and gentleman in addition to providing a well-rounded intellectual orientation. Instruction is normally divided into academic subjects, military instruction, and physical training, approximately half of the time being taken up by academic subjects. Faculty members are partly civilian, either tenured professors or instructors from civilian institutions. At the Military Academy students are selected for combat arms branches such as infantry and cavalry early, usually during the first year of instruction. Graduates of the Naval Academy selected for naval aviation attend pilot training at the Naval School of Aviation, which is of 20 months' duration. The Air Force Academy, co-located with the military aircraft industry at Córdoba, affords an excellent curriculum leading to commissioning as an aviator or aerospace engineer.

There is also an impressive system of advanced schools for career officers, specialized for each service or joint, including intermediate-level institutions and senior war college for those selected for promotion to colonel or captain. Courses are normally of one year's duration. In addition, the navy maintains a post-graduate school. The highest college is the National Defense College, with a curriculum devoted not only to matters of national security but also to questions of political interest.

NOTES

1. Jesús de León Toral et al., *El ejército Mexicano* (Mexico City: Secretaría de la Defensa Nacional, 1979), p. 512; Lyle N. McAlister, Anthony P. Maingot, and Robert A. Potash, eds., *The Military in Latin American Sociopolitical Evolution: Four Case Studies* (Washington, D.C.: Center for Research in Social Systems, 1970), pp. 218–21; Center for Advanced International Studies, *The Politi-*

cal and Socio-Economic Role of the Military in Latin America (Coral Gables: University of Miami, 1972), 3: 124.

2. McAlister, Maingot, and Potash, *Sociopolitical Evolution*, p. 220.

3. Center for Advanced International Studies, *Political and Socio-Economic Role*, p. 154; and interviews with officers about their backgrounds.

4. Edwin Lieuwen, *Mexican Militarism: The Political Rise and Fall of the Revolutionary Army, 1910–1940* (Albuquerque: University of New Mexico Press, 1968), pp. 92–94; McAlister, Maingot, and Potash, *Sociopolitical Evolution*, pp. 205–6.

5. León Toral, *El ejército Mexicano*, p. 512; McAlister, Maingot, and Potash, *Sociopolitical Evolution*, p. 218. This information was also verified through discussions with various officers.

6. George W. Grayson, "No Presidential Sashes—yet—on Mexico's Military Men," *The Christian Science Monitor*, September 17, 1982; Edward J. Williams, "Mexico's Central American Policy, Apologies, Motivations and Principles," Strategic Issues Research Memorandum (U.S. Army War College, March 15, 1981), p. 25.

7. Williams, "Mexico's Central American Policy," p. 25.

8. Richard Adams, "The Development of the Guatemalan Military," in *Militarism in Developing Countries*, ed. Kenneth Fidel (New Brunswick, N.J.: Transaction Books, 1975), pp. 139–40.

9. Col. Boris Rebbio Porta España, "Educación militar superior en el ejército de Guatemala," *Revista Militar* (Guatemala) (January-June, 1977): 14–16.

10. Renato Pereira, *Panama: fuerzas armadas y política* (Panama: Ediciones Nueva Universidad, 1979), p. 112.

11. Steve C. Ropp, *Panamanian Politics: From Guarded Nation to National Guard* (New York: Praeger, 1982), p. 46.

12. Pereira, *Panama*, p. 112.

13. The classic work on the Venezuelan military academy and several personal interviews with its author provide the background for this section; see Martin Garcia Villasmil, *Escuelas para la formación de oficiales del Ejército* (Caracas: Oficina Técnica, Ministerio de la Defensa, 1964). Another more recent commandant, General José Antonio Olavarría, and the new commandant, General Carlos Julio Penalosa, have also been invaluable collaborators with respect to this section of the present work and nearly all of the author's work on the military in Venezuela, General de División Alberto Muller Rojas, now controller general and former director of education for the armed forces of Venezuela, has been a sagacious and cooperative source for much of the material on military education reported throughout this work.

14. Gene E. Bigler, "Armed Forces Professionalization and the Emergence of Civilian Control over the Military in Venezuela," mimeo (Caracas: Instituto de Estudios Superiores de Administración, 1975), Table 1.

15. Carlos A. Gallanti C., *La movilidad social promovida por el sistema educativo militar* (Caracas: Institutos de Estudios Avanzados de Defensa Nacional [IAEDN], Curso XII; tesis, 1983).

16. Gary Hoover, *Venezuela* (Washington, D.C.: World Education Series, American Association of Collegiate Registrars and Admissions Officers, 1978) and the outstanding series of publications by the Oficina de Planificacion del Sector Universitario and the Consejo Nacional de Universidades.

17. J. Mark Ruhl, *Colombia: Armed Forces and Society* (Syracuse: Syracuse University, 1980), pp. 32–33.

18. Gustavo Gallón Girardo, *La república de las armas* (Bogota: Centro de Investigación y Educación Popular, 1981), p. 75.

19. Lyle N. McAlister, "Peru" in McAlister, Maingot, and Potash, *Sociopolitical Evolution*, p. 32.

20. Luigi Einaudi and Alfred C. Stepan, *Latin American Institutional Development: Changing Military Perspectives in Peru and Brazil.* (Santa Monica: Rand Corporation, 1971), p. 56.

21. McAlister, Maingot, and Potash, *Sociopolitical Evolution*, p. 33.

22. Liisa North and Tanya Korovkin, *The Peruvian Revolution and the Officers in Power, 1967-1976*, Occasional Monograph Series, no. 15 (Montreal: Centre for Developing-Area Studies, McGill University, 1981), pp. 81–82.

23. McAlister, Maingot, and Potash, *Sociopolitical Evolution*, p. 33.

24. Luis Valdez Pallete, "Antecedentes de la nueva orientación de las Fuerzas Armadas en el Perú," *Aportes* 19 (January 1971): 169–75.

25. North and Korovkin, *Peruvian Revolution*, pp. 78–79.

26. Carlos A. Astiz and José Z. García, "The Peruvian Military: Achievement Orientation, Training, and Political Tendencies," *Western Political Quarterly* 25 (December 1972): 671, Table 4.

27. McAlister, Maingot, and Potash, *Sociopolitical Evolution*, p. 34.

28. McAlister, Maingot, and Potash, *Sociopolitical Evolution*, p. 35.

29. North and Korovkin, *Peruvian Revolution*, pp. 80–81.

30. Liisa North, *Civil-Military Relations in Argentina, Chile, and Peru*, Politics of Modernization Series, no. 2 (Berkeley: Institute of International Studies, University of California, 1966), p. 51.

31. McAlister, Maingot, and Potash, *Sociopolitical Evolution*, p. 35.

32. Astiz and Garcia, "Peruvian Military," p. 672–77.

33. Astiz and Garcia, "Peruvian Military," p. 675, Table 6.

34. Astiz and Garcia, "Peruvian Military," p. 668; Einaudi and Stepan, *Latin American Institutional Development*, p. 405.

35. Einaudi and Stepan, *Latin American Institutional Development*, pp. 404–5.

36. Luigi Einaudi, "U.S. Relations with the Peruvian Military," in *U.S. Foreign Policy and Peru*, ed. Daniel A. Sharp (Austin: University of Texas Press, 1972), p. 44.

37. Einaudi and Stepan, *Latin American Institutional Development*, p. 406.

38. Einaudi and Stepan, *Latin American Institutional Development*, pp. 6–7.

39. Alfred C. Stepan, *The Military in Politics: Changing Patterns in Brazil* (Princeton: Princeton University Press, 1971), p. 41.

40. Stepan, *Military in Politics*, pp. 31–34.

41. Stepan, *Military in Politics*, p. 40.

42. *Estado de São Paulo*, February 6, 1981, p. 6.

43. Stepan, *Military in Politics*, p. 42.

44. Stepan, *Military in Politics*, p. 38.

45. *Veja*, November 30, 1977, p. 103.

46. Stepan, *Military in Politics*, p. 51.

47. *O Globo*, March 19, 1979, p. 8.

48. Ana Lagoa, *SNI: como nasceu, como funciona*. (São Paulo: Editora Brasiliense, 1983), pp. 64–65.

49. *Area Handbook for Argentina* (Washington, D.C.: U.S. Government Printing Office, 1974), pp. 335–38.

3

The Officers:
Career Patterns

In Latin American militaries, because of the importance of training and professionalism, early promotion is largely on a basis of merit plus seniority. Seniority usually prevails for the first step or two, thereafter playing a smaller part. Merit is a variable mixture, academic achievement at schools being more important in some countries, such as Peru and Brazil, character and rated performance in others, as in Venezuela. Politics also enter into the picture, perhaps especially in Mexico and Panama. In the upper echelons, of course, more or less political considerations are likely to prevail everywhere.

Most Latin American armed forces have strict up-or-out rules, permitting only a limited number of years in grade; this leads to a circulation of command and also serves considerably to reduce the potential of the armed forces for political intervention. Officers probably do not have time to build up enough of a personal following to increase the temptation to reach for personal power. On the other hand, the fact that the leading officers are subject to rapid turnover makes for more interesting, if briefer, careers, after which retirees probably qualify for important civilian posts.

The selection of high officers is legally more or less under the control of the president of all countries. However, if he intervenes for political or personal reasons in ways injurious to the professional ethics of the forces, he may lose more by alienating those left behind than he gains by putting his friends in positions of influence. Unless he is prepared to risk antagonizing the armed forces, the president himself must heed the military code. He may, however, use the rules to his advantage; thus, he may in most countries force any general into retirement by promoting a junior over him.

A common effect of promotion procedures is to increase the numbers of higher-grade officers. On the one hand, this means that officers are often overqualified for their work and in many cases have tasks that would be left to noncommissioned officers (NCOs) in the U.S. army. On the other hand, prospects of quick advancement through training encourage the proliferation of schools and courses.

MEXICO

Upon commissioning, an officer embarks on what often proves to be a diversified career. After graduation from a military academy, he serves two years as a second lieutenant. If he receives favorable evaluation reports, he is automatically promoted to first lieutenant and remains in that grade for a minimum of three years. After five years, the officer has the option of resigning his commission or continuing in the service.[1]

There are three basic requirements for promotion above first lieutenant. First, an officer must serve a minimum time in each grade. Secondly, he must pass a competitive examination for the subsequent grade. Finally, he must be rated favorably by his superior officers. If he follows the rules and impresses the right people, he can probably attain the rank of general.

After serving as first lieutenant for three years, an officer is eligible for advancement to the rank of second captain (*capitán segundo*). For this, he must pass a two-day competitive comprehensive examination. Next, his overall performance is evaluated, and a decision is made as to whether or not he should be promoted. Finally, officers are placed on a promotion list in the rank order of their test scores. Those who do not make the cutoff have to retake the examination the following year.[2]

Promotions to first captain, major, and lieutenant colonel follow the same general plan. The minimum time requirement for first captain is 8 years in service, 11 years for major, and 14 for lieutenant colonel. Selection for the rank of colonel is based on the recommendation of a board of senior officers, and the list is subject to approval by the Senate. There is also a time-in-service requirement for selection to colonel. Promotion to the rank of general follows the same pattern although there is no minimum years-in-service criterion.

Promotion to colonel and general is based ostensibly on merit, but personal connections and military politics influence the decision. The president gives final approval to the general officer list.

In the postrevolutionary period, it was commonplace to combine military service with political office: state governors were generally military officers. However, the number of military men with political careers began to decline rapidly by 1940, and this trend has continued to the present day.[3]

The death and/or retirement of many revolutionary officers, as well as the rise of a new generation of military men trained during the Cárdenas years (1934–40) and World War II, brought about a more stabilized and military-oriented career pattern.

Numerous variables, such as individual capabilities, personal preferences, position vacancies, and timing, affect an officer's career. After graduation from the Heroic Military College or one of the three specialty schools (communications, war materiel, or health service), a new second lieutenant normally serves three years with a tactical unit. Following this initial assignment, an officer is usually scheduled for attendance at one of the application schools (*escuelas de aplicación*). Subsequent assignments following this schooling may take the officer back to a unit, to a military zone headquarters, or to National Defense Headquarters (Mexico's version of the Pentagon) in Mexico City to perform low-level staff work. Most often, the officer returns to duty at the unit level. The Superior War College (*Escuela Superior de Guerra*) comes next for those first and second captains who have met the prerequisites for admission.

With graduation from the Superior War College, an officer begins his advanced career. The *diplomado de estado mayor* (DEM), as he is called, is normally assigned back to the field to serve in a military zone headquarters. After one year in the military zone, most officers are reassigned to one of the principal staff sections at Defense Headquarters. By this time, most officers have reached the grade of lieutenant colonel and continue to serve at Defense Headquarters. A few begin to move in a faster track and serve as battalion or cavalry squadron commanders. Other lieutenant colonels move on to instructor and administrative positions at the various military schools, hoping for an opportunity to command.

At the colonel level, types of assignments remain the same, with increased responsibilities. For example, colonels command certain brigades and cavalry regiments, serve as chiefs of staff of a military zone, or manage staff directorates at Defense Headquarters. A few may also be selected to attend the National Defense College, as are certain general officers. Generals can serve as brigade commanders, commanders of military zones, chiefs of functional directorates at Defense Headquarters, or directors of military schools. In colonel and general officer assignments, military politics often come into play.

Generals usually seek subordinates whom they have worked with in the past and consider loyal. Therefore, the chief of a functional directorate at the National Defense Headquarters normally determines which senior officers will be working in that directorate. Considerable personnel turbulence within the general officer ranks occurs at the outset of each presidential *sexenio*. The secretaries of defense and navy are personally selected by the president; they give key assignments, such as military and naval zone commands, to those whom the president and the secretaries of defense and navy consider to be extremely loyal and whose philosophies coincide with their own. Once these positions are filled, the new commanders bring in their loyal subordinates. These high-ranking officers can expect to have significant influence for the next six years or until a new secretary of defense (or navy) is named. This system parallels the *camarilla* or political clique that predominates within the Mexican political system.

In the upper echelons of the military hierarchy, contacts are often more valuable than technical competence. This *personalismo*, which permeates the military and society in general, is also an essential element in the relationship that exists between the president and the secretary of defense. At lower levels, the emphasis in the armed forces command structure is hierarchial. The commander wields absolute power, and little happens without his express approval. As a result, Mexican officers, for the most part, only react on direct orders from the commander and avoid much individual initiative.

A few "plums" may intersperse the career. These include duty with the Presidential Guard (*Guardia Presidencial*), which consists of several battalion-size units and a staff that report directly to the presidency. This elite unit is primarily responsible for the safety and security of the president and other high-ranking political leaders. Other sought-after positions include attaché duty in foreign embassies and attendance at foreign military schools. These assignments are especially attractive because of the perquisites, extra pay, and allowances, as well as the opportunity to travel and/or live abroad. In the past, desirable positions were used as rewards for loyalty. More recently, however, greater emphasis has been placed on ensuring that reasonably qualified personnel are selected to fill them.

GUATEMALA

Upon graduation from the *Politécnica*, Guatemalan officers are commissioned as second lieutenants and given their posts, usually outside the capital. A few of the best may be assigned to the Honor Guard battalion in Guatemala City. After 2 years, second lieutenants are promoted to first lieutenants. Subsequent promotions tend to come regularly every 4 or 5 years. There is some weeding out above the level of major, but the majority of officers can expect to reach the rank of colonel in about 20 years.[4]

While promotion patterns up to the rank of colonel are relatively even, important distinctions appear early in an officer's career. Class rank and branch of service help to establish these distinctions, as do the ties of *centenario* and, on occasion, family and regional influences. Political reliability is also important. The ambitious officer must seek certain kinds of positions; to do so, he must profess correct politics, depending upon who happens to be in control at the moment.

Service in favored units, such as the Honor Guard, the parachute or Kaibile battalions, or at the Politécnica, especially in a command position, is highly prized. Study abroad can also be an important step on the road to power. Those who have attended particular schools, such as the United States Army Command and General Staff College, tend to forge common links. This was especially true during the presidency of General Kjell Laugerud, a Fort Leavenworth graduate. It was much less the case under his successor, General Romeo Lucas García, who had never studied in the United States and did not speak English (he had, however, studied in France). The president, General Mejía Victores, had studied in the United States and attended the Inter-American Air Force Academy (IAFA) in Panama. He also graduated from Mexico's Superior War College.

Command of troops is an important factor in a successful military career. The Guatemalan army has five regional brigade headquarters, but these have only one active duty battalion and, in theory, two reserve battalions. The brigade commander and his executive officer are both colonels, while the battalion commander is a lieutenant colonel, yet it is widely recognized that the latter is more important and powerful than the colonel serving as executive officer.

Appointment to general staff positions is also very important. Such an appointment places an officer close to the center of national power and provides valuable experience and contacts. It can also be dangerous, since one can easily become identified with an unsuccessful contender for power. President Mejía Victores's previous service included tours, while holding the rank of colonel, as deputy chief of the army general staff, as commander of the army general headquarters, and as minister of defense. From this post he took over the presidency in 1983.

While study abroad is usually advantageous, service as an attache is more likely to be a form of honorable exile. Following his fraudulent defeat in the 1974 presidential elections, General Ríos Montt was shipped to Spain as military attache. In such cases the individual may spend the rest of his active duty career abroad, returning home only after retirement. Another group of officers are simply shunted aside, being placed in a category known as *disponible* (available). This keeps them under military discipline and available for duty, should their services be required; they continue to receive full pay and benefits but are effectively cut off from power.[5] Following the 1982 coup, former President Lucas and many of his supporters were placed in this category.

While most **Politécnica** graduates can expect to eventually be promoted to colonel, only a very few reach the rank of brigadier general. There was a period in the mid-1960s when there were no generals on active duty. In 1968 five colonels were promoted to brigadier general. and there has generally been about that number on active duty since then. As of April 1984. President Mejía Victores and Army Chief of Staff Rodolfo Lobos Zamora were the only active duty generals, although many others were *disponible.* The highest rank in the military, major general, is rarely conferred.

The relatively rapid rise to colonel, the almost total lack of possible promotions beyond that, and the necessity of waiting 30 years to retire at full pay produce a top-heavy structure, with many colonels performing tasks more suited to a major. There is within this group of colonels, however, a clearly defined pecking order. Seniority and class rank are important factors, but so too are career patterns, the influence of *promoción* and centenario ties, education abroad and, most of all, past and present positions as a troop commander.

Guatemalan officers have been notoriously underpaid throughout the twentieth century. Current salaries are somewhat better, but most higher officers still find it desirable to supplement their salaries in various ways. Unit commanders control the profits from the PX, a potential source of considerable income. Another means of earning extra money is obtaining a military position with a *sobresueldo*, or additional salary, often attached to posts which carry some civil responsibility. The number of such posts, however, is limited. Another more common tactic, which reached epidemic proportions in the Lucas era, is to engage in private business ventures while on active duty. The more powerful an officer, the greater the ease with which he can procure financing, partners, and, at times, virtual monopoly status for his efforts. The military has its own bank, the *Banco del Ejército*, which provides favorable financing for officers. The military also has interests in diverse enterprises, such as a cement factory and even Guatemala City parking lots.[6] Officers who go into private business can profit from contacts with military business, from their ability to avoid customs and other taxes, and from whatever local political power may attach to their positions. A final method of making money is through the acquisition of land, especially in newly developed areas. At times officers may be given land by local landowners seeking influence, protection, or some special favor. Others have benefited from government land development programs and from the distribution of national lands.[7]

As previously noted, officers can retire after 20 years, but they get full pay on retirement after 30 years. The 1983 Army Law (Executive Decree–Law 149–83) provides for compulsory retirement for disability, age, or, most commonly, the completion of 33 years of service. The government can, of course, suspend mandatory retirement in individual cases, such as those of individuals in high political positions.

PANAMA

Career patterns within the Defense Forces have been partially determined by organizational structure. Prior to 1983, this structure was traditionally modelled on that of the United States army, with a general staff divided into five sections (G–1 Personnel, G–2 Intelligence, G–3 Operations, G–4 Logistics, and G–5 Civic Action). Instead of constituting separate service branches, the Panamanian air force and navy were subject to control by the G–3. At the top of the organizational pyramid was the commander-in-chief, who directly controlled the military zones, infantry companies, and a number of other military units.

An entering lieutenant is likely to be assigned to police duty, one of the ten zone commands, a rifle company, or staff work in any of the other guard dependencies. Rotation from unit to unit is frequent, and police and military duties are constantly interchanged. With promotion to captain, the career ladder narrows. Some assume company commands, and a select few will get command of a military zone. Generally, the zone commands are given to field grade officers (mostly majors), whose status is emphasized by the fact that they are referred to as *jefes* rather than *oficiales*, the term used for company grade officers.[8]

Command of a military zone is an important step in the career ladder, although a few of the peripheral and less populated ones are not considered important and can be assigned to captains or even lieutenants. A zone command gives an officer a quasi-autonomous political and economic power base. Many of the primary functions of the zone commander are non-military. For example, he is a member of the provincial coordinating council determining regional development strategies and allocating funds. There are also opportunities for gain through a variety of illicit activities. Most importantly, the zone commander could "deliver" a part of the country to top officers during a power struggle. For example, Manuel Antonio Noriega as commander of the military zone in Chiriquí Province provided a base for Omar Torrijos to return triumphantly from a brief exile in 1969.

Next in progression toward the top of the organizational pyramid have traditionally been the members of the general staff. The assistant chiefs of staff (G–1, G–2, and so on) are uniformly lieutenant colonels. These *jefes* comprised the inner core of collective leadership of the guard before 1983 and were important national figures who exercised power far beyond the narrow purview of their military duties. They served during the Torrijos years as a "shadow cabinet," setting national policy largely by defining the limits of Torrijos's reform movement.[9] Within the general staff, some positions are inherently more important than others. G–2 Intelligence was the base upon which the current commander of the Defense Forces, Noriega, built his power.

The path to the top during the last three decades has been fairly clear. Necessary conditions for an officer to emerge as commander in chief include:

1. Graduation from a military academy. Only one of the top 10 officers in the National Guard in 1978 came up through the ranks, although former enlisted men were better represented in the top 20.
2. Service as commander of an important military zone. This allows for the development of critical political contacts.
3. Command of an important section of the general staff.

As in other Latin American countries, political considerations become increasingly important as an officer ascends the career ladder. From the 1940s through the 1960s, the position of commander in chief was held by two officers who both had very close contacts with the urban commercial elite. José Antonio Remón was something of a maverick and a populist but stayed within the confines of traditional elite circles. His family was part of the aristocracy, although it had fallen upon hard times, Remón's successor, Bolívar Vallarino, also had close ties to the aristocracy, and guard activities under his direction tended to reflect elite interests. Similarly, the ascent of Omar Torrijos was facilitated by his ties to the new emerging middle class, both in the transit zone and in rural areas. The commander of the armed forces thus tends to reflect both current institutional standards of professionalism and societal relations.

To the extent that career patterns in the military have been determined by organizational structure, they will be somewhat modified (particularly at the top) by the passage of the Military Organic Law in 1983. This law changed the name of the military from the National Guard to Defense Forces of the Republic of Panama. Eight separate service branches now operate under the leadership of the Forces' commander in chief. They are the National Guard, Air Force, Naval Force, Panama Canal Defense Force, Police Force, Traffic Directorate, Department of Investigation, and Department of Immigration. Included here are institutions (such as the Department of Immigration) that normally operate in other Latin American countries as dependencies of ministries other than defense. The Panamanian Defense Forces are unusual in terms of their range of functions and organizational differentiation.

A modification of rank structure accompanied establishment of the Defense Forces, with the addition of three new general officer grades (general of the forces, corps general, and division general) to the existing grade of brigadier general (the rank held by Omar Torrijos). Expansion of the "supergrades" occurred not only because of the new service branches but because of the maturation of the military perspective within the National Guard and the continued quest of this institution for regional status and equality.

This alteration of military rank structure moves the institution farther away from its police origins. Traditionally, as with most police organizations, personnel was heavily concentrated at the enlisted level and at the lower ranks of the officer corps. As late as 1970, over 50% of the officers were second lieutenants and over 85% were first or second lieutenants.[10] The drift of the officer corps toward a rank distribution more like that of Venezuela or Brazil (as a result of further militarization) suggests that the social gap between officers and enlisted men may rapidly increase.

The 1983 Military Organic Law also addressed the increasingly controversial issue of retirement. As the academy-trained officers of the 1950s discovered when Torrijos died in 1981, the traditional 25-year limit to a service career placed a premature cap on their political careers and ambitions. The new law kept the door open to continuation of a high position by stating that officers "will have the right to retire" after 25 consecutive or 30 nonconsecutive years of service.

VENEZUELA

Officer careers in Venezuela are conditioned by the centrality of education; formal regulations on time in rank, career length, and evaluation, all of which influence promotion; and the patterns of benefits and opportunities, which influence career choices and in turn create unfilled openings for lower-ranking officers and intense competition for fewer positions among higher ranks.

The Organic Law of the Armed Forces establishes the following minimum times in rank for promotion and maximum ages in rank prior to mandatory retirement. The normal age range for obtaining each rank is given in the final columns.

Rank (or Naval Equivalent)	Minimum Years for Promotion	Maximum Age	Normal Age to Obtain Rank
Second lieutenant	3	32	21–23
Lieutenant	5	37	26–28
Captain	5	42	31–35
Major	4	46	35–40
Lieutenant colonel	4	50	39–45
Colonel	4	54	43–49
Brigadier general	3	57	46–51
Major general	—	59	49–52

Prior to the 1983 changes in the Organic Law, an officer's career was limited to a maximum of 30 years. Each year a fairly large number of officers were forced to retire at 51 or 52 years of age. The 30-year career limit was instituted in 1958 as a means for establishing greater civilian control over the military by permitting very little time—often only a year—to officers in the highest posts.[11] Thus eight men have held the position of minister of defense over the last eight years, and rotation has been nearly as rapid in positions such as inspector general, commanding general, and even some major unit commands. Assignments to other prominent command posts, service academy direction, and so on were also commonly of only a year or two in duration.

By the Organic Law, as revised in 1983 and taking effect in 1985, the maximum period for service is extended to 33 years, and the president will have authority to grant extensions up to the maximum age in rank. However, retirement may be required for an officer in any rank who fails to be promoted to the next higher rank for 3 years after becoming eligible. Early voluntary retirements, prior to the 30-year limit, have been relatively uncommon in Venezuela for officers who have reached the rank of major. Consequently a quota has been instituted for mandatory retirements in each higher rank.

The three-year prolongation of careers falls short of officer hopes, but it may reduce some of the instability in higher posts and permit the time that has often been considered lacking for program development, reform, and continuity. It will also help prevent some officer deficiencies in the short term as the Venezuelan armed forces continue their recent and now more gradual pattern of expansion under Plan Carabobo. On the other hand, deceleration of turnover and slower ascent to key posts may prove frustrating.

The lengthening of careers will not alleviate the pronounced tendency of subaltern officers to leave service, which results in a fairly high percentage of vacancies with respect to authorized positions (at times as high as 40%) at the level of lieutenant and captain. Thus junior officers who remain in service often have various interesting opportunities, and there is competition in their recruitment to unit, staff, and other positions. Deficiencies are much fewer in the ranks of major and lieutenant colonel, usually 10–20%, but some commanders must still compete for key subordinates. In contrast, usually 100% of the positions designated for the superior ranks are actually filled by colonels and generals, so that competition is keen among the contenders, and the dispensers of the highest positions may be more selective.

With relatively few exceptions, which will be discussed below, promotion and assignments are based strictly on a merit system. Evaluations are both competitive and comparative. The stress created by such evaluations is intentional and meant to help in identifying leadership potential under the stress of command. A very broad set of criteria is used to assess performance. These criteria include professional attitudes; moral qualities; intellectual qualities; self-management, including physical fitness and financial responsibility; and command performance. Each officer receives 18 scores within these five categories and a point total from panels of superior officers. He has access to this information about himself and others as well.

Emphasis on education notwithstanding, intellectual achievement is only one of five sets of qualities evaluated. Formal school performance and educational attainment are far less important in determining advancement in Venezuela than they are said to be in Brazil, Peru, and elsewhere in Latin America. The Venezuelan pattern, more like that of the United States, has produced only one or two first-in-class cadets who have reached the post of minister of defense in the whole democratic period.

One reason for the relatively high retention rate of officers in Venezuela—as many as 40% of some cadet graduating classes have completed 30 years of service in spite of the anti–Pérez Jiménez purges, numerous coup attempts, and the guerrilla warfare of the 1958–67 period—is that pay and benefits have been quite generous. General Juan Vicente Gómez recognized the importance of officer remuneration early in his rule and kept his officers well-paid or provided them access to personal enrichment. However, the salaries of junior officers had eroded to the level of urban laborers within a few years after his death. Rómulo Betancourt became cognizant of this factor in planning the civil military coup of 1945 and seems to have shared his insight with other civilian leaders of the democracy since 1958.[12] Thus by 1960 Venezuelan officers had pay levels sufficient to provide a standard of living comparable to that of their United States counterparts. In the Venezuelan context, with a per-capita income of about one-fifth or one-fourth that of the United States, this made for a fairly luxurious standard; but it was in line with that of successful professionals, businessmen, and upper-level bureaucrats.

Inflation since the late 1970s and economic problems since 1981 have, however, eroded the military standard of living, along with that of many comparable middle-class civilians, especially at the entry and junior levels. However, special duty premiums, health, housing, military stores, education, credit, recreational facilities, retirement, and other benefits are good at all levels, but they are relatively more important at mid-career and above.[13]

Thus a variety of factors contributes to the distribution of officer ranks in Venezuela from 1974–84, estimated as follows: generals, 1.5–4%; colonels, 7–17%; lieutenant colonels, 10–22%; majors, 11–20%; captains, 10–19%; first lieutenants, 19–24%; and second lieutenants, 15–20%.

There is considerable variability from one branch to another and in the same branch over time, especially in the navy and air force. For instance, the National Guard (FAC) has regularly had the lowest percentage of superior officers (colonel and general), usually from 8–10%; the army generally follows with 11–14%; and the air force and navy commonly have 16–20% of their officers in the highest ranks. The tendency of those who reach major to stay until mandatory retirement results in the high percentages of higher-ranking officers in Venezuela.

The relatively flat distribution of percentages in rank and high proportions of superior officers are often cited as examples of non-modernized military institutions. Such was definitely the case in Venezuela in the *caudillo* period. While it would be a mistake to draw the same conclusion today, promotion to colonel and general is the step where politics may intervene, as it formerly did throughout the ranks. Rumors and innuendos about political interference by the president or the political parties through the Defense Committee of the Senate have been fairly common over the last 20 years. In many cases any action at all by the president or Senate, which both have constitutional authority with respect to promotions to ranks of colonel or higher, is interpreted as politicking. Yet interviews with several ex-ministers of defense and an examination of the records of the proceedings of the Defense Committee for a number of years indicate that relatively few officers have been taken from or added to the military-generated promotion list.

COLOMBIA

As addressed in the previous chapter, promotion to the higher grades frequently depends upon attendance at senior service schools. General staff duty on one of the service staffs or on the joint staff is also extremely important for promotion, particularly to general or admiral. As in most military organizations, considerable time spent in command is a requirement for promotion. Foreign assignments such as military attache, particularly in the United States, appear to be career-enhancing.

It is generally accepted that promotions are the responsibility of the armed forces themselves and that the civilian politicians should not intervene except at the very highest level; and the forces have sought to defend their autonomy in this regard when it has been infringed. The political importance of the military, however, has inevitably led presidents from time to time to seek to alter its complexion by advancing officers sympathetic to their views. Thus Alfonso López Pumarejo sought to reduce the Conservative coloration of the officer corps and thereby provoked a coup attempt in 1944. Much more grossly, Laureano Gómez at the beginning of the 1950s tried to get rid of Liberal officers and make the army the instrument of his semi-Falangist faction of the Conservative party, thereby pushing many Liberal officers and men into antigovernment violence. More recently, President López Michelsen (1974–78) tried to place his followers in key positions at the cost of early retirement of young officers, producing a serious protest.

PERU

As stated in Chapter 2, the typical officer spends a good deal of his time in one school or another and knows that his advancement is in large measure dependent upon his performance in such training assignments. Upon graduation from the Military Academy, the new officer is commissioned a second lieutenant. Specialization school courses are required for promotion to major or captain. Without being accepted by and successfully completing the War College, he has almost no chance to be promoted to general officer; and during the 1960s and 1970s, at least, study at the Center for Higher Military Studies (CAEM) was also a virtual requisite, at least in the army. Other possibilities for promotion through alternative training exist, as with the Intelligence School or specialized training abroad or for special skills, especially in the air force. While friendship and family ties can also make a difference, the upward movement in officer ranks is largely achievement-oriented.[14]

Most army officers enter the Military Academy from public schools at age 18 or 19. They typically serve for 30 years and retire at full pay with substantial perquisites in their early fifties. One intra-military career pattern worthy of note is the special role played by members of the Army Intelligence Service before, during, and after the 1968 coup. The five key colonels with General Velasco, who were called to organize the takeover and draft its plans for govern-ment (Plan Inca), were all members of the Intelligence Service and were influential in the first years of the military government. In fact, they went well beyond the "programmatic consensus" reached with-in the military through training at CAEM, study, article publication, and the like. Many of the most radical group within the army in Phase One of the military regime (1968–75) had a career experience which kept them somewhat apart from the rest of the institution.[15]

The career of General Juan Velasco Alvarado was typical, at least up to the time of his becoming president. Born in Piura in 1910, he was among eleven children of a minor public employee. His family has been described as "working class" and his childhood one of "dignified poverty." In 1929, after attending public primary and sec-ondary schools, he stowed away on a coastal steamer to Lima. Arriving too late for admission to Los Chorrillos (the military acad-emy), he enlisted as a private. The next year he won entrance to the military academy through competitive examination. Graduating at the head of his class, he shunned politics and rose gradually through the ranks, becoming a division general in 1965. His assignments included teaching at the Superior War College and Chorrillos—where he later served as superintendent—and serving as military attache in

France.[16] Velasco was commander in chief of the Army and chairman of the joint command at the time of the coup on October 3, 1968.

BRAZIL

The army is organized in 4 regional commands (headquarters in Rio, São Paulo, Pôrto Alegre, and Recife), plus the Amazon military command (headquarters in Manaus) and the Planalto military command (headquarters in Brasilia), the last administered by a three-star general. Within these 6 areas, 12 military regions are administered by two-star generals. In 1984, the officer corps consisted of 131 generals and 14,152 career officers, thus apportioned:[17]

Rank	1964 (%)	1984 (%)
General	1.0	0.9
Colonel	4.2	3.9
Lieutenant colonel	9.7	10.6
Major	15.7	14.9
Captain	29.9	26.9
First lieutenant	23.1	20.1
Second lieutenant	16.4	22.7

Upon graduation from the Army Military Academy (AMAN), the newly commissioned lieutenant spends approximately ten years in grade before promotion to captain, which is contingent upon successful completion of the Junior Officers' Training School (EsAO). Promotion to major and to colonel is by merit and seniority, with strict minimum and maximum time limits. In 1978 four unified "evaluation criteria" were adopted by the army to assess merit for promotion: (1) moral aptitude; (2) military conduct; (3) military vocation; and (4) good civilian conduct.[18]

The first post-1964 military president, Marshal Humberto Castelo Branco, greatly strengthened the up-or-out promotion/retirement rules in the mid–1960s, thus increasing the president's ability to shape the high command. Promotions through the rank of colonel are nonpolitical and decided by the internal command structure. Promotion to general is political in that the high command develops a three-name list for each vacant slot, and the president then chooses one. Before 1980, an officer could be passed over three times before being forced into retirement; currently, once means retirement.[19]

Obligatory retirement ages are 59 for a colonel and 66 for a four-star general. For a colonel to spend the maximum time allowed as a general (12 years), he would have to be promoted to one-star general at age 54; if he squeezed in under the wire at age 59, he would have but 7 years remaining. Recently, the president has replaced about one-fourth of the high command each year. In five years, President João Batista Figueiredo replaced all 12 members of the high command with personal friends (many were colleagues in the class of 1937 and 2 are his own brothers).[20]

In addition to promoting classmates, friends, and brothers, President Figueiredo used another criterion—membership in the select and powerful "intelligence community." With the promotion of General José Ramos de Castro to the high command in March 1984, 5 of the 12 slots were held by generals who had occupied high positions in the National Information Services (SNI), which Figueiredo directed during the Geisel government (1974–79), prior to becoming president. In addition, Castro was named to command the Second Army in São Paulo.[21]

Normally, officers may spend up to two years in nonmilitary functions in the civilian bureaucracy but must then return to active duty or go into the reserve. Thus, when General Rubén Ludwig was appointed education minister in December 1980, he would have had to resign by December 1982 if he had not gone back on active duty as chief of the president's Military Household in August 1982. Officers who served more than two years with the SNI had been exempted from this requirement, but after 1983 they were forced to choose between return to active duty or retirement. Generals may serve in such "aggregation" functions to age 70.

Obviously, politics is very important in military promotions, especially at the upper levels. However, political manipulation of promotions may undermine the president's support within the officer corps. It is clear that many senior officers between 1961 and 1964 resented President João Goulart's using political criteria excessively for promotion to general.[22] In 1964, 122 officers were immediately expelled from the armed forces.

The attrition of officers is a problem for Brazil in its deepening industrialization. Officers with highly specialized and technical skills, seeing promotions distant and inflation eroding salaries, may find the attractions of private or state enterprise irresistible. The most highly qualified go earlier, leaving their more mediocre colleagues behind. Highly qualified junior officers are recruited to high-paying technical positions, and the colonels pushing age 59 look for a sinecure on the directorate of a state or private enterprise or within the civilian bureaucracy. In 1983, Walder de Goes was able to identify some 8,000 retired military officers occupying civilian positions on the federal level of the public sector (state enterprises and federal bureaucracy).[23] This was one of the main forces holding back the transition to civilian rule in 1984–85.

A new and fully legitimate way qualified officers (both as an "aggregate" function and retirement occupation) utilize skills acquired while on active duty is in the booming Brazilian arms industry.

CHILE

Promotion in the Chilean military services depends on rank in the graduating class (*promoción*) of the service military school, subsequent performance, and successful completion of advanced courses. Officers are continually evaluated by their superiors on their moral, educational, professional, and administrative qualities, and, as described in the previous chapter, they return for additional education and training periodically throughout their careers. Promotions are on an up-or-out basis; for example, after a certain amount of time in grade an officer passed over for promotion is retired. In the case of the army, the top officers are selected at an annual meeting of all the generals, the *junta calificadora*. As a commanding general, President Pinochet is an *ex officio* member of this body, but he normally appears only at the beginning and end of its discussions. Recommendations are made by the vice-commander, currently (1985) Lieutenant General (only Pinochet is a full general) Julio Canessa Robert, in accordance with the president's wishes. Pinochet, as commander, can reject the advice of the generals but normally accepts it. However, unlike his civilian predecessors, he has substantial input in the process as the commanding general and can assure that its outcome is satisfactory. A similar procedure takes place in the other services.

It is possible to retire on a reduced pension after 20 years of service and on full pension after 30 years. (Theoretically the full pension is the equivalent of full pay, but because of the loss of various allowances, it amounts to about 75%.) Officers must retire at the end of 40 years of active service, and the retirement system has enabled President Pinochet to remove potential rivals. He and the other members of the ruling junta are exempt from the requirement of compulsory retirement, as are a few other top generals in key positions, such as General Canessa, and Humberto Gordon, the head of the National Information Center (CNI). There is an increasing age gap between Pinochet and his military associates and the other generals and admirals. In the case of the navy, as of 1985, Admiral Merino, the navy member of the junta, was 15 years senior to the next ranking admiral. While the gap is not as great in the army and air force, General Canessa is said to have been a student of Pinochet when he taught at the *Escuela Militar.*

When a top military commander is retired and another promoted to succeed him, all those with more seniority than the new commander retire. This enabled Pinochet to eliminate a large group of air force generals who supported General Gustavo Leigh when he publicly opposed Pinochet in 1978. Making somewhat dubious use of a 1974 Decree Law governing the "incapacity" of members of the junta to exercise their functions, Pinochet removed Leigh as air force representative on the junta and appointed an officer far down the seniority list as his successor, thus forcing out a number of more senior officers.

There are limits to the president's appointment powers. In 1970, the Statute of Democratic Guarantees—which was added to the 1925 constitution as a condition of Christian Democratic support for the election of Salvador Allende as president in the congressional runoff—provided that promotions and appointments could only be made from graduates of the armed forces' "specialized institutional schools." The 1980 constitution provides that the president may appoint military commanders only from the five officers who are highest in seniority, and they can be removed before the end of their four-year terms only with the consent of the military-dominated National Security Council.[24]

The generals or admirals of each service meet regularly as the Council of Generals or Admirals. In 1985 there were 41 army generals, a considerable increase from the Allende period, which some have attributed to Pinochet's desire to dilute the power of individual generals. The corresponding numbers in the navy and air force were 21 and 22. When Pinochet was under opposition pressure as a result of the monthly demonstrations in 1983 and 1984, he met often with the army Council of Generals for what were billed as briefing sessions but in fact were efforts to assure the generals' continuing support. That support was most important in the first part of 1984 when revelations of Pinochet's involvement in a dubious real-estate transaction raised questions about the army's continuing loyalty.

Leading officers of the services also serve two-year terms on the national defense staff, which draws up war plans and strategy. The chairmanship is rotated among the services.

After retirement top officers often take positions in state agencies or serve as ministers or "delegate-rectors" of the universities. However, they are expected to sever their connections with the military and no longer have any influence within the service. None of the present military commanders participated in the actual plotting of the 1973 coup, and besides the three members who remain from the 1973 junta, retired Rear Admiral Patricio Carvajal, the minister of defense, is the only one of the coup plotters who continues in a significant policy position.

ARGENTINA

Attendance at service colleges is mandatory for an officer's advancement. The senior war colleges are devoted to addressing national problems, and their graduates go on to fill key command and staff positions. Entrance to the National Defense College, the most senior of the war colleges, is highly competitive, and the graduates, many of whom are civilians, are destined to fill high positions in their services and the government. In addition to schooling, however, officers must progress through command assignments to achieve the highest ranks. The regularity of career patterns, with advancement by criteria of merit and seniority, has contrasted with the lack of a well-ordered civil service and has augmented the military scorn for officeholders and patronage-minded politicians. Foreign duty is likely also to be helpful to an officer's career.[25]

Career patterns, however, have been greatly affected by the military's involvement in politics. Selection boards were established in the first year of this century to replace the practice of presidential patronage. However, President Hipólito Yrigoyen (1916–22, 1928–30) meddled extensively in the promotion system, as also did Perón during his first administration, with a resultant degradation of professionalism.[26] In the turbulence after 1943, with recurrent purges, internecine quarrels, and early retirement of many officers, younger men increasingly came to the top. Time-in-grade requirements were reduced; after 1944, a man might become general in 28 years; after 1950, after only 22.[27] Although pensions have been adequate (90% after 30 years), officers facing early retirement commonly seek to prepare a civilian occupation. This has meant for many the procurement of civilian degrees as qualifications, as in accounting or law, while others take a great interest in state-related enterprises.

The future structure of the Argentine military under the civilian government of Raul Alfonsín is unclear at this time. However, the future Argentine military is likely to be smaller, more directed toward external threats than the maintenance of internal order, and more subject to civilian direction.

NOTES

1. Lyle N. McAlister, Anthony P. Maingot, and Robert A. Potash, eds., *The Military in Latin American Sociopolitical Evolution: Four Case Studies* (Washington, D.C.: Center for Research in Social Systems, 1970), p. 225 and discussions with officers.

2. Information from discussions during a year of attendance at the *Escuela Superior de Guerra*.

3. Roderic A. Camp, *Mexico's Leaders, Their Education and Recruitment* (Tucson: University of Arizona Press, 1980), pp. 56–57; McAlister, Maingot, and Potash, *Sociopolitical Evolution*, pp. 223–25.

4. This is a long-standing trend. See Richard Adams, "The Development of the Guatemalan Military," in *Militarism in Developing Countries*, ed. Kenneth Fidel (New Brunswick, N.J.: Transaction Books, 1975), pp. 153–57.

5. Eugene E. Keefe, "National Security," in *Guatemala: A Country Study*, ed. Richard F. Nyrop (Washington, D.C.: U.S. Government Printing Office, 1984), p. 192.

6. Keefe, "National Security," pp. 127–28; Gabriel Aguilera Peralta, "The Militarization of the Guatemalan State," in *Guatemala in Rebellion*, eds. Johnathan L. Fried, Marvin E. Gettleman, Deborah Levenson, and Nancy Peckenham (New York: Grove Press, 1983), pp. 117–18.

7. Adams, "Development of Guatemalan Military," p. 127.

8. Richard F. Nyrop, ed., *Panama: A Country Study* (Washington, D.C.: U.S. Government Printing Office, 1982), p. 190.

9. Steve C. Ropp, *Panamanian Politics: From Guarded Nation to National Guard* (New York: Praeger, 1981), p. 45.

10. Carlos Núñez, "Panama: El reformismo de los militares," *Pensamiento Crítico* 41 (June 1970).

11. Gene E. Bigler: "Professional Soldiers and Restrained Politics in Venezuela," in *New Military Politics in Latin America*, ed. Robert Wesson (New York: Praeger, 1982), p. 180.

12. Rómulo Betancourt, *Venezuela: política y petróleo*, 3rd ed. (Caracas: Editorial Senderos, 1977), p. 551.

13. The idea that military loyalty to the civilian democracy is mainly a function of petrodollar munificence is very widespread and equally exaggerated. The military in Venezuela tends to fare about as well as do other middle-class segments of society. However, personnel expenditures for the Venezuelan military tend to run proportionately below those of other Latin American militaries.

14. Carlos A. Astiz and José Z. García, "The Peruvian Military: Achievement Orientation, Training, and Political Tendencies," *Western Political Quarterly* 25 (December 1972): 672–77.

15. Alfred C. Stepan, *The State and Society: Peru in Comparative Perspective* (Princeton: Princeton University Press, 1978), pp. 145–47.

16. David P. Werlich, *Peru: A Short History* (Carbondale: Southern Illinois University Press, 1978), p. 304.

17. Alfred C. Stepan, *The Military in Politics: Changing Patterns in Brazil* (Princeton: Princeton University Press, 1971), p. 50; *Estado de São Paulo*, January 16, 1982, p. 5.

18. *Jornal do Brasil*, May 26, 1978, p. 6.

19. Robert Wesson and David V. Fleischer, *Brazil in Transition* (New York: Praeger, 1983), p. 126; *Estado de São Paulo*, December 28, 1980, p. 6. Access to the rank of general is also contingent upon successful completion of the ECEME three-year course.

20. Ibid.

21. *Visão*, April 9, 1984, p. 18. Traditionally, a new promotion to the army high command is posted to a bureaucratic or lesser command position before being assigned to command one of the four armies.

22. Stepan, *Military in Politics*, p. 165.

23. Walder de Goes, "O novo papel das forças Armadas do Brasil" (Paper presented at the Seventh Annual Meeting of ANPOCS, Aguas de São Pedro, SP, October 26–28, 1983).

24. *Textos comparados de la constitución política-1980 y de la constitución política-1925.* (Santiago: Instituto de Estudios Generales, 1980), p. 80, art. 93.

25. Alain Rouquié, *Pouvoir militaire et société politique en République Argentine* (Paris: Fondation Nationale des Sciences Politiques, 1978), p. 678.

26. *Area Handbook for Argentina* (Washington, D.C.: U.S. Government Printing Office, 1974), pp. 329–37.

27. Rouquié, *Pouvoir militaire*, p. 631.

4

Foreign Influences

As is to be expected of lesser powers, Latin American armed forces have been considerably shaped by foreign influences. Thus they have until rather recently procured equipment and munitions almost entirely from abroad. But to depend on foreign supplies means to accept foreign personnel to oversee their installation and probably train in their use. It usually also entails sending a mission to the supplying country for instruction, not only in regard to the particular weaponry acquired but probably in military arts generally. Acquisition and use of arms from a particular source, especially a superpower, presumably also create some disposition to adopt the military doctrines of that power and may, moreover, cause a country to either reflect or favor a political philosophy more or less sympathetic to the arms supplier. That arms supplier, since World War II, has almost always been the United States.

Latin American countries have also depended heavily on foreign military expertise. This was true from the days of early professionalization, the latter part of the nineteenth century and later, when missions were solicited to assist in the reorganization and systematization of the armed forces. Foreign missions came mostly from Germany, France, and Britain (the last for the navy). The outcome of World War I reduced the German presence (although it was substantially restored in several countries in the 1920s and 1930s) and brought the United States onto the scene as the largest single source of military training and doctrines. World War II confirmed the results of World War I and made the United States the overwhelmingly dominant foreign influence—through military advisors, training at U.S. schools or with U.S. forces, and, of course, the supply of weaponry. There were U.S. missions in virtually all Latin American capitals, thousands of Latin American officers passed through Fort Bragg, the School of the Americas in Panama, and other institutions, and nearly all of the military equipment of Latin America was procured from the United States.

This situation corresponded to the dominant economic and political position of the United States in the postwar Western world, especially in this hemisphere, and U.S. leadership in the Cold War. It began to change with the weakening of the U.S. position in the Vietnam war, détente, and, in the latter 1970s, U.S. policies of restricting arms sales and deliveries to Latin American nations. The Nixon administration sought to discourage the expenditure on arms of resources badly needed for economic development; subsequently, during the Carter administration, military assistance was suspended to countries violating human rights on a large scale—including Guatemala, El Salvador, Brazil, Chile, Uruguay, and Argentina—either by the U.S. action or by the Latin American country taking the initiative when accused of human rights violations.

The results were foreseeable. Peru, denied modern U.S. planes, bought French Mirage jets and subsequently acquired Soviet tanks, with which came Soviet advisors. Many countries went shopping for arms, to West Germany, Sweden, or elsewhere, as an assertion of independence and because of the difficulty of relying on the United States for their needs. Argentina, Brazil, and to some extent other countries undertook to produce their own armaments to the extent of their technological capabilities. In the case of Brazil, this was rather far; Brazil even became a significant competitor in the world munitions market, offering personnel carriers, light planes, and many other items. Training was not so much diversified as nationalized, with the proliferation of specialized schools. A landmark of declining U.S. influence was the closure in September 1984 (because of failure of negotiations with Panama) of the 38-year-old School of the Americas at Fort Gulick.

Thus the overweening influence of the United States has to a considerable extent crumbled away, partly because of policies of this government but perhaps more because of the evolving world situation, in which U.S. economic preeminence has been much reduced and the disposition of even resolute anticommunists (such as the

Brazilian military leadership) to follow the U.S. lead has much diminished. This does not mean that the United States is not still far ahead of any other country. And the influence of the global adversary has not grown correspondingly; it remains confined to Cuba, latterly Nicaragua, and some continuing presence in Peru. The gainers have been friends and more or less close allies of the United States, including France, Israel, West Germany, Brazil, and other countries within the Latin American community.

While U.S. influence has obviously declined, it is unclear just how weighty any foreign presence really is. Contacts may cause friction as well as a disposition to follow the wishes of the foreigners, and the relationship between arms supply and foreign policy is not clear and direct. Peru seems to have been rather little influenced by the Soviet Union's having become for some years the prime military supplier. It is probable, although not to be taken for granted, that officers with U.S. training are more positively inclined toward this country than are those of a different background. It is disputed whether training in the United States inculcates the attitudes (prevalent among U.S. personnel) of military professionalism and acceptance of civilian authority. It is important that close relations between armed forces at least facilitate information when it may be needed.

MEXICO

Since the Revolution, the Mexican armed forces have been careful to remain free of any substantive foreign influence. This tradition derives from Mexico's highly independent foreign policy. Moreover, the absence of an external security threat has obviated the need for sophisticated armed forces which might require extensive foreign assistance. In the years immediately following the Revolution, the best officers were sent to military schools in Western Europe to obtain experience and knowledge which they could apply to improve the Mexican military education system in Mexico. Gradually, fewer officers went to Western Europe, and most of them began attending schools in the United States.[1]

Since World War II, the U.S. military has exerted more influence on the Mexican armed forces than any other foreign military force. However, while the Mexican economy is inextricably linked to that of the United States, the same cannot be said of its armed forces.

The Mexican Revolution generated a feeling of nationalism within the military. Alfred Stepan emphasizes that it was a military elite that founded Mexico's ruling party in 1929.[2] In the first decades after the Revolution, the armed forces were very careful to avoid U.S. influence, especially during the Cárdenas administration. During World War II, however, the forces of both countries became more closely aligned. After the war, Mexico continued to send troops to the United States for training, and United States influence appeared in the organizational structure of the Mexican forces. Nevertheless they have kept an independent and nationalist spirit.

In 1951, the United States proposed defense assistance pacts to eight Latin American countries including Mexico, offering military assistance if the recipients would assume certain defense responsibilities within the hemisphere. Only Mexico refused. Mexico again demonstrated its military independence in the early 1960s when the Kennedy administration proposed multilateral military action against Cuba.[3] Eric Nordlinger contends that most military officer corps envision themselves as leading nationalists, identifying with the nation.[4] This is true in Mexico not only because of the tradition of the Revolution but also because of anti-Yankee sentiment lingering since the nineteenth century.

U.S. military assistance programs that have been utilized in Latin America since the end of World War II include Military Assistance Program (MAP) grants of arms and equipment, a Foreign Military Sales (FMS) credit program, grants issued for military training provided under the International Military Education and Training Program (IMET), and special funds furnished under the Security Support Assistance program to threatened pro-U.S. governments.[5] Since 1950 Mexico has received no MAP grants and since 1968 has neither sought nor obtained any FMS credit. There has been a concerted effort to avoid taking "handouts" from the United States.[6] In Latin America, only Costa Rica, Haiti, Panama, and El Salvador received less U.S. military assistance than Mexico during the period 1950–78.[7] Mexico has also avoided engaging in any long-term bilateral defense agreements with the United States. Military relations with the United States are characterized as having "remained cordial . . . but . . . more symbolic than substantive."[8]

However, Mexico and Brazil are the only Latin American nations which have a U.S. defense attache with the rank of brigadier general. All the other defense attaches are of the rank of colonel or below.

Moreover, certain benefits accrue to both nations as a result of this relationship. Professional and social contact between the U.S. military attache personnel and Mexican officers occurs on a regular basis. Exchange programs for service personnel of all ranks take place at frequent intervals throughout the year.[9]

In the area of training, the U.S. influence far outweighs that of any other nation. However, from FY 1950–78, only 906 Mexican military personnel attended U.S. military schools in the United States or Panama, and there has been no consistent trend recently.[10] During that period only Costa Rica and Haiti sent fewer.

In the past, Mexican officers have attended military schools in Argentina, Brazil, France, Great Britain, Italy, Peru, and West Germany, but only at the rate of one or two officers a year.[11] Mexico has sent a number of observers and/or training missions to the USSR, Cuba, and other Eastern bloc nations in recent years but has yet to establish formal training agreements with any of these countries. Diversity in foreign training serves to reinforce Mexico's independent posture with regard to military matters.

A final indicator of foreign military influence is arms trade. During the period 1975–79, Mexico imported approximately $70 million worth of arms. The principal suppliers were Great Britain ($40 million), the United States ($10 million), and France ($10 million). The remainder came from countries such as Brazil, Israel, and Spain. Mexico has sought diversification; it anticipates producing more arms domestically and increasing purchases from Latin American suppliers such as Brazil, although arms imports from the United States are expected to increase over the next few years because of Mexico's military modernization program.[12] Geographic proximity also offers training advantages and reduced transportation costs as well as accessibility of spare parts.

GUATEMALA

Although highly nationalistic, the Guatemalan military has always been dependent on foreign weapons, equipment, and training. In 1873, when General Justo Rufino Barrios established the *Escuela Politécnica*, Guatemala's military academy, Spanish officers were brought as faculty.[13] Later, French and Chilean officers served at the Politécnica. From the 1930s on, the United States has been the dominant external influence. In World War II Guatemala promptly declared war on the Axis powers, putting itself in line for U.S. training and lend-lease equipment.

In 1944, junior officers, with wide popular support, toppled the government and inaugurated a controversial ten-year effort to remake Guatemala's social, political, and economic structures. This kept the military in turmoil and introduced deep ideological and generational splits into the officer corps. From 1950–54, the Arbenz administration moved steadily to the left, producing clashes with domestic elites, the United Fruit Company, and the U.S. government. The Guatemalan military was unhappy with many of Jacobo Arbenz Guzmán's policies and at the same time resented U.S. pressures. Events came to a head in 1954, when Arbenz received a boatload of Czechoslovakian arms and reports began to circulate of government plans to create workers' and peasants' militias as a counterbalance to the army. When a small exile force, organized and equipped by the Central Intelligence Agency (CIA), invaded from Honduras, the military refused to defend the government. While not unhappy to see Arbenz fall, many officers strongly resented the dominant role of the U.S. ambassador in selecting a successor government.[14]

Following the fall of the Arbenz government, U.S. ties with Guatemala's military were rapidly increased. In 1955 a military assistance agreement was concluded and U.S. army and air force advisory missions were dispatched to Guatemala. Grant military aid (MAP) and sales of military equipment on a credit basis, which had been halted from 1950–54, were quickly restored.[15] The training of Guatemalan officers and enlisted men at schools in the United States and in the Canal Zone was also resumed. By 1966, $2,526,000 in military equipment had been provided to Guatemala, the highest total for any Central American nation in the 1954–66 period.[16]

In recent years, Guatemala has sought to lessen its dependence on the United States and diversify its sources of arms and training, a trend given impetus by the virtual severance of U.S.-Guatemalan military ties during the Carter administration. From 1980–83, sales totalled only $1.4 million.[17] The Guatemalans have begun efforts to manufacture their own armored cars and have built a small-arms ammunition factory, the latter reportedly with Austrian assistance.[18]

The United States, however, remains the major source of foreign supplies. In January 1983 the Reagan administration, despite strong

Congressional criticism, authorized the sale of $6.4 million in helicopter spare parts, A–37B ejection capsules, radios, and other equipment.[19] The Guatemalan government's fiscal crisis prevented it from taking full advantage of this opportunity, but for FY 1985 the Reagan administration requested $10 million in FMS financing for Guatemala and $300,000 in IMET funds to train 36 Guatemalans in the United States and 108 abroad, largely in Panama.[20]

From 1978 through 1983, almost no Guatemalan officers received such training, resulting in a generational gap which may influence the military in future years. But 1983 witnessed a small-scale resumption of the training of Guatemalan officers in the United States, and approval of the FY 1985 request will restore training programs to near earlier efforts.

An important element of U.S. military influence has been the Military Assistance Group (MAG) stationed in Guatemala. In addition to administering the Security Assistance Programs, the officers and enlisted men assigned to Guatemala have undertaken such diverse tasks as working with the parachute and commando battalions, teaching English to cadets at the Politécnica, and assisting in obtaining translations of U.S. manuals. During the late 1960s, U.S. special forces advisors reportedly played an important role in the successful counterinsurgency campaign in Zacapa. The strength of the MAG reached 29 officers and men, in separate army and air force missions, in 1970.[21] Since then, it has declined until in recent years only 3 officers have been assigned to Guatemala. The U.S. military presence was recently increased by an exchange officer, but his involvement in counterinsurgency training created considerable negative publicity in the United States, underlining the obstacles to closer relations between the United States and the Guatemalan military.

U.S. influence and assistance have played a significant role in modernizing the Guatemalan military. The United States has, among other things, helped to create a central maintenance facility, improve recruit training centers, develop civic action programs, organize the engineer battalion, and create the airborne battalion.[22] Much of the equipment is still of U.S. origin, including most of the artillery, trucks, jeeps, and helicopters; the ten A–37Bs that form the heart of the combat capability of the air force; most of the transports and trainers; almost all of the navy's small complement of ships; and even a few World War II-era tanks.[23]

In recent years, the second most significant external influence has been Israel. Its involvement began to grow in the 1970s with the purchase of ten Aravas for light transport duty with the air force. Even more significant was the decision to adopt the Israeli assault rifle and light machine guns. The disruption in military relations with the United States reportedly led to the introduction of Israeli advisors in small-unit and counterinsurgency tactics. The Israelis also helped develop the Army School for Electronics and Communications, which was opened in the presence of the Israeli ambassador at the end of 1981.[24]

Other sources for equipment and training have been France (three Aérospatiale CM-170R Magisters purchased for the air force in 1971), Belgium (light tanks), Yugoslavia, Italy, Switzerland, and Taiwan. Training has been provided by Taiwan, Italy, France, Germany, Austria, and numerous Latin American nations.[25] The Taiwanese probably make the greatest effort in this area, but the impact of these nations combined does not approach that of the United States or Israel.

A nonfactor in foreign involvement of the Guatemalan military is membership and participation in CONDECA, the Central American Defense Council. With active support from the United States, CONDECA was founded in 1963. Guatemala took an active part, hosting meetings and participating in numerous joint military exercises in the 1960s and 1970s. CONDECA went into a decline in the 1970s and virtually collapsed following the 1979 Nicaraguan revolution. In 1983 efforts began to revive it. Guatemala at first played an active role, and newly installed President Mejía Victores hosted a September organizing meeting.[26] Interest, however, declined afterwards. That the revived CONDECA was aimed against Nicaragua and might involve Guatemalan participation in what would be essentially a U.S. operation aroused nationalist resentment among many officers, already suspicious over reports of U.S. influence in Mejía Victores's rise to power. Guatemala may also have hoped that CONDECA would provide access to U.S. aid, enhance its international image, and even provide support regarding Belize. None of these hopes was realized, and Guatemala lost interest.

PANAMA

In the literature on military organizations, there has been a tendency to equate foreign training with foreign influence and even to quantify this relationship by counting the number of foreign training missions, officers and enlisted men trained by country, and so forth. This perspective is vastly oversimplified. Training missions can certainly imprint organizational structures, operating procedures, and even goals on military institutions. However, high levels of external influence can also cause resentment and engender a search for ways of asserting national autonomy. Military organizations, as demonstrated by the Panamanian example, may resist the imposition of alien value structures.

From 1904 to the present, Panama's police/National Guard/ Defense Forces have relied heavily on the United States for training. Training in police methods was given by U.S. instructors, and a North American served as police commander from 1917–27. With conversion of the police into a National Guard, this trend continued. Large numbers of Panamanian officers and enlisted men participated in the training programs offered by the United States at the U.S. Army School of the Americas (Fort Gulick), the Inter-American Air Force Academy (Albrook Air Force Base), and the Small Craft Instruction and Training School (Rodman Naval Base).

The continuity of U.S. training masks substantial changes that have taken place within the military institution in conjunction with its "renationalization." Particularly important were the changes during the Torrijos years, which made the National Guard more independent of the United States both from an ideological and (to a somewhat lesser degree) technical standpoint. When Omar Torrijos came to power, U.S. intelligence operatives worked in and with the institution. The coup of 1968 had to be kept secret from the United States, and Torrijos moved quickly after taking power to sever these ties. More importantly, he began to create training centers and other units whose aim was not so much to provide narrowly technical skills (still available from the United States) but rather national ideological perspectives. U.S. military personnel stationed in Panama argued that these facilities were not cost-effective, missing the point that cost-effectiveness rationalized and perpetuated U.S. control.

One of these training centers was the Tomás Herrera Military Institute, established in 1974 at Rio Hato. Modelled on a Peruvian military high school, it was designed to supply the National Guard with personnel proficient in developmental fields such as agronomy and to imbue students with a national developmentalist mentality. A secondary function was to provide a corps of cadets who could be rallied should the Torrijistas be challenged either from within the military or without.[27] The other institution (previously discussed) was the National School for Political Capacitation (ESCANAP), which gave the National Guard a means of dissemination of views on national policy.

While levels of U.S. training have remained high, this is somewhat deceptive as an indicator of influence because the Defense Forces have established institutional mechanisms for the development and inculcation of their own nationalist ideas. The Defense Forces rely on the United States only for the more mechanical and technical aspects of training. Furthermore, officer cadets are being trained in the more "independent" academies of Latin America and enter the Defense Forces less influenced by U.S. military doctrine.

In regard to materiel, until 1968 Panama's military equipment was exclusively of U.S. manufacture; but General Torrijos purchased Belgian rifles and machine guns and Israeli submachine guns and mortars.[28] Although there has been continuous pressure for heavier and more advanced equipment, including fighter planes, the United States has effectively argued that these capabilities are unnecessary given the heavy U.S. military presence in the area. Now that the Defense Forces have a responsibility for external defense, the rationale for denying them heavier arms and more sophisticated equipment has become less persuasive.

VENEZUELA

During the nineteenth century, after the war for independence, contact with and influence from foreign militaries was minor and incidental. But foreign military advisors were brought in to assist the major reform of the armed forces (1910–14) undertaken by General Juan Vicente Gómez. Gómez, who was advised by General Francisco Linares Alcantara, the first Venezuelan West Point graduate, recruited a Chilean officer, Colonel Samuel McGill, who had been militarily educated by the first Prussian military mission to that country just after the turn of the century. McGill occupied many posts, from chief of cadet training at the new military academy, to chief of military instruction, to director of the general staff.[29] Over several years of service, he gradually completed the Prussianization of the armed forces. To this date, military cadets and officers still use the goose step. Uniforms and weapons, Prussian ideas on organization, the use of gymnastics training, ceremony, and discipline were incorporated into the Venezuelan army.

Prussian-Chilean influence was not, however, exclusive, since the reform effort opened the armed forces to other outside influences as well. About a dozen officers were sent to military academies in Colombia and Peru before 1920. Several other foreign officers, especially Chileans, were also imported to provide fundamental military training to senior officers and noncommissioned officers (NCOs).

Once the reforms were in place and Gómez was convinced that his forces were invincible, foreign contacts were dropped except for some intermittent assistance from France after World War I. The French assisted in the establishment of the Military Aviation School and Service in 1920 (later sending instructors), supplied aircraft throughout the 1920s, sent a full military mission for a few years, and finally replaced weapons earlier acquired from Prussia. The nadir of foreign training was reached during Gómez's last five years (1931–35), when only a single soldier was sent to the United States to study aerial photography.[30] The rejection of interchanges, including scholarships and missions, seems to have been provoked by repeated conspiratorial incidents by graduates of foreign programs.

General Eleazar López Contreras, who succeeded Gómez in 1936, made a significant effort at military modernization, including technical training, weapons acquisition, and military academy study abroad. A U.S. naval mission arrived in late 1941, after General Isaías Medina Angarita succeeded to the presidency. Medina, a graduate of the first class at the Military Academy under McGill, sent more officers to foreign schools, especially to the Superior War College at Los Chorrillos in Peru. The first contingent in 1942 was an especially ambitious and capable but professionally frustrated group who later became known as the Peruvian generation. Their capacities and professionalism were enhanced by contact with the officers who were carrying out the professional revival in Peru after the debacle of the War of the Pacific (1879–83); but their frustrations mounted after their return to an institution still dominated by old *Gomecistas*, corruption, outdated doctrines, poor organization, low pay, and few chances for promotion.

The Peruvian generation included Marcos Pérez Jiménez, Felipe Llovera Páez, Julio César Vargas, and Martín Márquez Anez. By 1943

all the members of this group were involved in a *logia militar* movement on the Argentine model, known as the Patriotic Military Union
or UPM. A little over two years later the UPM instigated a conspiracy
with the Acción Democrática party (AD) and then overthrew Medina
on October 18, 1945. The officers alleged that their purpose was to
combat incompetence and corruption in the government so that they
would be free to modernize and professionalize the military as they
had seen the Peruvians doing. They brought AD into the plan because they had no wish to govern but wanted to provide a basis for
civilian reform of the regime.

The three years of AD rule from 1945–48 was a time of intense
professional renewal, a large build-up of new materiel, and intense
foreign contacts, especially with the new U.S. mission. The removal
of all officers above the rank of major in November 1945 also allowed
for rapid ascent of the Peruvian generation. In November 1948, most
of the Peruvian generation participated in the overthrow of the AD
government. The new junta was led by still another internationalist
officer, Lieutenant Colonel Carlos Delgado Chalbaud, who, although
not a member of the Peruvian generation, was a French-trained engineer and graduate of St. Cyr and the Fort Leavenworth staff college.

Thus the leadership of the officer corps in the late 1940s was
exposed to more foreign contact than any comparable group of that
time. The praetorianism of some of this group was influenced by their
overseas experience and their interventionist colleagues abroad, but
it seems probable that exposure to a militaristic philosophy merely
accorded with existing predispositions. Similarly, foreign influence,
especially the increasing cooperation with the United States, has also
been suggested as a source of the commitment to democracy expressed by officers at the time; but the proselytizing of AD and the
political atmosphere of the period may have been more significant.[31]

In any event, the new leaders wanted to share their overseas
experience. Only about 50 officers had studied abroad up to 1945,
but dozens were sent from 1946 to 1948 and almost 600 from 1949
to 1957. Of these, about 35% studied in the United States, and
smaller numbers went to Italy, Peru, England, and France. Several
hundred NCOs and ranks were also sent overseas for training for the
first time in the 1950s.

Since the return of civilian rule in 1958, a pattern of high foreign
contact has been maintained, but the predominance of U.S. military
training has definitely increased. The Inter-American Defense System,

especially its War College in Washington, UNITAS fleet exercises, and the School of the Americas in Panama became the more important foreign sources of ideas about military doctrines and missions. U.S. prevalence in overseas training is most apparent in the distribution of officers who took foreign courses, excluding minor cases, from 1960 to 1973, as shown in the following table.

Country	Army	Navy	Air Force	Total
Belgium	60	—	—	60
Brazil	68	5	31	104
France	82	10	21	113
Germany	15	2	3	20
Italy	17	15	6	38
Peru	38	5	4	47
Spain	35	10	—	45
United Kingdom	25	25	43	93
United States (including Canal Zone)	1,011	142	863	2,016
Total	1,351	214	971	2,536

About three-fourths of army training was in U.S. schools, close to two-thirds of naval training, and almost nine-tenths of air force training. Data are not available for the National Guard (FAC), but the officers of that branch received relatively little overseas training until the latter half of the 1970s when rather intensive, large-scale programs for National Guardsmen were developed in Spain. The frequency of overseas training has diminished in recent years with the increase of advanced educational programs in the country. The number of Venezuelan soldiers now trained in the United States has shrunk, and many are paid for by Venezuela. The small U.S. military group in Venezuela is now seen as mainly a support group for the transfer of military hardware. In 1980, 28 army officers and 2 NCOs completed training programs abroad, but 316 officers and about 200 NCOs (including cadets or ranks) completed their courses within the country. Moreover, the quality of the Venezuelan military educational system is such that increasing numbers of foreign students attend courses at the military academies and advanced schools.

Contact with the Inter-American Defense System has been especially significant and somewhat controversial in three ways since the late 1950s. First, the idea of military subordination to civilian democratic authority has been promulgated by the United States through the institutions in this system, but there is some controversy as to how far the United States was responsible for the ideas expressed. Second, while some members of U.S. military missions and Venezuelan leftists felt that U.S. counterinsurgency training was a major factor in defeating the guerrillas of the early 1960s, Venezuelan officers have criticized the program as being inapplicable or ineffective. Thirdly, some Venezuelan officers who studied at the Inter-American Defense College during the late 1950s and early 1960s brought back geopolitical and Cold War ideas; but older officers, to support their geopolitical and national security doctrines, emphasize the Venezuelan experience with guerrillas, border problems with Guyana and Colombia, and Cuban support for subversion.

Another source of foreign military influence is through weapons acquisitions and the training for use and maintenance that may accompany them. Germany and then France dominated weapons sales to Venezuela up to World War II, although purchases from the United States had increased greatly by the 1930s. In the postwar period U.S. predominance in supplies to all Venezuela's service branches reached its peak. By the early 1950s, Venezuelan weapons acquisitions began to be diversified, especially for the air force and navy, with major purchases from the Canadians, British, French, and Italians. The U.S. share was raised by the 1982 sale of F–16s, but the recent devaluation of the bolivar and the continuing use of French armor and Mirage aircraft, Italian frigates, diverse British equipment, and materiel from a variety of other sources will probably help Venezuela maintain a diversified arsenal.

COLOMBIA

The first foreign military mission in Colombia was an unsuccessful French mission in 1895, at a time when foreign military missions (British, French, German, and Italian) were just beginning to be popular in Latin America. A three-man Prussian-trained Chilean military mission invited to Colombia in 1907 was more successful. It oversaw President Rafael Reyes's reform, which inaugurated the modern Colombian armed forces. A second Chilean mission in 1909 assisted the foundation of the War College. Other Chilean missions came in subsequent years. From 1921–24 a French air mission aided in establishing the Colombian air force. There was a Swiss mission from 1924–27 and a German mission from 1929–34. The Colombian navy was established in 1936 along with a naval academy, under the auspices of the army. A British naval mission served in Colombia from 1936 until the end of 1938. The British naval mission left a mark on Colombian navy traditions and uniform insignia that persists to this day.

A Colombian complaint was that these foreign missions, particularly the air missions, attempted to completely reorganize the Colombian military establishment without regard to Colombian problems and to sell military equipment that Colombia did not want. It was in this environment that the United States was invited to send a naval mission, which arrived in 1938, replacing a British mission whose contract was running out. It was supplemented by an air corps mission. The U.S. missions must be termed a success story. Until the late 1920s there were few countries in the Western Hemisphere more hostile to the United States than Colombia, as a result of the way in which Panama gained independence and the Hay-Bunau-Varilla Treaty. In a little more than 20 years, U.S.-Colombian military relations went from decidedly hostile to exceptionally cordial. The U.S. naval mission in Colombia, established in 1938 and still there today, was an important contributing factor.

The initial naval mission, consisting of 8 officers and 13 chief petty officers, established a close relationship with the Colombian navy as well as the Colombian government. Cooperation extended to other areas, such as intelligence cooperation on the eve of and during World War II. An early concern was for Japanese activities on the west coast of Colombia.

U.S. missions were able largely to displace the many German and Italian missions in Latin America prior to the beginning of World War II. With the approach of war, service-to-service talks were conducted in nearly all Latin American countries including Colombia. A U.S. army mission was established in Colombia in 1942. The wartime agreement included access to bases. Colombia maintained internal security and contributed to the convoy effort in the Caribbean. During the Korean War, Colombia was the only Latin American country to send combat troops and warships to Korea—3,000 men (1,000 at a time), a fifth of the army. There was some belief that President Gómez used this tactic to get Liberal officers out of the country. However, these small forces performed well.

Over the years several thousand Colombian military personnel have attended the army School of the Americas and air force and navy schools in Panama. Others have received training in the United States at the Command and Staff Colleges and War Colleges, the Naval Postgraduate School, other graduate schools, and various functional schools related to equipment purchased under the Security and Assistance Program.

In recent decades, the United States has given extensive assistance to the Colombian forces in their effort to repress more or less Communist-led and Cuban-assisted guerrilla movements. U.S. aid was especially prominent in the civic action program of the 1960s, whereby the army sought to undercut the guerrilla movement by conducting literacy campaigns, building schools and clinics, restoring communications, and assisting agriculture.

Contrary to the situation in other Latin American nations, the continuity of military-to-military relations has never been broken. The United States remains the main source of armaments, although Brazil and Argentina have provided some supplies in recent years, including armored vehicles. Aircraft are mostly of U.S. origin, although France and Israel have supplied a few. Colombia has consistently supported hemispheric defense. The navy and air force regularly participate in the annual UNITAS exercises in which units of the U.S. navy along with those of Latin American nations circumnavigate South America, conducting air and naval exercises. Other joint/combined exercises have been aimed at counterinsurgency and infiltration.

PERU

There have been foreign military missions in Peru almost continuously since 1896, when President Nicolás de Pierola invited a French military mission in order to train an army defeated in battle (the War of the Pacific, 1879–83) and torn by internal conflict. The mission stayed until the late 1930s, beginning with the establishment of Peru's first military college for officers in 1896 and forming over the period a truly professional but still interventionist army.[32] The French also established the first Peruvian school of aviation, but they were replaced by an Italian air mission in the 1930s, a U.S. marine training contingent in 1940, and the U.S. air force in 1946. In the 1930s there was a German military mission contracted by President General Oscar R. Benavides (1933–39).[33] While there had been a U.S. naval mission in Callao since 1922, the first U.S. army mission was established in 1945. Since the mid-1970s, the Soviet Union has maintained a substantial military mission in Peru to assist in training and maintenance of Soviet military equipment purchased by Peru beginning in 1973.[34]

Between 1945 and the late 1960s, there were close ties between the Peruvian and the U.S. military establishments. The size of the U.S. military mission varied but peaked in 1966, with 66 officers and enlisted personnel. U.S. military grant assistance to Peru between 1950 and 1955 was third in size in Latin America, totalling $59.3 million, or about 6% of Peru's military expenditures.[35] From 1955–79 all forms of U.S. military aid and sales to Peru came to just over $261 million.[36] Some 49% of all general officers between 1960 and 1965 had received foreign military training, 75% of them in the United States, 30% in France, and 10% in Italy, Great Britain, and Belgium. (The total is more than 100% because some officers received training in more than one foreign country.) Between 1947 and 1967 the United States trained 324 Peruvian officers and 127 enlisted men at the School of the Americas at Fort Gulick in the Panama Canal Zone. Through 1975, the United States trained 2,455 Peruvians there, fifth in number in Latin America, along with 930 in the United States and another 3,349 in Peru itself.[37]

Relations deteriorated in the late 1960s, after the United States rejected Peru's request for F–5 fighters and Peru turned to France for Mirages. When seizures of U.S. fishing boats by Peruvian authorities led to a cutoff in U.S. arms sales, the reduced U.S. military mission (totalling 38) was expelled from Peru in July 1969.

From this date the Peruvian military sought to diversify its sources of military equipment and training. From 1977–81, the number of Peruvian military personnel trained at the School of the Americas declined rapidly from 543 to 14.[38] Through 1979, a total of 780 Peruvian military personnel were trained in the Soviet Union.[39] The Peruvians obtained just over $1 billion in materiel during the period 1974–78: $650 million from the Soviet Union, $90 million from the United States, $70 million from France, $60 million from the Federal Republic of Germany, $40 million from Italy, $10 million from the United Kingdom and $90 million from other countries.[40] This pattern made Peru one of the most diversified countries in Latin

America in terms of foreign sources of arms, as well as by far the largest single importer of arms in all of the Western Hemisphere (accounting for one-fourth of total foreign arms purchases by Latin America in the 1974–78 period).

The impact of foreign training and assistance is difficult to assess. To the degree they help a country to professionalize its armed forces, in the Latin American political context a more professional army is better equipped to become involved in politics when the circumstances require. Both the French military missions of the 1896–1938 period and the U.S. missions of the 1945–69 era contributed to greater, not lesser, military intervention in politics through their improving of the professionalism of the armed forces in general. U.S. training and assistance, it is argued, are "a mechanism for the transfer of organizational technology, which increases the professionalism of the military and increases its involvement in politics."[41]

Another view is that

seen against the background of substantial and improving Peruvian military educations, the assessment of the impact of . . . American training would suggest that it is relatively marginal on most matters of day to day behavior, and that its effects must be sought at the level of technical skills and general values rather than in support of specific U.S. policies or operations. . . . U.S. training, while often producing admiration for many things American, is more likely to provide critics than supporters of U.S. policies toward Latin America.[42]

In partial support of both perspectives, interviews of a small sample of Peruvian officers in 1976 suggest that

United States training appears to be moderately associated with belief in more interventionist role definitions, particularly with the doctrine of "national security and development." However, of the several career characteristics found to be correlated with Peruvian role definitions, U.S. training appears to have less impact than participation in civic action programs or branch of service.[43]

In addition, "most of the Peruvian officers interviewed denied that their U.S. training had influenced their beliefs. . . . Most argued that the vast differences in the two societies made the American irrelevant."[44] Given the presence of over a hundred Soviet military advisors in Peru in recent years and the training of hundreds of

Peruvian military officers and enlisted men in the Soviet Union since 1975, it would probably be possible to make almost precisely the same arguments concerning the rather marginal impact of Soviet training in the 1970s and 1980s as those one makes for the U.S. training of the 1940s through 1960s. With the professionalization of the Peruvian military largely accomplished, the kinds of impacts likely to occur in the future, whatever the source of training and assistance, are likely to affect only the periphery rather than the core of Peruvian military concerns.

BRAZIL

Prior to World War I, German influence was very strong in Brazil, as it was in other South American nations. After the Treaty of Versailles, the French predominated, only to be challenged by the Germans in the mid-1930s. When Brazil broke with the Axis powers in 1942 and sent troops to participate with the U.S. forces in the Italian campaign, foreign influence came to be dominated by the United States until 1977, when President Ernesto Geisel abruptly canceled the 1952 U.S.-Brazilian military agreement. After 1977, the Brazilian military sought diversified foreign contacts, especially in Western Europe (France, Great Britain, Germany, and Italy), but did not totally abandon relations with the United States.

After the Franco-Prussian War and the consolidation of the German national state, the Prussian army became a model for many South American countries. Many junior officers spent two-year periods in Germany from 1900 to 1914, and their new ideas regarding the "modernizing" role of the military and the necessity of a strong centralized government were embodied in the publication *A Defesa Nacional*, which began circulation in October 1913.[45] This influence was intense during the presidency of Marshal Hermes da Fonseca (1910–14). The "Young Turks," as they were called, led a very active campaign for professional improvement of the Brazilian army.

Due to the results of World War I, Brazil requested a French military mission in 1919. A mission of 26 officers, led by General Maurice Gamelin, arrived in 1920. It concentrated its efforts on the technical and intellectual training of junior officers at the recently established Junior Officers' Training School (EsAO) in Rio and on the reorganization of the general staff. This training assisted in the demise of the old military elite and paved the way for the rapid promotion of junior officers after the 1930 revolution.

Many officers thus trained in the 1920s became active in the semifascist *Integralista* movement in the 1930s and mobilized support for the Third Reich. General Goes Monteiro, who had been a model student of the French mission, as chief of Army general staff in 1938 negotiated a five-year U.S. $100 million arms barter deal with Germany. Had not the war broken out the following year, this would have involved a German military mission.[46] The rapid victories of the German war machine in 1939 and the collapse of the western front in 1940 were admired by Brazilian army officers, but there was little carry-over in terms of acceptance of Nazi ideology. Anti-British sentiment was strong for two reasons: (1) British interdiction of German arms shipments to Brazil; and (2) U.S. lend-lease shipments to Britain, which were seen as an impediment to U.S. arms sales to Brazil.

In January 1942, Brazil hosted the Rio Conference of Latin American Nations and used this forum to break formally with the Axis powers in return for U.S. arms sales.[47] This paved the way for the equipping and training of three divisions of the Brazilian Expeditionary Force (FEB) to join with the U.S. Fifth Army campaign in Italy in 1944, and to an intimate relationship lasting 35 years.

After the war, a U.S. military advisory mission was sent to Rio to help in the organization of the Superior War College (ESG). Until 1977 it maintained a liaison officer at the school. In 1952, a formal military agreement was approved by the Brazilian Congress, despite heated nationalistic rhetoric.[48] This agreement provided for sales and transfers of U.S. arms and training for Brazilian officers in the United States. Stepan questions the assumption of U.S. influence over Brazil's adoption of a counterinsurgency ideology, with data showing reduced Brazilian participation at U.S. army schools of this type. Of the 112 Latin American graduates from Fort Bragg, only 2 were Brazilians; and of the 16,343 officers going through the Panama School, only 165 were Brazilians. Master strategist General Golbery do Couto e Silva stated that "the ESG was preoccupied with local and revolutionary warfare in the 1950s, when the U.S. army was essentially worried about nuclear warfare."[49]

However, of the 102 line generals on active duty in January 1964, 28 had attended U.S. military schools; of the 10 line generals in the Humberto Castelo Branco "core group," 8 had had such training.[50] An important connection between senior Brazilian and U.S. officers in the early 1960s was their service together as junior officers in the Italian campaign in 1944. General Vernon Walters, U.S. military attache in Rio de Janeiro from 1962–67, was a key figure in U.S. influence during this period. The basic elements of U.S. influence were the military agreement and the joint Brazilian-U.S. defense commission.

In 1965, the Brazilian army again sent an expeditionary force into a joint operation with the U.S. army, a 1,000-man contingent for the Dominican Republic "peace-keeping" effort. Requests for Brazilian participation in joint operations in the Korean and Vietnam wars were politely declined.

By the early 1970s, U.S. influence over the Brazilian army had waned. More sophisticated weapons were denied, and Brazil turned to Western European suppliers. The military agreement and joint commission were abruptly and unilaterally cancelled by the Geisel government in March 1977 in reaction to U.S. pressures against the 1975 German-Brazilian nuclear agreement and the State Department's report to Congress on the condition of human rights in Brazil. Even the Brazilian navy, which had long participated in joint operations, cooled its relations with the U.S. navy and sought equipment and technology from Great Britain and West Germany. Brazilian officers visiting or in training in the United States were recalled.[51] The Carter government attempted in vain to rally support for its cereals export boycott of the USSR in 1980 by sending a high-ranking general to Brasilia. Similar efforts by General Vernon Walters to win Brazilian participation in a "South Atlantic Treaty Organization," which would include South Africa, also failed.

Following these "low-profile" years from 1977–81, the Reagan government named Rio-born Langhorne Motley ambassador to Brasilia. Motley had served as an air force officer with the general staff of the southern command in the 1960s in Panama and knew some officers personally. His patient efforts of "direct diplomacy" with the military, bypassing normal foreign office channels, coupled with an emergency U.S. treasury "bridge loan" of $1 billion in September 1982 (saving Brazil from technical bankruptcy), improved relations enough to permit the formation of five "joint study groups," including a military study group, during President Reagan's visit to Brazil in November of the same year.

A very general "memorandum of understanding" on possible "discussions of doctrines" and "exchanges of intelligence data" was signed during Secretary of State George Shultz's visit in February 1984. The memo also discussed the possibility of technology transfers to the Brazilian arms industry, to be studied on a case-by-case basis with certain safeguard or reserve clauses against sale to "inconvenient third countries." A formal military agreement, however, was vetoed by Army Minister Walter Pires.[52]

The Brazilian navy was displeased by the U.S. navy's policy of clearing its relations with all South American navies, thus placing Brazil on a par with Paraguay or Bolivia. The only concrete offer in the February 1984 meetings was a pair of old surplus ships, one of which would have to be cannibalized to make the other seaworthy. Instead, the Brazilian navy decided to buy designs and technology for landing ships for $25 million to be built at the navy arsenal in Rio.[53] Relations in this area remain far below their pre-1977 status.

Two final points emphasize continued U.S. influence over Brazilian military strategies as related to foreign policy. First, Brazil assumed the role of "friendly neighbor and tutor" with Surinam, which helped bring the latter "back into South America" and diminished Cuban and Soviet influence. Second, in August 1983, information given by Ambassador Motley to General Medeiros of the National Information Services (SNI) persuaded the Brazilian government to "interdict" and search four Libyan transport planes en route to Central America. Instead of "medical supplies" listed on the cargo manifests, Brazilian Air Force (FAB) officers found light arms, ammunition, and several small aircraft.

British influence with the Brazilian navy was strong prior to World War II and since the mid-1970s has regained some ground lost to the United States. The Falklands/Malvinas crisis put strains on this relationship and that with the FAB. Striving to maintain sympathetic neutrality in support of Argentina, while not offending Britain, the FAB accommodated numerous "forced landings" in Rio and other air fields in Southern Brazil of Royal Air Force (RAF) planes en route to or from the Falkland Islands. The FAB was very interested in the recent EMBRAER sale of 250 Tucano jet trainers to the RAF.

Israel is also influential with a segment of the Brazilian army. This relationship is most intense with officers associated with the intelligence community, who have had training in Israel or been attached to the Brazilian Embassy in Tel Aviv. Given Brazil's dependence on Middle Eastern oil suppliers and the volume of Brazilian exports to this region, the "Israeli connection" is kept very discreet.

Planning and strategy of the Brazilian army are differently influenced by Argentina. Because of geopolitical competition dating from the nineteenth century, Brazil's Third Army has always been heavily garrisoned along the southern border, and arms purchases and technological upgrading have been one of the results of this rivalry. Brazil's nuclear strategy is also linked to Argentina's lead in this area. Brazilian military strategists (especially the air force and navy) were sobered by Argentina's performance during the Falklands/Malvinas episode. Both nations are aware that this rivalry is exploited by First World powers, and thus they have reached, in the areas of nuclear and military technology and economic mutual defense, a level of rapprochement not attained over the last 50 years. Although currently low-key, the Brazilian/Argentine rivalry continues to be projected into relations with the so-called "client states," Bolivia, Paraguay, and Uruguay. Reevaluation of this rapprochement is currently in progress because of the recent regime changes in both Argentina and Brazil.

CHILE

After victory in the War of the Pacific (1879–83), the Chilean government decided to modernize and professionalize military training, and it initiated the first German mission to Latin America. Emil Körner, a Prussian captain, was hired to organize the *Academia de Guerra* (War College or Command and Staff School) and to advise on the improvement of instruction in the *Escuela Militar.* Körner remained in Chile, serving as the chief foreign advisor to the army from 1886 until his retirement in 1910. Under his influence a three-year War College curriculum modelled on the German *Kriegsakademie* was introduced. It achieved such renown that Colombia, Ecuador, El Salvador, and other countries sent officers there at the beginning of the twentieth century. (It is from this period that the practice of goose-stepping at Chilean military parades dates.)

Körner brought a number of European instructors to Chile, most of them German, and Chilean officers pursued advanced courses in Germany. The Chilean navy, on the other hand, looked to Britain for its models and training; and when the Chilean air force was created, it was trained principally by Americans. Thus to this day Chileans say that they have "an American air force, a British navy, and a Prussian army."

Körner was involved directly in Chile's brief civil war in 1891, taking the side of the Congress in its conflict with President José Manuel Balmaceda. When the Congress was victorious, partly due to his efforts, his continuing influence was assured. His students became the middle-level officers who intervened repeatedly in Chilean politics in the 1924–27 period, leading to the emergence of Carlos Ibáñez as plebiscitary president from 1927 until his forced resignation in 1931. While the Chilean army officers' social attitudes do not seem to have been derived from their German-influenced training, it is possible that their impatience with the compromises and corruption of the Parliamentary Republic (1891–1975) stemmed partially from the sense of professional competence and technical superiority that had been imparted by their schooling.[54]

Direct German influence was not as obvious after World War I, but in the 1930s a number of officers went to Germany and Italy for advanced training. Some officers were sympathetic to the Chilean Nazi movement in the late 1930s, and there was a military plot against the Popular Front government in 1939. However, this seems to have been more related to Chile's politically polarized politics and to military opposition to Marxist influence than the result of specific training programs.[55]

There was a pro-German element in Chile during World War II, but there is no evidence that it had strong support among the Chilean military. After World War II, the dominant foreign influence became that of the United States. In 1951 a U.S. military aid program was established and Chileans began to receive training in the Panama Canal Zone and in the United States.

About 7,000 members of the Chilean military have been trained at U.S. facilities since the end of World War II, and it has received about $175 million in aid.[56] Military aid from the United States continued during the Allende period even after most other new loan flows from the United States ceased. Since 1976 there has been a human rights–related prohibition by the U.S. Congress on military aid, training, and sales to Chile. Chile, however, continues to be an active member of the Rio Treaty of Mutual Assistance and participates in annual joint naval maneuvers with the United States off the Chilean coast. Pursuant to the congressional cutoff, the U.S. Military Assistance Group was withdrawn in 1980, but the relations with the U.S. attaches of each of the services remained friendly and cooperative. U.S. training of Chilean officers has ceased, and by 1985 only one member of the Council of Generals had received training in the United States. Resumption of U.S. aid has been conditioned by Congress on presidential certification of improvement in human rights, as well as on Chilean actions to bring to justice the murderers of Orlando Letelier in Washington in September 1976. Chilean officers now go to other countries for training, especially Brazil. The lack of U.S.-manufactured ejection fuel for F-5 fighters and A-37 Cessna trainers has created serious problems for the air force. Human rights questions at times have also created difficulties for arms purchases from Great Britain and Austria.

Even before the U.S. cutoff of military aid, Chile was attempting to diversify its sources of military equipment. The army has tanks from the United States, Israel, and France; the air force has British Hawker Hunters, French Mirage jets, and U.S. F-5s; the navy's ships are principally of U.S. and British manufacture and it has purchased submarines from West Germany. During the Allende period, senior generals went to the Soviet Union to inspect military equipment, but strong opposition within the military prevented any program of military assistance from being initiated.

Other Chilean arms sources include Brazil, Spain, and South Africa (with which exchanges began in 1982). Chile also has its own small but growing arms industry, producing radar systems, anti-aircraft cannon, rocket launchers, armored cars, small ships, and training planes. In 1984 the revelation that Chile was exporting cluster bombs to Iraq caused something of a political scandal. At times the Chilean government has attempted to develop closer relations with the Arab countries, even in one case voting with them on an anti-Israeli resolution in the United Nations. However, the closest military ties continue to be with the United States and Brazil.

ARGENTINA

Argentina as a nation has been heavily influenced by France, Germany, Great Britain, Italy, and the United States. Much of this influence has, of course, carried over to the military. Great Britain exerted a strong influence in Argentina, particularly in the nineteenth century, being heavily involved in the meat-packing industry and in building of railroads. The influence of the United States was also apparent. In addition to the South Atlantic Squadron, which operated in the area, the United States sent consular agents to Argentina even before full diplomatic representation was established, and President Domingo Sarmiento (1868–74) contracted U.S. school teachers to establish an elementary education system patterned after that in the United States.

With the beginning of professionalism of the Argentine military in the Sarmiento presidency and in the wake of the Paraguayan War (1865–70), the Argentine military was equipped with U.S. Remington rifles. The beginnings of U.S. influence were soon superseded, however, by German influence, which had appeared in Chile in the 1880s. However, the prestige of the Chilean military plus the high reputation of the German army after the Franco-Prussian War caused several Latin American countries to seek a German military mission and German equipment. A formal German military mission was established in 1899 by President Julio Roca, partly because of the excellent performance of the Chilean army trained under the Körner mission. Germany became a steady arms supplier, and the Superior War College, founded in 1900, was under German influence from the beginning. This made for a rather awkward situation, with Germany as the major arms supplier to both Argentina and Chile, which at this time were engaged in an arms race and nearly went to war several times over the Andean boundary.[57]

The decision to establish a German military mission was by no means automatic or unanimous. There were great misgivings in Argentina regarding foreign influence. There was also a desire to establish an Italian legion because of the large Italian population; and because of the strong British influence in Argentina, serious consideration was given to a British military mission. The decision for a German military mission allegedly was confirmed by the poor performance of the British army in the Boer War (1899–1902). A British naval mission came at the turn of the century, however, and the navy was generally equipped with British ships (as was Chile's navy).

U.S. naval influence began with the cruise of the Great White Fleet (1907–08), during which some destroyers made a brief stop in Buenos Aires. It was not until the Taft administration, around 1910, that the United States joined the naval arms competition in Latin America. President Taft saw selling arms to Latin America as an opportunity to assist U.S. shipbuilders. Therefore, a roving naval attache was posted in Latin America, and U.S. navy visits were made to several South American countries, including Argentina, Brazil, and

Chile. At this time Brazil was engaged in a major naval modernization program, which Argentina saw as a threat. To counter it, Argentina contracted for two battleships from the United States, which were received in 1914.[58]

During this period the United States also commenced a program of training foreign officers on U.S. navy ships. Argentina took advantage of this program while its battleships were being built. Additionally, Argentina as well as Chile sent naval commissions to the United States. Although the United States did not send advisors to Argentina for several years, in 1914 the precedent for U.S. military missions was set. The U.S. navy provided advisors to the Brazilian Naval War College in that year. This ultimately led to legislation which established U.S. naval missions in Latin America and set the pattern for all U.S. military missions.[59]

At the beginning of World War I, the Argentine army was heavily influenced by Germany, and the navy was essentially British with the beginnings of U.S. influence. Argentina remained neutral, while eight Latin American nations declared war on the Central Powers and four broke diplomatic relations. Although there were enclaves of support for Germany in Argentina, sympathies were mostly for the Allies, particularly France. After the United States entered the war, a U.S. navy task force was based in Brazil to patrol the South Atlantic. One of the tasks of its commander, Admiral Caperton, was to encourage Argentina to join the war on the side of the Allies. Caperton visited Argentina and was cordially received, but President Hipólito Yrigoyen was determined that Argentina would remain neutral.

After World War I, German missions returned to Argentina and an Italian air mission was established. In the 1930s the United States became concerned by Nazi and, to a lesser extent, Italian-fascist influence in Argentina and several other countries of Latin America. To counter this, U.S. military missions were expanded.

In November 1934 three U.S. navy officers were assigned as advisors to the Argentine Naval War College. The mission, whose members operated under renewable one-year contracts, was apparently quite successful. It left Argentina in 1941 but was subsequently reinstated and remained throughout World War II. This modest beginning resulted in a long-term association between the U.S. and Argentine navies. In 1938 an army air corps mission was also established in Argentina.[60]

With the commencement of hostilities in Europe in 1939 and Nazi victories in 1940, preparation for war in the Western Hemisphere was greatly accelerated. The first and second Foreign Ministers' Meetings of Consultation were held in Panama in 1939 and in Havana in 1940. The Panama conference proclaimed neutrality for the Americas and defined a neutrality zone. The Havana conference convened after France fell in 1940 and adopted the Declaration of Reciprocal Assistance and Cooperation for the Defense of the Americas. A major concern was preventing territories in the Americas belonging to occupied European nations from being taken over by the Axis powers. Putting the doctrine of Reciprocal Assistance and Cooperation in military terms, the U.S. military conducted a series of service-to-service talks with Latin American nations between August and October 1940.[61]

Satisfactory bilateral agreements were eventually made with all hemispheric countries except Argentina. Argentina reserved the right to maintain its neutrality and to trade with the Axis powers as well as the Allies in order to maintain a good commercial position in the event the United Kingdom fell. The Argentine delegation felt that the United States would provide sufficient protection if the Western Hemisphere became actively engaged in war. Pro-German feeling in the Argentine officer corps was so strong that the overthrow of President Ramón Castillo in 1943 was motivated in large part by the belief that he wished to align Argentina with the United States.

A U.S. naval force subsequently known as the South Atlantic Force operated out of Brazil, as in World War I. But a source of major concern was the neutrality of Argentina and its tilt toward the Axis powers. There were repeated reports of Argentine and Spanish ships assisting enemy submarines by providing positions of Allied merchant ships. Argentina was also a beehive of espionage activity. Nevertheless, U.S.-Argentine navy-to-navy relations were maintained. The small U.S. naval mission remained at the Argentine Naval War College and nearly 100 Argentine naval personnel were trained in the United States. Further, Argentina was an active member of the Inter-American Defense Board. Unsuccessful efforts to get Argentina to side with the Allies centered on a dispute over the quantity of arms Argentina would receive. The United States sought to make Argentina responsible for the safety of Allied shipping using the Straits of Magellan. Argentina objected that it would be drawn into the war.[62] Prior to the end of the war, Argentina finally broke with the Axis powers.

Following World War II and during the first Perón administration, U.S.-Argentine military-to-military contact was minimal. But there was a great upsurge of U.S. influence in the revulsion against dictatorship after Perón's downfall in 1955. The period 1955–78, especially the period of the Alliance for Progress, was the time of greatest U.S. military influence in Argentina. U.S. missions were invited, and many Argentine military personnel were trained at schools in the United States as well as at the School of the Americas and the Inter-American Air Force Academy in Panama. The Argentine military, especially the navy, became equipped primarily with U.S. equipment. In the earlier part of this period, surplus World War II and Korean War materiel was particularly easy to obtain from the United States. In the later 1960s, as the equipment supplied by the United States became obsolete and as U.S. supplies became scarce due to the Vietnam War, Argentina as well as many other Latin American countries began to look to other sources.

Argentina's return to European weaponry was accelerated during the late 1970s by U.S. restrictions on arms sales because of human rights violations, culminating in the cutoff of all security assistance in 1978. Since the 1960s Argentina had also begun developing its own arms industry, so that by the late 1970s it had an export capability in light armored vehicles and small aircraft. Argentina has produced armaments under both coproduction and licensing arrangements with Germany, Italy, France, and Great Britain (prior to the Falklands/Malvinas War), and it has equipment from all these plus the United States.[63] However, much of the military hardware, such as the Pucara attack aircraft, is of Argentine design.

During the long period of U.S. influence, a system of inter-American military conferences was developed. The Conference of American Armies is held annually, as is the Conference of Chiefs of American Air Forces. The Inter-American Naval Conference is held every two years, and specialized conferences in such areas as communications and intelligence are conducted annually, with Argentina a regular participant.

The United States and Argentina have also participated in several joint naval exercises. The most significant of these have been naval control of shipping exercises and the annual UNITAS exercise. These have been both bilateral and multilateral. Since the late 1970s, Argentina has usually declined to participate, frequently citing maintenance difficulty due to lack of spare parts for its U.S.-supplied ships.

Security of the South Atlantic, a concern for the United States in both world wars, again became a concern in the late 1970s. The combination of key petroleum routes from the Middle East through the South Atlantic, increasing Soviet presence in the South Atlantic, and Cuban presence in Africa were causes for concern for U.S. strategic planners, a concern exacerbated by recognition that the U.S. navy lacked means to protect these sea lines of communication.

At the outset of the Reagan administration a concerted effort was made to recertify Argentina for security assistance. Additionally, a series of service-to-service talks was instituted with Argentina concerning the South Atlantic and other areas. These initiatives were halted as a result of the Falklands/Malvinas War and the major setback in U.S.-Argentine relations. With the advent of the Alfonsín government, Argentina was certified for security assistance and foreign military sales are now being made on a case-by-case basis. But much was lost during the period when security assistance was cut off, and it remains to be seen how much U.S. influence will be restored.

NOTES

1. Center for Advanced International Studies, *The Political and Socio-Economic Role of the Military in Latin America* (Coral Gables: University of Miami, 1972), 3: 128; Edwin Lieuwen, *Arms and Politics in Latin America* (New York: Council on Foreign Relations, 1961), p. 111; Lyle N. McAlister, Anthony P. Maingot, and Robert A. Potash, eds., *The Military in Latin American Socio-political Evolution: Four Case Studies* (Washington, D.C.: Center for Research in Social Systems, 1970), p. 228.

2. Alfred C. Stepan, *The State and Society: Peru in Comparative Perspective* (Princeton: Princeton University Press, 1978), p. 91.

3. Guillermo Boils, *Los militares y la política en México (1915-74)* (Mexico City: Ediciones El Caballito, 1975), pp. 159–60; Edwin Lieuwen, *Mexican Militarism: The Political Rise and Fall of the Revolutionary Army, 1910-1940* (Albuquerque: University of New Mexico Press, 1968), p. 145; Thomas E. Weil, ed., *Area Handbook for Mexico* (Washington, D.C.: U.S. Government Printing Office, 1975), pp. 374–75.

4. Eric A. Nordlinger, *Soldiers in Politics: Military Coups and Governments* (Englewood Cliffs: Prentice Hall, 1977), pp. 65–66.

5. Michael Klare, *Supplying Recession* (New York: The Field Foundation, 1977), p. 31; Lars Schoultz, *Human Rights and the United States Policy Toward Latin America* (Princeton: Princeton University Press, 1981), pp. 211–17.

6. Boils, *Los militares*, p. 163; Judith Alder Hellman, *Mexico in Crisis* (New York: Holmes and Meier, 1978), pp. 127–28.

7. Schoultz, *Human Rights*, p. 215.

8. Center for Advanced International Studies, *Political and Socio-Economic Role*, p. 130.

9. McAlister, Maingot, and Potash, *Sociopolitical Evolution*, pp. 108, 228.

10. Department of Defense Security Assistance Agency (DSAA), *Foreign Military Sales, Foreign Military Constructions Sales and Military Assistance Facts* (Washington, D.C.: Data Management Division, Comptroller, DSAA, 1982), pp. 77-78.

11. McAlister, Maingot, and Potash, *Sociopolitical Evolution*, p. 229.

12. *DMS Market Intelligence Report* (Greenwich: DMS, 1982), Mexico Summary, p. 3.

13. Ernesto Chinchilla Aguilar, *Formación y desarrollo del ejército de Guatemala* (Guatemala: Editorial del Ejército, 1964), pp. 23-29.

14. For details of this period see Richard H. Immerman, *The CIA in Guatemela* (Austin: University of Texas Press, 1982); and Stephen Schlesinger and Stephen Kinser, *Bitter Fruit* (Garden City, N.Y.: Doubleday, 1981).

15. U.S., Congress, House, *Human Rights in Guatemala* (Hearing before the Subcommittee on Human Rights and International Organizations and the Subcommittee on Inter-American Affairs of the Committee on Foreign Affairs, 97th Cong., 1st sess., July 30, 1981), pp. 34-39.

16. Don L. Etchison, *The United States and Militarism in Central America* (New York: Praeger, 1975), pp. 96-98.

17. "Into the Fray: Facts on the U.S. Military in Central America," *The Defense Monitor* 13 (No. 3, 1983): 5.

18. *Defense and Foreign Affairs Daily*, January 12, 1983, p. 1.

19. *Defense and Foreign Affairs Daily*, January 12, 1983, p. 1; John Felton, "Military Sale to Guatemala Draws Criticism," in *Congressional Quarterly Weekly Report* (January 15, 1983): 93.

20. U.S., Department of Defense, *Congressional Presentation: Security Assistance Programs, FY 1985*, pp. 369-71.

21. Gabriel Aguilera Peralta, *La integración militar en Centroamérica*, (n.p.: INCEP, n.d.), p. 39.

22. Brian Jenkins and Céasar Sereseres, "U.S. Military Assistance and the Guatemalan Armed Forces," *Armed Forces and Society* 3 (August 1977): 577.

23. International Institute for Strategic Studies, "The Military Balance, 1983-84," *Air Force Magazine* 66 (December 1983): 53.

24. Eugene E. Keefe, "National Security," in *Guatemala: A Country Study*, ed. Richard F. Nyrop (Washington, D.C.: U.S. Government Printing Office, 1984), p. 193; *Manchester Guardian Weekly*, January 10, 1982; Flora Montealegre and Cynthia Arnson, *Update #1: Background Information on Guatemala, Human Rights and U.S. Military Assistance* (Washington, D.C.: Institute for Policy Studies, 1982), pp. 13-14.

25. Col. Boris Rebbio Porta España, "Educación militar superior en el ejército de Guatemala," *Revista Militar* (Guatemala) (January-June 1977); 10-11; Montealegre and Arnson, *Update #1*, pp. 13-14.

26. Richard Millett, "Praetorians or Patriots? The Central American Military," in *Central America: Anatomy of Conflict*, ed. Robert Leiken (Elmsford, N.Y.: Pergamon Press, 1984), pp. 88–89.

27. Steve C. Ropp, *Panamanian Politics: From Guarded Nation to National Guard* (New York: Praeger, 1982), p. 50.

28. John Keegan, *World Armies* 2nd ed. (Detroit, Mich.: Gale Research Company, 1983), p. 459.

29. Samuel McGill, *Poliantea: memorias del Coronel McGill* (Caracas: Editorial de la Presidencia de la Republica, 1978).

30. Angel Ziems, *El Gomecismo y la formación del ejército nacional* (Caracas: Editorial del Ateneo de Caracas, 1979) is the major general source on the Gómez period.

31. Winfield J. Burggraaff, *The Venezuelan Armed Forces in Politics, 1935–1959* (Columbia: University of Missouri Press, 1972).

32. Frederick M. Nunn, "Professional Militarism in Twentieth Century Peru: Historical and Theoretical Background to the Golpe de Estado of 1968," *Hispanic American Historical Review* 59 (August 1979): 391–418.

33. American University, Foreign Area Studies, *Peru: A Country Study*. (Washington, D.C.: U.S. Government Printing Office, 1981), p. 223; Liisa North, *Civil-Military Relations in Argentina, Chile, and Peru*, Politics of Modernization Series, no. 2 (Berkeley: Institute of International Studies, University of California, 1966), p. 49.

34. U.S., Arms Control and Disarmament Agency (ACDA), *World Military Expenditures and Arms Transfers, 1969–1978*, (Washington, D.C.: ACDA, 1980), p. 162; Central Intelligence Agency (CIA), National Foreign Assessment Center, "Communist Aid Activities in Non-Communist Less Developed Countries, 1979 and 1954–79" (A Research Paper, ER-80-10318U, October 1980), p. 15.

35. Luigi Einaudi, "U.S. Relations with the Peruvian Military," in *U.S. Foreign Policy and Peru*, ed. Daniel A. Sharp (Austin: University of Texas Press, 1972), pp. 38–39.

36. American University, *Peru*, p. 260, Table 12.

37. Einaudi, "U.S. Relations," pp. 44–45; North American Congress on Latin America (NACLA), "U.S. Training Programs for Foreign Military Personnel: The Pentagon's Proteges," *Latin America and Empire Report* 10 (January 1976): 15, 28.

38. U.S. Army School of the Americas (USARSA), "USARSA Graduates," mimeographed (Ft. Gulick: USARSA, 1981).

39. CIA, "Communist Aid Activities," p. 16, Table A4.

40. ACDA, *World Military Expenditures*, p. 162, Table 4.

41. John Samuel Fitch, "The Political Consequences of U.S. Military Assistance to Latin America" (Paper prepared for presentation to the 18th Annual Convention of the International Studies Association, St. Louis, Mo., March 16–20, 1977), p. 1.

42. Einaudi, U.S. Relations," pp. 46–47.

43. William R. Salisbury, "Special Career Experiences and Role Definitions Among Peruvian Officers" (M.A. Thesis, University of Florida, 1977), cited by Fitch, "Political Consequences," p. 10.

44. Fitch, "Political Consequences," p. 34, note 33.

45. Georges-Andre Fiechter, *Brazil since 1964: Modernization under a Military Regime* (New York: Halsted Press, 1975), p. 39; Edmundo Campos Coelho, *Em busca de identidade: o exército e a política na sociedade Brasileira* (Rio de Janeiro: Forense-Universitaria, 1976), pp. 78–79.

46. Frank D. McCann, Jr., *The Brazilian-American Alliance, 1937-1945* (Princeton: Princeton University Press, 1973), pp. 111–13.

47. McCann, *Brazilian-American Alliance*, pp. 253–58.

48. Stepan, *The State and Society*, p. 129; Thomas E. Skidmore, *Politics in Brazil, 1930-1964: An Experiment in Democracy* (New York: Oxford University Press, 1967), pp. 106–7.

49. Cited by Stepan, *The State and Society*, pp. 130–31.

50. Stepan, *The State and Society*, pp. 131, 240.

51. Robert Wesson and David V. Fleischer, *Brazil in Transition*, (New York: Praeger, 1983), pp. 160–61.

52. *Jornal do Brasil*, February 5, 1984, p. 21; February 7, 1984, p. 16; and February 19, 1984, p. 8.

53. Ibid.

54. On the role of foreign military missions in Latin America, see Frederick M. Nunn, *Yesterday's Soldiers* (Lincoln, Neb.: University of Nebraska Press, 1983), as well as Nunn's earlier works on the Chilean military, *The Military in Chilean History* (Albuquerque: University of New Mexico Press, 1976), and *Chilean Politics, 1920-1931: The Honorable Mission of the Armed Forces* (Albuquerque: University of New Mexico Press, 1970).

55. See Alain Joxe, *Las fuerzas armadas en el sistema político de Chile* (Santiago: Editorial Universitaria, 1970) and North, *Civil-Military Relations*.

56. Hugo Fruhling, Carlos Portales, and Augusto Varas, *Estado y fuerzas armadas* (Santiago: FLACSO, 1982), p. 21.

57. Brian Loveman and Thomas M. Davies, Jr., eds., *The Politics of Antipolitics* (Lincoln, Neb.: University of Nebraska Press, 1982), pp. 100–4; Anthony W. Gray, Jr., "Seapower and the Latin American Wars (Unpublished paper, The American University, Washington, D.C., 1972).

58. G. Pope Atkins, "Lecture on German Military Influence in Argentina" (Unpublished paper, The American University, Washington, D.C., November 1974).

59. Anthony W. Gray, Jr., *The Evolution of U.S. Naval Policy in Latin America* (Ann Arbor, Mich: University Microfilms, 1982), p. 42.

60. Gray, *Evolution of U.S. Naval Policy*, pp. 98–99.

61. John Child, *Unequal Alliance: The Inter-American Military System, 1938-1978* (Boulder, Colo.: Westview Press, 1980), pp. 15–20.

62. Gray, *Evolution of U.S. Naval Policy*, pp. 140, 142, 175–99.

63. International Institute of Strategic Studies, "The Military Balance, 1982–1983," *Air Force Magazine* 65 (December 1982): 135.

5

Interservice
Relations

The army is the dominant service in all Latin American countries, primarily because it is the largest but also because it is on the ground. Navies may hold a few bases, and the air force can potentially bomb the presidential palace, but the army controls the capital and the country. Navies and air forces have on occasion been rather influential, particularly in Argentina, Brazil, and Chile, and to a lesser degree in Peru. However, they are commonly called "junior" services and are not in a position to effect a coup; at most they can press the army to act and help insure its success.

Usually the branches work rather closely together. There is a supreme command in the ministry of defense or its equivalent, and probably a joint staff at the top level. However, the services are organized more or less independently, as in the United States, and there may be corresponding friction. In large part, this is typical bureaucratic politics: squabbling over budget shares, who is to get the latest arms, and how the turf is to be divided; and it is probably not much more significant than such friction in other branches of the government. Rivalry may be intense, however; in Brazil a few shots were fired over the control of planes for a carrier in 1964. Moreover, as was shown in the preceding chapter, armies and navies may be subject to different and conflicting foreign influences.

There may also be differences among the services for more basic reasons. The army is the more politically potent, and this is likely to cause resentment in the other services. On the other hand, the navy and air force are inclined to be more elitist. They have more equipment per person, require higher technical standards, spend more time in training, and ordinarily are composed only of volunteers, not conscripts. Career personnel are correspondingly a larger part of the service. It may be also that a larger percentage of naval officers are of upper-class background, and there is more of an aristocratic tradition among naval and air force than army officers, with more social distance between officers and enlisted ranks.

Presumably as a result of such differences, the navy, or at least its hierarchy, has usually been inclined to be more anticommunist or more antipopulist than the army. Repeatedly in Brazil, for example, the navy has taken the lead in pushing the hard line; and in Argentina the navy was in the forefront of the fight against Juan Domingo Perón in 1954 and usually against Peronists subsequently. In Peru, the navy held back from the more radical tendencies of President Velasco Alvarado (1968–75). In Chile, the navy was most determinedly against Salvador Allende in 1973, and it took the initiative in demanding his overthrow.

How costly the differences among the services may be in terms of duplication or inefficiency, we can hardly guess, as these are subjects much less investigated and publicized in Latin America than in the United States. Perhaps the greatest significance of interservice differences is somewhat to diminish the ability of the armed forces to act politically as a solid body.

MEXICO

The Mexican armed forces comprise approximately 95,000 in the army, 24,000 in the navy, and 4,500 in the air force. Paramilitary forces include about 22,000 police and 120,000 rural militia. The president is commander in chief. The army and air force are under the secretary of defense, the navy under the secretary of the navy. The former is more influential approximately in proportion to the size of the force he commands.

In 1939, the marine force was separated from the national defense secretariat and placed under a new ministry of the navy. Both the ministries of national defense and the navy are organized along similar lines, with several military zones or territorial commands, a service staff, and functional bureaus and departments. In 1944, the bureau of military aviation was upgraded to the Mexican air force, but control of the air force remained with the ministry of national defense.[1]

There has been an ongoing struggle by the secretary of defense to unify all three services under one defense ministry, which naturally would be controlled by the secretary of defense, an army general. Political leaders oppose such unification for fear that it would make the secretary of defense too powerful.[2] They have found a natural ally in the navy, which obviously enjoys its autonomy. The air force may be the real loser in the present system, since it is a kind of stepchild to the army. While it is semiautonomous operationally, its budget is ulitmately controlled by the secretary of defense, who shows favoritism toward the army.

The military budget is the chief focus of friction among the services. Until the late 1970s, it was extremely limited (0.7% of the GNP).[3] This created fierce competition for scarce resources, and one service's gain appeared to come at the expense of a competing service. When the modernization program resulted in a larger military budget, competition continued because each service aggressively tried to upgrade its needs. Traditionally, the navy has received proportionately more than the army, to the displeasure of army circles. The final arbiter on budgetary decisions as well as all major decisions dealing with the armed forces is the president, so both secretaries are constantly trying to sway the president on their behalf. Nonetheless, it is difficult to gauge the degree of friction within the upper echelons of command, given the closed nature of the military institution in Mexico. Only those high up in the military chain of command would be privy to these disagreements.

Within the services there exist petty jealousies between different branches, as are not uncommon to military institutions. In the army, the competition is the most intense between the infantry, which is by far the largest sector of the army, and the cavalry, which is considered the elite element. The present secretary of defense and his predecessor were both cavalry officers, and, as a result, the cavalry has been favored over the past few years. This has been especially evident in the recent conversion of all cavalry regiments from horse to mechanized units. Although this was an essential improvement, it was viewed as preferential treatment by officers in other combat arms, who assumed that money allocated toward improvements in the cavalry would mean less money for their own needs.

Similar frictions are common in the navy and air force also. There are differences of opinions and philosophies between naval officers and merchant marine officers as well as between pilots and administrative officers in the air force. However, it is safe to assume that any differences between the secretary of defense and the secretary of the navy would be amicably resolved before either officer would allow these disagreements to harm permanently the institution of the military, the object of first loyalty.

GUATEMALA

The armed forces of Guatemala have about 20,000 in the army and only 960 in the navy, plus 600 in the air force, supported by some 12,000 in the national police, including 2,000 in the treasury police.

The Guatemalan Army Law of December 1983 declares that "The Guatemalan Army is one and indivisible . . . comprised of integrated air, sea and ground forces." This affirms the traditional position of the military, which confines the air and naval arms to the status of subordinate forces within the army. Officers in the other branches, including the military police, virtually never rise above the rank of colonel and are not considered for the key posts of deputy chief of staff, chief of staff, or defense minister. As might be expected, this is the source of some resentment, especially in the air force. Suspicion of air force desires for separate status runs strong among the high command, a suspicion reinforced by the role of the air force in the internal splits and conflicts which wracked the armed forces in the early 1960s.[4] As a result, air force missions, equipment, and ammunition are tightly controlled from above. This contributes to strain and does nothing to stem sentiment within the air force for separate status, but the air force lacks power to force attention to such issues.

There is much less evidence of such friction with the young and weak navy or with the military police. There are also past and potential conflicts with private paramilitary organizations, although these have also often worked closely with the military. The December 1983 Army Law declares that "to organize para-military or militia forces outside the institution is prohibited. The organization of such forces is a punishable act." The degree to which this will be enforced remains to be determined.

PANAMA

Prior to 1983, Panama's air force and navy operated under the jurisdiction of the G–3 for the National Guard and were thus dependencies of it. In 1983 the National Legislative Council created the Defense Forces of the Republic of Panama, strengthening the independent organizational existence of army, navy, and air force units, administered through a joint staff.

The origins of the Panamanian air force can be traced back to 1964 when the National Guard purchased its first airplane (a Cessna 185) from the United States. Omar Torrijos was one of the first National Guard officers to fly in this plane and immediately sensed the advantage of an air arm for both military and political purposes. When Torrijos came to power, the Panamanian Air Force (FAP) was established, and the general used FAP aircraft to build political support in the countryside and neutralize the influence of the urban commercial elite.

The first generation of FAP officers included many pilots who did not receive their flight training from a military academy. In the initial group of 23, there were 2 graduates of the Mexican military academy and 3 of the Argentine academy.[5] During the 1970s, air force officers were subject to the same rotation policies as other members of the National Guard. There seems to have been a conscious effort to ensure that a separate service mentality and bonds of loyalty did not emerge among air force personnel. Nonetheless, there are strong suggestions of the gradual emergence of a truly independent branch with its own general staff and political outlook. First, the air force officer corps grew rapidly under Torrijos from 23 in 1969 to 60 in 1978. Second, both the air force's commanding officer and new pilots entering service (particularly from the Argentine military academy) were trained as fighter pilots. At some future time, the air force will demand fighter planes, perhaps creating a rift with other branches.

The Panamanian navy was formed at the same time as the air force, as a separate Department of Marine Operations (*Departamento de Operaciones Marinas*). The commander held the same rank as the commander of the air force (major) and graduated from naval training school in Mexico. There are presently a dozen officers on naval assignment who received training in Peru, Mexico, and Argentina. The navy cannot be considered comparable to the air force as a potentially powerful branch. It engages primarily in coastal patrol and has little political potential. Most of the enlisted personnel come from the merchant marine school that serves Panama's large flag-of-convenience fleet.

In the short run, tensions within the Defense Forces are likely to relate to differences between officers recruited from the ranks and more recent graduates of Latin American military academies, who view the traditional police functions of the Forces as beneath their dignity. With such a large contingent of "police officers" still remaining in the organization, the academy-trained army, air force, and navy officers probably have more in common than they have dividing them. However, there is a continuing trend toward strengthening of military components at the expense of police units. The academy-trained officers will soon (if they have not already) completely establish their hegemony, and at that time feuds over force structure, budgetary allocations, and the like will probably break out among them.

VENEZUELA

The major organizational reforms of the Venezuelan armed forces after the return of civilian rule in 1958 were designed to eliminate army predominance over other branches. Measures taken included restructuring the general staff into a joint general staff; putting cadet training under the control of the separate branches; starting a new academy for the National Guard (FAC); terminating the system of two years of joint instruction for all the services (known as the Basic School); formalizing command and educational autonomy for the branches; and promoting more officers from outside the army to the posts of minister of defense, inspector general, and chief of the joint general staff.[6] The reason was, at least in part, that army predominance was seen as the major source of military conspiracies. But these measures, although justified at the time on these grounds—the almost exclusive army origins of coup attempts up to 1957 were well known—in reality were probably a product of navy and air force resentment over the army officers' role in the Pérez Jiménez regime; and the sudden prominence of Admiral Wolfgang Larrazábal, president of the junta, and Air Force General Castro León, minister of defense, along with the prominence of officers who accompanied them after Pérez Jiménez fell, did not help to diminish such resentment.

Up to 1958 and since then to a lesser extent, the dominance of the army within the armed forces has been more a product of size, location, tradition, and so on than of explicit attempts by that branch to subordinate the others. When Juan Vincente Gómez came to power in 1908, he had an army background, the navy was minuscule, and the other services were nonexistent. He built up the navy somewhat, although the dry docks constructed for it were more often used late in his regime to build armored cars than to work on ships. He also established an air service in 1920, but it remained part of the army, as was the case in most militaries of the 1930s and 1940s.

Presidents Eleazar López Contreras (1936–41) and Isaías Medina Angarita (1941–45) were also army men, but the first also established (1936–37) the National Guard or Fuerzas Armadas de Cooperación (FAC), and both greatly expanded the other services. López also eliminated the *Sagradas* (holy ones), a special police unit within the army made up of loyalists from Gómez's home state of Tachira who had terrorized the military and civilian population. By creating the National Guard as a paramilitary force and attaching it to the Ministry of Interior Relations, López removed the police and civil security functions from the armed forces. He also emphasized the specific defense functions of the branches, but army (and a few navy) officers still occupied the non-flying command positions in the air force, which lacked an academy for other than flight training.

During the period of vigorous professionalization from 1945–48, the air force gained further autonomy. Its own officers were put in command; and complete military instruction was given by its own academy until about 1953, when the Basic School took over the first two years of training for all the branches. The National Guard was converted formally into the FAC, placed under the Ministry of War Defense—as the War Ministry was renamed—and given paramilitary duties in both defense and police work; but the police function itself was the primary responsibility of the Interior Ministry. Carlos Delgado Chalbaud, who served as defense minister, and Marcos Pérez Jiménez, the chief of the general staff, centralized the military at this time; but they did so in order to professionalize all the armed forces and not to subordinate the junior branches.[7]

Army officers achieved more prominence (serving as ministers, governors, and so on) during the Pérez Jiménez regime than they had had since the 1930s, but this was because they had been the dictator's cronies. There was no favoritism for the army. The navy got a fleet of destroyers and other ships, and the air force got squadrons of the latest jets and other aircraft, while the army was subordinated, along with the other branches, to the new *Seguridad Nacional* or National Security (SN), which operated from the Interior Ministry under the dictator's civilian crony, Pedro Estrada. With over 5,000 men by 1957, the SN, in the tradition of the Sagradas, had become a nonuniformed, terroristic paramilitary force about half as large as the army and larger than the FAC.

The idea of the prominence of the army as maker of coups should have been dispelled by the role of air force and naval officers and units in the various coup attempts, from the air force rising of January 1, 1958 to the naval and marine revolts of several years later. Once the various branches had attained a size large enough to encourage personal ambition and political involvement, adventurism was about as frequent in one branch as another.

Relations between the branches seem to have been good during the democratic period. There is much camaraderie between officers of the different branches who started reaching the highest ranking posts a few years ago—the classes of 1955 to 1960—because they were together in the Basic School. Furthermore, officers seem to form quite cordial relations with mates from other branches in special courses and schools (Command and Staff College, the War College, and so on) and in many assignments (such as the Presidential Military House) that require interservice collaboration. It is also increasingly common to have one or two colleagues from other branches (and a few foreigners) in courses in the advanced command schools of each branch. In addition, the services borrow ideas and innovations freely from one another.

Rivalry between the services could be stimulated by fiscal, materiel, or other favoritism for one branch or another. Any difficulties of this nature that may have occurred during recent years have not found their way into the public domain, but there have been at least superficial grounds for resentment. For instance, the army's share of the total armed forces budget dropped from 27 to 19% from 1971–74, while the air force experienced almost the reverse. There have also been periods in which one or another service was favored in new hardware: the navy got six frigates during the late 1970s and early 1980s and the air force has been getting its F–16s, but the FAC and army have received nothing comparable for over a decade. Similarly, there is a fairly stable tendency for the shares of the budget to follow the rank order of the sizes of the branches. Thus the army, with about 40,000 men, gets the largest budget; the FAC, which is only slightly larger than the navy (15,000 in comparison with 13,000), comes next, and then the navy; and the air force, with only about 6,000 effectives, gets the least money. However, the air force received over Bs. 14,000 per airman, more than four times the army's Bs. 3,000 per soldier.

Informal observation suggests that the major problem of internal discord within the armed forces arises less from interservice rivalry than from generational differences, contrasting levels of professional dedication, and varying degrees of politicization and partisan loyalty. The generation gap in the Venezuelan armed forces is not predominantly an age issue but is more the product of different experiences that age cohorts have had and what is viewed by some officers as a resulting qualitative difference. Officers who entered the academy from about 1950 to 1957 did so at a time of relatively high military prestige. However, the prestige of the military was greatly reduced by the popular revolt against Pérez Jiménez and civilian repudiation of the numerous coup attempts from 1958 to 1963. The quality of cadet classes which entered the academies from 1959 to about 1966 was much lower than that of previous classes, and the classes were much smaller as well. The military triumph over the guerrillas and the achievement of university-level status and quality by the academies restored the appeal of a military career; cadet classes from about 1970 improved greatly in quality and numbers. The result has been growing generational consciousness within the officer ranks.

The issue of professionalism in the military is rarely discussed openly with outsiders, but there is ample reason for concern. More scandals involving officer corruption, drug trafficking, congressional inquiries, and so on have come to light in recent years than at any time under the democracy.[8] Officers seem increasingly to be distinguishing between the more and less professionally dedicated of their peers and sorting themselves out informally into groups along these lines. Such behavior, along with generational differences, also has been associated with various political movements in the military in the past, such as the Patriotic Military Union (UPM), several conspiracies in 1958-59, and so on. And while there is no evidence that there is any more partisan behavior than before (see Chapter 7), there are some signs that the perception of partisan political behavior in the ranks is adding to the concern over corruption by officers.

Thus there is the potential for reinforcing cleavages that could raise the level of conflict and potentially involve the military in politics.

COLOMBIA

The army consists of approximately 57,000 personnel (including 28,000 conscripts) as of 1983. It has headquarters in Bogota but is divided into ten regional brigades and one training brigade. It also has approximately 70,000 reservists.[9] The superiority of the army derives from its size, its location, and its tradition.

The navy consists of approximately 10,000 personnel (including 3,000 marines). The main elements of the Colombian fleet are based at Cartagena, which is the principal naval base and the headquarters of the fleet commander, although the commander of the navy and his staff are based in Bogota. Ships include German submarines, Italian midget submarines, destroyers of U.S. and Swedish origin, and coastal and riverine patrol craft. Colombia is also buying modern corvette-class ships from Germany.

The air force, which has grown from small beginnings in the 1920s to approximately 6,000 personnel, is also headquartered in Bogota with bases throughout the country. The air force is equipped with 28 combat aircraft and 10 armed helicopters, with additional aircraft on order. Aircraft types include Mirages, AT–33s, several types of helicopters, C–130 and other transport aircraft, and training aircraft.[10]

The 50,000-man National Police also comes under the Ministry of Defense and under certain circumstances comes under the control of the armed forces. The National Police equipment includes 30 helicopters and 9 Coast Guard craft. The army gets the lion's share of the budget and is by far the dominant service. The country is organized into military zones, nearly all commanded by army officers; the coastal zone, centered in the department of Atlántico, and the department of Amazonas are commanded by navy admirals. Much of the internal security of the jungle regions and the river systems is entrusted to the navy.

Because of a limited budget, the military has maintenance problems. The navy and air force have particularly suffered as a result of their proportionally small share of the budget. The crises in the past have also hampered military operations, due to fuel shortages and the high cost of fuel. Stringency naturally increases interservice rivalries. However, these rivalries are ameliorated by the fact that officers of all services attend the General Staff Course at the Colombian War College when they are in the grade of major or lieutenant commander.

The minister of defense is not a commander but an administrator, a senior army officer supervising the three services. The president exercises control of the armed forces through the commanding general of the armed forces, who is, like the minister, an army general. The commanding general is assisted by a chief of staff who heads the joint general staff, located in Bogota. This staff is organized into five sections: D1–Personnel, D2–Intelligence, D3–Operations, D4–Logistics, and D5–Civil Concerns. The commanding general of the armed forces exercises command over all three services. The president is also advised by the Supreme Council of National Defense (including ministers of defense, interior, foreign affairs, and finance) and by a High Military Council. The three services are rather closely integrated under the general leadership of the army. In the antiguerrilla effort, the chief business of the armed forces in recent years, the navy and air force have operated under army direction.[11]

PERU

The most recent figures available show an army 75,000 strong, a navy of 20,500, and an air force of 40,000, the total officers presumably coming to approximately 13,550. Of these, 7,500 correspond to the army, the largest and most politically active of the three services.

The army, as the dominant branch of the armed forces, consumes the most resources, dominates in the military decision-making process, and has been historically the most politically active service. Of the 1979 military budget for personnel costs, 44% went to the army, as compared with 31% for the navy and 25% for the air force.[12] Both the army and the air force have received extensive Soviet military assistance since 1973, with substantial budgetary implications. The navy has also undergone remodernization, but not with Soviet equipment. It has received several new submarines from Germany, along with frigates and other ships from Italy in the late 1970s and early 1980s. Total military expenditures as a percentage of central government expenditures were estimated at 26.5% in 1978.[13] This was quite high by Third World standards and suggests that all the services were substantially remodernizing their forces and equipment, even in the face of growing economic difficulties. Hence the three services agreed on the basic need to borrow substantial amounts of money (over $1 billion in 1974–78 alone) for importing military equipment.

Class differences among the three services have already been noted, along with the substantial immigrant background among the air force officers. There also appear to be many family ties across as well as within the services. At least 35% of the brigadier generals in active service in 1971 had brothers who were or had been officers in some branch of the Peruvian armed forces.[14] Thus the understandable differences in perspective and outlook among the armed forces, caused by varying class backgrounds and distinctive aspects of service training, are subsumed to a degree by family ties, general agreement on the need to modernize the armed forces, and various formal arrangements for intermingling of the services, as in the Center for Higher Military Studies (CAEM).

The joint command illustrates the commingling. Set up in 1957, it advises the president on military matters, monitors national intelligence reports, and supervises the operation of CAEM. It consists of the chiefs of staff of the army, navy, and air force and their assistants, and its presidency rotates annually among the three services.

In relation to the political role of the armed forces, the dominance of the army is apparent. With the exception of Admiral Lizardo Montero in 1881–82, officers holding the presidency (52 of 78 presidents) have been from the army only. But the political activities of the army have been couched in recent years in terms of unity of the forces. The 1962–63 military government was at least formally an all-service junta, even though the senior army officer was the "first among equals." General Juan Velasco Alvarado, four other generals, and four colonels (all from the army) planned and executed the 1968 overthrow of the Belaunde government. The conspirators initially bypassed several senior army officers and the leadership of the navy and the air force. A desire to preserve the unity of the armed forces induced these bypassed elements to participate in the "institutional government."[15] But differences surfaced from time to time, usually in terms of a conservative/progressive division, which placed most of the more conservative navy men on the outs with the more radical-reformist army, even as they found allies among highly placed individuals of the army and air force.[16]

Another aspect of intermilitary differences is the role of the 25,000-strong Civil Guard. It declared a strike for higher wages in

February of 1975, resulting in the first modern example of one armed service fighting another—the army battling and defeating the guard in Lima. This crisis contributed to the collapse of the Velasco government in August and its smooth replacement through what turned out to be a conservative coup led by General Francisco Morales Bermúdez. A similar strike in 1982 by the Civil Guard was settled quickly by the civilian government, who simply raised the police force's wages to levels equivalent to military pay (a boost of some 66% on the average).

BRAZIL

The army totals about 183,000, the navy 47,000, and the air force 92,000, supplemented by paramilitary organizations including some 185,000. The three branches are quite separate but integrated in four arenas: the Armed Forces General Staff (EMFA), the National Security Council (CSN), the Military Cabinet of the President (*Casa Militar*), and the Armed Forces High Command (ACFA).

The EMFA is the most important arena in terms of interpreting interservice views about policy. Directly responsible to the president and chaired on a rotating basis by a four-star officer who has ministerial standing, the EMFA's main role is planning and coordination, while the ACFA deals more with day-to-day problems. The EMFA chief has authority to call meetings of the Council of Chiefs of Staff (CONCEM).[17]

The ACFA is composed of the ministers of the three branches, their chiefs of staff and the EMFA chief. It concentrates on policy problems of general interest to the three services. The chief of the Military Cabinet, the president's institutional link to the three branches, coordinates their policy inputs to the president.

Up to the Paraguayan War (1865–70), the navy was the emperor's favorite service; but since then the army has been by far the senior of the three branches, both in terms of men under arms and tradition of political involvement. During the First Republic (1889–1930), three army generals occupied the presidency, and all five presidents during the 1964–84 period were generals. During the Medici government a naval officer, Admiral Augusto Rademaker Grunewald, was recruited as vice-president. Active duty and reserve officers occupying positions in the direct and indirect federal administration have overwhelmingly been from the army. Perhaps this is why the junior services were more emphatic in their support for political liberalization and a return to a civilian political regime under the rule of law in 1984.

Historically, there have been important interservice differences. The new republic had barely gotten off to a shaky start when the navy rebelled against army domination of the presidency since 1889, calling for a return to a constitutional monarchy. The army was forced to request aid from the civilian politicians, and, in the process, *paulista* political leader Prudente de Morais ascended to the presidency.

The navy has long been aristocratic in its recruitment of officers, who have tended to be of North European extraction. In the post-1945 period, the newly created air force tended to be the most vociferously anticommunist of the three branches and to be associated with the conservative, neo-liberal UDN political party. On the other hand, the army, being the largest branch, tends to represent a much broader spectrum of socioeconomic and ethnic backgrounds as well as ideological and political beliefs.

The first significant split between the three branches after 1945 occurred prior to and during the chaos following Getulio Vargas's suicide in August 1954. The air force had taken the lead in the campaign for Vargas's ouster. On August 5, a gunman eventually linked to the presidential guard attempted to assassinate Deputy Carlos Lacerda, an archenemy of Vargas; but his bodyguard, Air Force Major Rubens Vaz, was killed instead. The air force began its own inquiry, and on August 22 a group of air force officers issued a manifesto calling for the president's resignation. This pressure from the air force mobilized navy support, which proved too much for the army. A majority of generals joined in, and two days later the president shot himself.[18]

In November 1955, there was a more intense air force-navy versus army split regarding the legitimacy of PSD-PTB coalition's victory in the presidential elections the month before and the impending inauguration of President-elect Juscelino Kubitschek in January 1956. The Kubitschek-Goulart alliance was seen by the 1954 conspirators as a return to power of the Vargas clique, and, with interim President Carlos Luz, they began plotting a divide-and-conquer strategy toward the army. Army Minister Henrique T. Lott learned of the conspiracy and was able to unite the army behind the "legalist" concept of obeying the constitution. In a swift preemptive coup, Lott deposed the interim president, who was duly impeached by the Congress and replaced by the Senate president, a Kubitschek loyalist. Navy and air force ministers denounced Lott's action as "illegal and subversive," and the conspirators fled to a rebel cruiser, the *Tamandaré*, in Rio's Guanabara Bay, and escaped to open sea. The rebels' plan to set up a government in São Paulo was thwarted by Governor Jânio Quadros, who refused to allow the *Tamandaré* to dock at the port of Santos.

Kubitschek suffered minor air force revolts in 1956 and 1959, where young rebel officers took control of some remote bases in an effort to spark a chain reaction of uprisings at coastal installations. Both incidents were quickly crushed, and the rebels received amnesty.[19]

A year later, in December 1956, the air force and navy became embroiled in a conflict which dragged on for eight years. Kubitschek purchased a surplus British aircraft carrier, which was refitted and christened the *Minas Gerais.* A feud developed over whose planes were to land on the ship's flight decks, the air force pointing out that the navy had no suitable planes.[20] The matter reached a climax in late 1964 under President Castelo Branco, who reputedly favored a unification of the three branches under a Ministry of Defense. Junior air force officers machine-gunned a navy helicopter, forcing the resignation of Air Minister Nelson Freire. In January 1965 the president decreed a solution, specifically delineating lines of authority between the two branches. The navy turned its planes over to the air force, which in turn transferred its antisubmarine helicopters to the navy. Neither branch was entirely satisfied.

The crisis of October 1965 that nearly removed Castelo Branco from office was partially based on an interservice split. Army hardliners led by General Albuquerque Lima and naval officers were organizing a coup which was thwarted by forceful intervention by Army Minister Artur de Costa e Silva. This forced the president to deepen the military regime with the assertion of dictatorial power. It also secured the army minister's position as successor.

The *Minas Gerais* question having been resolved only two years before, the new President Costa e Silva met some problems in choosing his military ministers. He chose Admiral Rademaker, well-known for his anti–air force sentiments; but his nomination of Air Brigadier Sousa e Melo (the son of an admiral) balanced this somewhat.

During the first two military governments a basic question of doctrine and strategy further divided the army and navy: whether to emphasize internal security and counterinsurgency or defense from extracontinental attack. Seeing its role and influence declining in the late 1960s, the navy attempted to refocus strategy on external defense.

The next round of interservice conflict occurred in August and September of 1969, during the succession negotiations following the incapacitation of President Costa e Silva. The civilian vice-president, Pedro Aleixo, was set aside, and the three service ministers assumed the government as a junta. There were differences regarding the general political philosophy of the interim government and the succession process. Admiral Rademaker and Air Brigadier Sousa e Melo took very hard-line positions, as opposed to the more moderate position of Army Minister Lyra Tavares. Both the navy and the air force were unhappy with the predominant role of the army during the first five years of military government and by army domination of the 1969 succession process. When Emilio Médici was finally chosen as a compromise candidate, he immediately named Admiral Rademaker as his vice-president and thus soothed the interservice conflict.

During both the Medici and Geisel presidencies, interservice frictions increased in the intelligence area. Although the National Information Services (SNI) had become the "national service," each branch maintained its own intelligence unit: army (CIEX), navy (CENIMAR), and air force (CISA). These three branch intelligence services became very jealous of each other's functions and competencies, to the point that each was closely watched by the SNI.[21]

The three service branches at times have had differences of opinion regarding foreign policy. In 1976, the Geisel government's recognition of the Cuban-backed Angolan regime was not well received by the navy and air force, nor was the decision by both the Geisel and Figueiredo governments not to participate in a South Atlantic Treaty Organization with South Africa. During the Falkland/Malvinas crisis, the air force and navy were more sympathetic to the British, because of pending negotiations of sales by EMBRAER to the Royal Air Force (RAF) and technology transfers to the Brazilian navy. The air force initially hindered negotiations with Libya in 1983 regarding the latter's four transport planes, impounded in Recife and Manaus and found to be carrying arms bound for Central America.

The 1984–85 presidential succession again polarized the services in a manner similar to 1955 and 1969 (army versus air force/navy) but in a reverse ideological connotation. Navy and air force officers were now overwhelmingly in favor of a return to the barracks, and internal survey research showed a majority to have been in favor of the civilian vice-president Aureliano Chaves as presidential aspirant in early 1984. These positions cost Navy Minister Maximiano da Fonseca his job in March 1984 and threatened the position of Air Minister Delio Jardim de Mattos several times. The air force and navy saw a return to civilian rule as a way out from 20 years of domination by the army, a means of increasing their appropriations, and a method of accelerating their ambitious reequipment programs. Key elements in the army high command, on the other hand, were very reluctant to relinquish power and appeared genuinely suspicious of civilian politicians taking command of the nation.

CHILE

In the Chilean armed forces, the junior services are relatively large in relation to the army. The navy and air force commanders have had significant influence in the post-1973 junta; however, the army, because of its greater size and presence throughout the nation, is clearly the most powerful branch. General Augusto Pinochet Ugarte was able to use this fact to establish his predominance over the junta in the first months after the coup, despite some initial discussion of the possibility of rotation of the presidency among the services. The navy, which controls the Valparaiso area and, to a lesser extent, the area around Concepción, has been less enthusiastic about the laissez-faire economic policies of the civilians in the Finance Ministry, preferring more state control over the economy. The air force has been effectively limited as a critic since the confrontation between Pinochet and General Leigh and his service supporters in mid-1978, while the national police have never been considered as having an important role in national decision making, partly because of social differences in what is still a very class-conscious society.

Cabinet ministry responsibilities were initially allocated to the different services. Each member of the junta in theory supervised several ministries, but in fact the ministers reported individually or in related groups directly to President Pinochet, and decisions were made by him. Thus the increasing personal domination of government policy by Pinochet prevented the development of feudal baronies by one or another service. Since the entry into force of the new constitution in March 1981, the members of the junta have concentrated on the preparation and evaluation of legislation in their respective areas rather than focusing on day-to-day policy.

Between 1974 and 1977 an independent center of power developed in the National Intelligence Directorate (DINA) under General Manuel Contreras. However, when Pinochet was under U.S. pressure as a result of the investigation of the Letelier murder, he removed Contreras and reorganized the DINA as the National Information Center (CNI), under a general who was a trusted confidant with more limited powers. The CNI, which is composed mainly of military men, continues to fight subversion and antigovernment activities, but it is more closely subordinated to Pinochet than was its predecessor. The question of the relation of the CNI to the Chilean legal system, especially to the courts and constitution, has become increasingly controversial.

ARGENTINA

At the end of the military government in 1983 the armed forces included: army, 125,000 (90,000 conscripts); navy, 36,000 (18,000 conscripts); and air force, 19,500 (10,000 conscripts). As in other Latin American countries, the army has traditionally been the dominant service, and the majority of the top positions in the joint military establishment have been occupied by army officers. The services are rather independent, however. With the modernization of the Argentine military at the beginning of the century, a modified German general staff system was established, but the joint staff system, as it has evolved, is ineffective, and the services do not work together as a whole. The minister of defense has always been an army officer, but this office has usually been weak.

During the period of the last military government, the joint service chiefs formed a military junta and chose the president from among the members. The president ruled at the pleasure of the junta, serving more or less as chairman of a board of directors. Presidents Juan Videla and Roberto Viola both relinquished their positions as commander of the army upon assuming the presidency. The system worked well from the standpoint of providing a system of checks and balances on the president. When General Leopoldo Galtieri became president in 1981, however, he retained his position as commander of the army.

The armed forces of Argentina have had more than the usual interservice and intraservice rivalries. These have been particularly strong in the past, especially in the army between infantry and cavalry, and between the aristocratic navy and the middle-class army. There have been strong ideological and political differences. During World War I, the German-trained army was pro-German, and the British-trained navy was pro-Allied, while the government was neutral. The navy has usually been the most "liberal" or constitutionalist of the services, while the air force has been the most nationalistic. The navy never supported Juan Domingo Perón and was neglected by him until very late. It attempted to overthrow him in June 1955, and it led the rebellion of September 1955. During following years, when the issue of accommodation with Peronism or struggle against it dominated Argentine politics, the navy was in the forefront of the irreconcilables.

After 1976, under the junta, the navy and air force had a relatively greater share of influence. This was to a great degree dictated by the need to work together during troubled times, as in the fight against subversion, in which the navy and air force played major roles along with the army. Admiral Eduardo Massera, who commanded the Argentine navy in the late 1970s, was particularly influential in national security policy. He was instrumental in developing Argentine strategy during the Beagle Channel dispute with Chile, which nearly erupted into war in 1978. Navy Commander Admiral Jorge Isaac Anaya was the driving force behind the decision to invade the Falklands/Malvinas.

As a result of that war, the army and navy leadership was discredited. The air force, whose performance in the war was best, emerged with the least criticism. In the wake of the war all of the services purged their key leadership; even the commandant of the National Defense College was removed. Bitterness was expressed by many air force officers, particularly toward the navy. It was felt that the air force had borne a disproportionate share of the load and that the navy had dragged them into the war but had not provided enough surface support. The same criticism was also leveled by the air force against the navy concerning the 1978 Beagle Channel crisis. In March 1985, President Raul Alfonsín named Air Force Brigadier Teodoro Waldner as head of the joint chiefs of staff, a position traditionally occupied by an army general, thereby exacerbating interservice rivalries.[22]

Major changes took place with the advent of the Alfonsín government in the areas of civilian control over the military and reorganization of the joint staff establishment. A civilian became minister of defense, and his position has been significantly strengthened. Many other key positions in the defense establishment are now occupied by civilians. A major problem, however, is the lack of a trained civilian defense bureaucracy. To leave behind a long tradition of semiautonomy of the armed services cannot be easy.

NOTES

1. Lyle N. McAlister, Anthony P. Maingot, and Robert A. Potash, eds., *The Military in Latin American Sociopolitical Evolution: Four Case Studies* (Washington, D.C.: Center for Research in Social Systems, 1970), p. 213; Edwin Lieuwen, *Mexican Militarism: The Political Rise and Fall of the Revolutionary Army, 1910-1940* (Albuquerque: University of New Mexico Press, 1968), p. 120.

2. Discussions with officers at the *Escuela Superior de Guerra*.

3. International Institute for Strategic Studies, *The Military Balance, 1978-1979* (London: Adlard and Son, Bartholomew Press, 1978), p. 68.

4. Richard Adams, "The Development of the Guatemalan Military," in *Militarism in Developing Countries*, ed. Kenneth Fidel (New Brunswick, N.J.: Transaction Books, 1975), p. 135.

5. Renato Pereira, *Panama: fuerzas armadas y política* (Panama: Ediciones Nueva Universidad, 1979), p. 151.

6. Gene E. Bigler, "Armed Forces Professionalization and the Emergence of Civilian Control over the Military in Venezuela," mimeo (Carcacas: Instituto de Estudios Superiores de Administración, 1975).

7. Winfield J. Burggraaff, *The Venezuelan Armed Forces in Politics, 1935-1959* (Columbia: University of Missouri Press, 1972), pp. 81-82.

8. In June and July 1984, a subcommittee of the Chamber of Deputies conducted an investigation that involved three ex-ministers of defense.

9. International Institute for Strategic Studies, "The Military Balance, 1982-1983," *Air Force Magazine* 65 (December 1982): 137.

10. Ibid.

11. Gustavo Gallón Girardo, *La república de las armas* (Bogota Centro de Investigación y Educación Popular, 1981), p. 35.

12. American University, Foreign Area Studies, *Peru: A Country Study* (Washington, D.C.: U.S. Government Printing Office, 1981), p. 223.

13. U.S. Arms Control and Disarmament Agency (ACDA). *World Military Expenditures and Arms Transfers, 1969-1978* (Washington, D.C.: ACDA, 1980), p. 63.

14. Carlos A. Astiz and José Z. García, "The Peruvian Military: Achievement Orientation, Training, and Political Tendencies," *Western Political Quarterly* 25 (December 1972): 671-72.

15. David P. Werlich, *Peru: A Short History* (Carbondale: Southern Illinois University Press, 1978), p. 305.

16. Liisa North and Tanya Korovkin, *The Peruvian Revolution and the Officers in Power, 1967–1976*, Occasional Monograph Series, no. 15 (Montreal: Centre for Developing-Area Studies, McGill University, 1981); Alfred C. Stepan, *The State and Society: Peru in Comparative Perspective* (Princeton: Princeton University Press, 1978).

17. Riordan Roett, "The Political Future of Brazil," in *The Future of Brazil*, ed. W. H. Overholt (Boulder, Colo.: Westview Press, 1978), p. 75.

18. Thomas E. Skidmore, *Politics in Brazil* (New York: Oxford University Press, 1966), pp. 140–41; Peter Flynn, *Brazil: A Political Analysis* (Boulder, Colo.: Westview Press, 1979), pp. 169–71.

19. Flynn, *Brazil*, p. 193.

20. Skidmore, *Politics in Brazil*, p. 171. Kubitschek's detractors hold that the purchase was a deliberate ploy to divide and distract these two junior branches, which had been conspirators in 1955.

21. Ana Lagoa, *SNI: como nasceu, como funciona* (São Paulo: Editora Brasiliense, 1983), p. 35.

22. *Christian Science Monitor*, March 13, 1985, p. 12.

6

Ideology and
Doctrine

In the language of the military, indoctrination is an approximate synonym for instruction; and the armed forces, built around schools· of various levels, almost inevitably give a good deal of attention to the imparting of values and philosophy as guides to action and rationalizations of the demands the forces lay on their people.

Military ideology has various aspects. Pride in the service and its traditions, especially its wars, is perhaps universally cultivated. For example, the War of the Pacific figures largely in the education of Peruvian cadets. It is not to be expected that any military organization should be modest about its past and present merits. Organizational pride of the national forces is inseparable, of course, from national pride and patriotism. The backbone of military ideology is, however, (except in Marxist-Leninist states) adherence to the military system itself, to its hierarchy and institutional integrity and well-being. This is of the essence; it is hardly to be denied that the greatest driving force of military politics is the self-interest of the organization, both materially (pay, benefits, and so on) and organizationally (fear of competition or of threats to the hierarchy).

Because of their devotion to the status and order of the institution, the armed forces are basically conservative; that is, they do not seek any upheaval of the basic power relationships (favorable to themselves) in society. They may become more or less allied with an oligarchy (as has usually been the case in Central America, for example), not only because they stand for order and discipline but also because they, or at least a few of their number, profit thereby, perhaps illicitly. They may be reformist because they see an inequitable socioeconomic order that weakens the nation through low productivity and the armed forces through the shortcomings of the uneducated and undernourished recruits. But they do not propose to give power to any new political forces.

The armed forces also seek to fix the role of the nation in world affairs and establish the military as the arm of the national will. These goals have encouraged the study of geopolitics, the projection of force abroad, which has been an academic specialty perhaps more in Latin America than anywhere else since the fall of the Third Reich. During the Cold War, various Latin American militaries assumed the mission of combatting communism at home and in the world; this ethos has remained strong until recently, especially in Central America and in the Southern Cone. In Brazil, anticommunism tended to give way to Brazilian *grandeza* in the early 1970s, and the main task of the armed forces shifted from antisubversion to national development until the military undertook to retreat from rulership in the late 1970s.

The broader purpose of the armed forces has generally been stated in terms of security, which has usually meant protection against considerable dangers of internal disorder rather than either protection from unlikely external attack or the attainment of unrealistic goals of national expansion. Security obviously means much more than keeping the guns ready; it rests on national strength, which requires social harmony and economic development. Hence, especially in the countries with more sophisticated higher training for officers, a doctrine of national security leads naturally to a doctrine of security and development. This has been most strongly the case in Brazil and Peru, where the military has not only undertaken civilian developmental projects (civic action) but has also assumed responsibility for guidance of the nation in the absence—as the officers have seen it—of competent civilian leadership.

The relevance of ideology is obviously greatest when the generals are in power and have to define their mission. Ideology then acts as something of a moralizer, giving (or presuming to give) purpose to the regime of force. The ideology is then elitist, sanctioning the government of the elect (or self-elected), as in "guided democracy," until the nation is sufficiently matured to permit full electoral democracy. This is the essence of Brazil's "Security and Development" doctrine.

If the military retreats from its wielding of power, this rationale ceases to be relevant. The opposite and less self-serving ideology is the acceptance of civilian supremacy under constitutional procedures as legitimated by free elections. The military generally swears to uphold the constitution, and officers have often cultivated an image of themselves as defenders of its sanctity. This may, of course, become a rationale for the overthrow of a president deemed to be in contempt of the constitution, such as was given for the ousting of João Goulart in Brazil in 1964 or Salvador Allende in Chile in 1973.

The armed forces may thus at one time regard themselves as called upon to guide the nation, making law by their fiat; at another time they may envision themselves as obligated to serve civilian leaders, while protecting the nation and preserving the established legal order. A nation's conversion to democracy has to be accompanied by a reversal of military ideology, as in Brazil, Peru, or Venezuela; and the democracy can be secure only so long as the armed forces support such a reversal, from the education of cadets through the highest war college.

MEXICO

A handsome volume on the history of the Mexican army published by the National Defense Secretariat describes the army as a genuinely popular product of a revolutionary movement that put an end to a long-standing unjust social order and illegitimate government.[1] As Samuel Huntington has suggested, the Mexican Revolution provided a "unifying social myth" that legitimized the political system that ultimately developed and flourished in the wake of the massive bloodshed of the Revolution.[2]

The present political system, unlike any before it, has been able to check militarism in Mexico and subordinate the energies of the military to the overall purposes of the state. The military as an institution has been subsumed by the political system that emanated from the Revolution. Therefore, the ideology of the armed forces is in many ways the ideology of the political system, since both had their origins in the Revolution; and both institutions are now integral parts of the Revolution mythology. It is the military's responsibility to guarantee the continuance of the political and economic system founded on the principles of the constitution of 1917.

The Defense Secretariat history also characterizes the Mexican military as a determining factor in the nation's peaceful development since the Revolution. The nation's general tranquility and stability derive from the military presence and fortitude exhibited over the past 50 years. The military, as an institutional pillar of the Revolutionary system, has further distinguished itself by its professional and apolitical nature. The military concerns itself primarily with defending national sovereignty and guaranteeing internal security and stability, which in turn enhances national development. The military firmly asserts that is is not a political actor.[3]

Officers envision themselves not only as guardians of the Revolutionary heritage but also as active participants in the accomplishment of the goals of the Revolution. In this regard, civic action has been a principal part of the military's overall mission, enhancing its image as "servant of the people."[4] Over the years, this image of a benign army serving the people has become part of the military ideology in Mexico.

The Mexican military has had a tradition of civic action since the end of the Revolution. In the early 1920s, the army participated in such tasks as building roads, constructing irrigation projects, and repairing railroad and telegraph lines. By 1926, civic action missions were incorporated into the newly created Organic Law of the Army, which legalized the army's organization, mission, and relationship to the state.[5] During the 1940s and 1950s, the depoliticization of the armed forces was accompanied by increased emphasis on their involvement with civic duties. To date, the military has performed this role very effectively, especially in remote rural areas where it has demonstrated both the power and usefulness of the Mexican system.

The effects of Mexico's noninterventionist foreign policy have carried over into the military. Although staunchly anticommunist, the military has adopted a basically defensive philosophy. It has been cautious to avoid even remote association with U.S. military objectives in the hemisphere. In deference to the ideology which evolved from the Revolution of 1910, the Mexican armed forces oppose any form of military intervention and would never interfere with what they perceived to be a social revolution taking place in another country.

Ideology is inculcated through a socialization process beginning the first day a cadet enters the military academy. It continues and is reinforced after commissioning by instruction at the various service schools, by the content of the many military journals and publications, by the influence of military ceremonies and addresses by military leaders, and, finally, by constant association with fellow officers. As Lyle McAlister observed, "universal military values . . . are given a peculiarly Mexican flavor, by associating them with glorious episodes in the nation's and the army's past."[6]

Questions have often arisen concerning the military attitude toward democracy. Civilians run the government, and the military plays a subordinate role within that government. Mexican officers readily acknowledge the difference between the Mexican system and democracy in the United States. They justify these differences by citing the cultural and economic differences between both countries but emphasize that the Mexican system has served their country well for over 50 years. They perceive their government as being democratic, especially when compared to the predominantly authoritarian and exclusionary political systems of their Latin neighbors.

The Mexican military's ideology overlaps with that of the ruling PRI party, which has a monopoly on ideology in addition to its monopoly on political power. The military supports the system established by the constitution of 1917, in which the PRI serves a vital role. The fact that the president authorizes military pay raises and allows the military to maintain a prominent role in the country reinforces the military's commitment to the PRI. Nonetheless, officers prefer to characterize themselves as apolitical. Most are careful to state that the military supports not the PRI but the constitution.

While the constitution of 1917 assigned the armed forces the responsibility of defending the sovereignty and independence of the country, maintaining its constitution and laws, and preserving its internal stability, it is the last responsibility that has received most of the military's attention over the last few decades. The most visible evidence of this commitment is found in the positioning of troops throughout the country. Approximately 40% of the army forces are located in the general vicinity of Mexico City and neighboring Puebla in order to cope with possible internal security problems in the Mexican heartland. There are no significant concentrations along the nation's land and sea borders.[7]

U.S. influence is considerable with regard to the content of doctrine, despite the independence of the Mexican military from U.S. policies. Mexican armed forces utilize U.S. military texts and training materials, and U.S. military tactical doctrine is taught in all military schools. The doctrine is often adapted to meet the Mexican capabilities, but care is taken not to modify the basic precepts. The military has also made improvements in training programs by the introduction of war gaming exercises, adapted from U.S. models, into some of the advanced military schools.

GUATEMALA

The 1983 Army Law declares that the army is the chief institution responsible for national independence, sovereignty, territorial integrity, and honor. This formulation, which appeared in earlier statutes, demonstrates the very high view that the military has of its own place within the state.[8] It does not regard itself as subordinate or even equal to any civilian political authority. At the least, it possesses, and believes itself entitled to exercise, a veto power over all basic governmental decisions regarding national security, as well as military matters such as budget, promotions, and discipline.

Guatemala's military is steeped in the tradition of the *fuero militar*, the colonial legal system which gave the military immunity from civil justice and established it as virtually a state within a state. Guatemalan officers are not tried by civil courts, and there have been virtually no cases of internal military justice being administered for offenses against civilians. The officer corps has also enjoyed traditional immunity from most taxes and customs duties and is not even subject to civil suits for debts or damages.

Since 1954 anticommunism has been a basic part of the army's ideology. Much emphasis is placed upon the foreign origins and anti-religious nature of communism, thereby appealing to both nationalist and religious sentiments. Definitions of communism and subversion, however, are usually vague, enabling the high command to define as communist anyone who threatens the status quo or the power and privileges of the military or who questions current government policies.

The principle of hierarchy has reasserted itself strongly since the fall of Ríos Montt in 1983. A major factor in his ouster was the resentment felt by senior officers over what were perceived as violations of this principle under his government. The chief infraction was, of course, the placing of junior officers in high positions, a practice that has now ended. Emphasis is placed upon the chain of command, with power concentrated at the top. The high command has been narrowed to the chief of state, the defense minister, and the chief of staff, who exercise ultimate control over promotions, assignments, operations, and budget. This emphasis on hierarchy has produced resentment and cynicism among many junior officers, but for the moment they seem powerless to change things.

Military indoctrination is heavily influenced by U.S. doctrine, with some adaptations based on Guatemalan experience. Israeli advice in counterinsurgency has also had some influence on doctrine. Much of the basic literature, however, remains simply Spanish translations of U.S. army documents and manuals.

PANAMA

Ideological development in the armed forces since the establishment of the republic has been conditioned by a number of factors, most importantly the functions that military men have historically been called upon to perform and the perspectives of key officers. From the 1920s through the 1950s, the institution did not really have an ideology but a mentality, an outlook that perhaps bore closer resemblance to that of the Chicago police than to other Latin American armies. This police mentality can be characterized as inherently conservative in relation to potential social turbulence and unrest. Yet the police were "sons of the people," blacks and mulattos whose outlook was also somewhat populist. Colonel José Antonio Remón successfully tapped these wellsprings of populist sentiment in his rise to power during the early 1950s.

In the Cold War, the National Guard took on a developmentalist coloration in keeping with the mentality of the Alliance for Progress. The armed forces were to be both the guarantors of national security and the instrument of economic change. Omar Torrijos and the small coterie of officers supporting him (especially Manuel Antonio Noriega and Roberto Díaz Herrera) were the major expositors of this developmental philosophy and created the National School for Political Capacitation (ESCANAP) for its propagation within the guard. It should be noted that this new mentality did not displace the old one but rather was superimposed upon it. Torrijos and his fellow developmentalists held the high ground within the guard, but they were always constrained by other members of the general staff such as

Rubén Darío Paredes, who espoused the visceral conservatism of the older generation.[9]

During the latter Torrijos years, a new mentality seems to have emerged from the increasing military professionalism of the guard and the influx of officers trained in Latin American academies. While developmentalism still occupies an important position within the hierarchy of institutional values, increasing importance has been placed on narrower defense interests. Clear doctrinal statements are still relatively rare, but those which have been made suggest that the Defense Forces are increasingly concerned with two national security scenarios: (1) a threat to the nation from the turmoil in Central America, and (2) fear that the United States theoretically might under certain circumstances attempt to secure militarily the canal area, invading Panama in the process.

These scenarios obviously pull officers in different directions with regard to geostrategic decisions such as the choice of international allies. Those who believe that the first scenario is the more likely stress the increased importance of good relations with the United States and of regional alliances such as the Central American Defense Council (CONDECA). Those who emphasize the latter call for strengthened relations with Third World powers. In spite of such differences of opinion, the Defense Forces are increasingly concerned with their role as the guarantor of national security.

It would be going too far to suggest that members of the Defense Forces currently share a common ideological outlook. The officer corps is composed of political factions and generations that have different professional training, threat perceptions, and mentalities. The many "police officers" who were promoted from the ranks continue to represent the conservative populist tradition associated with Remón. Yet in spite of their numbers, their second-class professional status means that they have not occupied the top positions and thus have not left their definitive ideological stamp on the military. General Torrijos willed his developmental legacy to Manuel Antonio Noriega and Roberto Díaz Herrera, both of whom graduated from the Peruvian military academy and can be characterized as Peruvianists in the tradition of Juan Velasco Alvarado. They will probably continue to espouse this developmental approach, gradually yielding to the more militarily professional instincts of their junior colleagues.

VENEZUELA

In the tradition of *caudillo* politics, the Venezuelan military until very recently required very little doctrine or ideology to define their mission. They used force to advance their caudillo's power, coercively controlled the populace, and defended against rival caudillos. Impassioned discourse, inflammatory editorializing, and a host of different colored factions within the political parties were all part of the free-for-alls of coalition formation and defense, but ideology per se was dismissed cynically by even the most partisan intellectuals. It was only after the control of the Gómez dictatorship had been consolidated (toward the end of the second decade of this century) that panegyrics to the dictatorship by Laureano Vallenilla Lanz began to form a doctrine of power.

Vallenilla's positivistic justification for the Gómez dictatorship also elaborated a role for the armed forces as the "necessary gendarme" for the maintenance of order, imposing a civilizing, democratic caesar. Very little advancement in military doctrine and ideology was made for the next two decades until the return of the Peruvian generation (see Chapter 4) initiated the drive for modernization and efforts to create a doctrine of military professionalism.

However, in the period of partisan conflict during Acción Democrática (AD) rule from 1945 to 1948, the politicization of every aspect of society threatened the very purpose for which the young officers had ushered AD into power in 1945. Thus the *golpe* of 1948 temporarily returned the military to their responsibility as needed gendarme of society and also forced them to find a way to reconcile this duty with their increasing commitment to professionalism.

A major architect of the new ideology was the son of Gómez's apologist, and the program that the young Vallenilla Lanz helped design to justify the Pérez Jiménez dictatorship was eventually dubbed the New National Ideal.[10] The major tenets of the new doctrine married the commitments of the earlier periods to civilizing order and technocratic professionalism and added some important elements from more recent experience. First, the increased nationalism that political liberalization had engendered earlier in the 1940s was retained.[11] Second, the geopolitical lessons about anticommunism and national defense in a hemispheric context that Venezuelan officers had learned in their new professional studies were incorporated. Third, the same technocratic modernization that the officers had already undertaken in the military was extended to the rest of society by creating a series of basic industrial enterprises (steel, hydroelectricity, petrochemicals, and so on) directly under military control (see also Chapter 7). The creation of the paramilitary Seguridad Nacional (SN) under the Interior Ministry at least relieved the armed forces of some of the repressive duties that they had served under earlier dictators.

With the return of democracy in 1958, some of the more perspicacious democratic leaders seem to have recognized the promise of the Pérez Jiménez approach to national development; they retained and even heightened some of its basic elements, especially nationalism, the commitment to technocracy, the leading role of the state in the economy, and the acceptance of a hemispheric geopolitical position, even though they vehemently repudiated the dictator. However, when the civil authorities replaced the armed forces at the center of the system, the utility of the ideology for the definition of the military's mission was put in doubt. Besides, the destruction of the dictator's security apparatus, the SN, and the creation of a system of civil liberties required that every vestige of caesarism should also be eliminated. How then define the role of the armed forces in the new democracy?

The answer came slowly, especially during the unstable years and repeated coup attempts of the late 1950s and early 1960s. The principal developers were Presidents Rómulo Betancourt, Raul Leoni, and Rafael Caldera. First, they nurtured the military commitment to technocracy, modernization, and professionalism. Second, they upheld the nationalistic commitment which had been growing during the 1950s by asserting more control over foreign investment, abetting the repatriation of many unwanted immigrants, reactivating several long-dormant border disputes, and expanding border development activities.[12] Third, they maintained the hemispheric geopolitical commitment but added to it both a commitment to democracy—the Betancourt doctrine—and a revival of the Bolivarian vision of hemispheric integration.[13]

The mission that would distinguish the Venezuelan armed forces doctrine from the corporatist, modernizing military nationalisms of bureaucratic-authoritarian regimes was supplied primarily by Fidel Castro. From the beginning of the guerrilla violence in Venezuela, Betancourt succeeded in defining the origin of the threat as external and inspired by a hostile foreign power. Venezuela was not under siege because underdevelopment, exploitation at the hands of international capitalism, and poverty were creating a revolutionary consciousness; rather, a band of fervent partisans committed to an alien (and antinationalistic) ideology were getting weapons, training, and financing from an enemy abroad. Thus Betancourt described the strategy of the hypothetical communist enemy, which was already an accepted part of the geopolitical doctrine, in a way that justified keeping the military out of politics.

This approach to counterinsurgency provided the basis for one of the most professional and successful antiguerrilla campaigns in the hemisphere and also facilitated pacification and the reincorporation of guerrillas into the system. The most important thing that guerrilla groups had to do to rehabilitate themselves was to cut their ties to the international conspiracy. A few officers have taken exception to this outcome over the years, but the consistency of the doctrine and the rapid disciplining of the objectors have brought acceptance of a system in which over a dozen ex-guerrillas have participated even in congressional oversight of the armed forces.

The partially geopolitical doctrine that worked so well in the 1960s was created in an ideological and institutional framework that allows for its evolution as conditions change. The constitution of 1961, Article 132, formally adds an important new ideological ingredient to the professional, nationalistic, developmental, hemispheric, and anticommunist framework that was carried over from earlier years. This addition is the concept of the virtue of the military's nonpolitical societal role (nonvoting, nonoffice-holding, nonpartisan, and nondeliberative) under civilian guidance and in support of democracy (assuring orderly elections and the sovereignty of elected authority). Acceptance of this fundamental of civil-military ideology is still somewhat uncertain in Venezuela, but it has been greatly reinforced by the evolution of the doctrine of military mission. The ideological framework of military mission allows for a definition of threat that focuses military attention on border regions, the oil industry, and communist subversion of the neighboring states where Venezuela's interests are at stake (territorial nationalism in Guyana and hemispheric and Bolivarian nationalism in Grenada and Central America).

The redefinition of military ideology must be carried over to professional reorientation—restructuring the army back and forth from a small-unit, mobile counterinsurgency force to a large-unit organization capable of incorporating large numbers of reserves on short notice in order to respond to border threats. Civilian political authority, to increase its acceptability, must participate in the process which leads to major decisions, and it must provide support for both continued professionalization and appropriate changes. These changes involve both an alteration in national security policy and a major overhaul of the conscription system (see Chapter 1).

New institutions to manage doctrine and ideology and civilian-military interaction had to be created. The two major innovations have been the National Security and Defense Council (CONASEDE) and the Institute for Higher Studies of National Defense (IAEDN), the former founded in 1976 and the latter in 1971. The system no longer relies on just the sagacity of democratic presidents but includes two high-level institutions involving cabinet-level civil-military interactions (CONASEDE) and the participation of academic, business, party, and other elites (IAEDN). In the few years the two institutions have been in operation, doctrine has both been more formalized and undergone more evolution than in the rest of the democratic period. There have been significant structural changes as well, including the new conscription law, revisions in the Organic Law, upgrading of the military academies, creation of the graduate studies institute, and development of the new force structure (Plan Carabobo).

The creation of IAEDN under the direction of strategy specialist General Carlos Celis Noguera helped crystalize the implicit ideology of civil-military relations already discussed and then led to the elaboration of a doctrine of national security and defense, which resulted in the founding of CONASEDE a few years later.[14] The two institutions have now established a framework of dynamic interactions through which doctrine, applications, structure, and civil-military relations can be constantly reviewed.

Furthermore, these two institutions, which use civilian staff and involve civilians—some of the teaching staff and course participants at IAEDN are civilians and some staff of the secretariat at CONASEDE are involved in the work of the civilian-led sectoral cabinets of the executive branch—have broadened the context of national defense discussion and raised the profile of the armed forces. This has created minor crises over leaks and publicity, but it has also legitimized the system and reduced the sensitivity of civil-military discussions.[15]

Editorialists may still proclaim the existence of military taboos, but when they continue to bandy the taboo subject about in public, it becomes apparent how open and flexible the system has become.

The actual doctrine of national security and defense, however, has undergone little change since the late 1960s. Venezuela is still clearly understood to be a vulnerable raw materials supplier within the Western Hemisphere defense system, and the major threat is still external communist aggression through subversion or support for domestic insurgency. Of course, an additional threat exists because of the subversion of neighboring countries, which may exacerbate existing border controversies and differences in national interests within the Western system. Thus Venezuela must diversify its external relations, sources of military supply, and access to technology in order to maintain its separate interests. These interests include: disputed borders, especially the Esequibo region of Guyana; protection of vital industries, especially oil; expansion of Caribbean relations; the fostering of inter-American integration; and the political and economic development of Venezuela and other countries.

The security and defense doctrine and the broader ideology which supports it have been fairly well-integrated with the civilian execution of foreign policy under democracy, but the military usually follows without much input. On one occasion, vigorous military disagreement may have forced the Herrera administration to change the terms of a tentative settlement of the Gulf of Venezuela dispute with Colombia. At other times, there have been expressions of military disagreement with the government; for example, grumbles erupt quickly whenever relations warm with Cuba, and military celebration of U.S. intervention in Grenada contrasted with the official condemnation. Military-civilian agreement prevails in domestic policy as well, especially with respect to the areas where the military is more greatly involved, such as civic action, vocational education, state-industry protection, border control and colonization, antinarcotics efforts, acceptance of austerity programs, and so on. Moreover, officers are probably more divided with respect to domestic policy preferences (as will be shown in Chapter 7) than they are with respect to foreign policy. Yet in both arenas, the military view has rarely become so distinct as to present a sense of corporate interest that differs from the national political program.

COLOMBIA

The Colombian military has a long tradition of abstinence from partisan politics. This began in the war for independence early in the nineteenth century, when most of the officers were Venezuelans, who were often resented as imperious outsiders. When independence was secured, the army had rather low prestige and little power; it was generally accepted that it was not to take part in high politics, the province of an upper class more interested in literature than soldiering.

In the many civil conflicts of the nineteenth century, however, the army assumed more or less political positions. It was consequently the aim of President Rafael Reyes (1904–09) to depoliticize it, stressing professionalism, technical skills, and service to the fatherland.

Reyes was decidedly successful, and the army held fairly consistently to an ideal of noninvolvement for nearly 40 years (until 1946), despite the fact that a large majority of officers favored the Conservatives over the Liberals in Colombia's perpetual political contest. Liberal President Alfonso López Pumarejo tried to counter these Conservative proclivities, and, in 1936 and during his second term in 1944, Conservative officers tried to overthrow him. But reluctance to take on a political role was stronger than partisanship for most officers, and the coup attempts were dismal failures. After the 1944 attempt, however, some of the most extreme Conservative officers were removed.

With rising political tensions under the Conservative government of Mariano Ospina Pérez (1946–50), and much more so under the radical Conservative government of Laureano Gómez (1950–53), many Liberal officers left the service or were expelled, making the army an instrument of partisan politics and repressing Liberal opposition to the Gómez dictatorship. Even military training was heavily politicized.[16] Again, however, dislike for political involvement prevailed over partisan inclination, and the army's reluctance to be used as a means of repression was a major factor pushing the army to overthrow Gómez in 1953.

Although the succeeding regime of General Gustavo Rojas Pinilla was not, strictly speaking, a military but rather a personal dictatorship, many officers took political positions, and the army acquired an increased sense of its role in the state.[17] Again, however, the military came to resent being used as an instrument of repression and in 1958 overthrew the rule of one of its own.

Upon ousting the regime of Rojas Pinilla, the military set up a junta that shortly turned power back to civilians. The army accepted, however, the role of combatting the insurgencies and guerrilla warfare that had plagued the country ever since the Bogotazo of 1948. In the 1960s, the violence, which had been between Liberal and Conservative forces in the countryside, became largely a struggle of communist groups (backed by Castro's Cuba) attempting to bring about social revolution.

In response, the military assumed a hard-line approach. In the 1970s this was formulated as a doctrine of "national security." This doctrine, propagated chiefly by the Superior War College, was borrowed from other Latin American countries, especially Brazil, where it had seen the most development. It postulated a Colombia engaged, like and with the United States, in a global struggle against communism (the Christian West against the Communist East) and called for ideological and psychological as well as conventional warfare. It also treated national security in terms of technical and industrial progress, economic solidity, social unity, and military power and gave the armed forces a mission of building up all these ingredients of national strength. It was unclear, of course, how much emphasis should be placed on different forms of combat against communist and guerrilla movements.

There was a current of opinion that it was necessary not only to shoot the guerrillas but to remedy social and economic causes that led peasants to cooperate with or join them. Thus Minister of War Alberto Ruiz Novoa in 1962 argued for more attention to social justice,[18] as did Generals Alvaro Valencia Tovar in 1975 and Landazabal Reyes in 1981. They were all silenced, however; and the dominant drive was for repression by military means.

As the guerrilla threat ebbed in the 1970s, the military turned its attention to external threats, which had been largely out of view since the conflict with Peru in 1932–33. Venezuela is the traditional national rival, and conflicting boundary claims in the Gulf of Venezuela (with supposed oil deposits) are a perennial cause of tension. Together with questions of illegal Colombian immigrants to Venezuela and some jingoistic manifestations on both sides, this territorial question led to a surge of Colombian nationalism in the early 1980s.

For the armed forces, this conflictual atmosphere required modernization of their generally rather poor equipment. There has also
been concern about the Nicaraguan claim to the small island of San
Andrés, a tourist spot where Colombia maintains a garrison.

In sum, the Colombian armed forces have a secular tradition of
noninvolvement in politics, although this has been somewhat qualified by the long task of dealing with armed subversive movements (as
discussed in Chapter 7). They see professionalism as best for their
status and prestige; and it is especially important that they be politically neutral in view of the traditional political division of Colombia
between the Conservative and Liberal parties. Their temper is anticommunist and basically conservative, however, despite some currents of social concern. Coming from a rising middle class, the officers
opt for stability, although it may mean defense of an essentially
oligarchic system.

PERU

The explanations for the turning of the Peruvian armed forces to
a progressive or radical ideology involve both intramilitary factors
and external influences from Peruvian society and abroad. The causes
include the influence of the Center for Higher Military Studies
(CAEM) in particular, military training in general, and the armed
forces' involvement in civic action programs in the late 1960s, which
enabled them to see first-hand some of the problems of their own
society. The military also perceived the effect of social and economic
issues on national security when they were called upon in 1965 to
fight small guerrilla groups in three different areas of Peru; and
during the 1950s and 1960s, the military was affected by the seeming
inability of civilian political parties to come to grips with the major
problems of the society. There was a growing disgust for foreign
exploitation of the country's resources, particularly in the case of
the International Petroleum Corporation, which had strong U.S. government support. The military felt, too, that it was being hemmed in
by its closest military ally, the United States, especially in that country's failure to provide for what the Peruvian military regarded as its
needs rather than what the U.S. military considered those needs to be.

There was consequently a growing recognition that the military's
past policy of supporting the status quo was not in the best interests

of the country. "The Army came to see itself as used by the rich [and] . . . decided that the policies of the rich were slowly but surely exciting a disastrous revolutionary condition and that the Army alone possessed the cohesion, expertise, and national standing necessary to avert the crisis."[19] Alienation from the so-called oligarchy increased in the late 1950s and early 1960s, and an independent ideology toward Peruvian social and political phenomena began to develop, generally expressed in the language of technology and planning. When one compares the journal *Revista Militar* of 1949–51 and 1962–64, one finds a dramatic increase in the number of articles oriented toward the army's relation to society and its role in relation to national development and modernization—from no articles (out of 95) to 15 (out of 98).[20] Another study of articles related to the "new professionalism of internal security and national development" in the *Revista de la Escuela Superior de Guerra* shows an increase from 1.7% of total articles in the 1954–57 period to over 50% in the 1963–67 period.[21] The new military ideology seeks to improve social and economic conditions to eliminate the basis of support of revolutionary groups.

CAEM's 1961 statement of the new principles of action for the armed forces reflects the emerging new ideology: "The final end of the state being the welfare of the nation, and the Armed Forces being the instrument which the State uses to impose its policy . . . in order to arrive at collective prosperity, the Armed Forces has as a mission to watch over the social welfare, the final end of the State."[22] With its modernization, the military became more independent of social groups, and its officers began to apply the emerging rational standards of their own organization to the society as a whole. They realized that the social and economic structure could not sustain the type of modern military institution into which the Peruvian Armed Forces was developing. "Developed in isolation from political groups, the new ideology reflects its bureaucratic origins: it can be reduced to a faith in the possibility of technological solution for Peru's 'developmental problems'."[23]

The core elements of the ideology of the military, as expressed by the reformers in the military government between 1968 and 1975, included the following: rejection of political parties and traditional elites; the uniqueness of the Peruvian Revolution as neither capitalist nor communist; stress on economic pluralism, humanism, and the full participation of the people; and fairness to all sectors, social harmony, peace, order, patience, and sacrifice. However, there was considerable diversity of perspective, and achieving an ideological consensus was difficult.

> While the moralism and concern for social justice provided the elan for the Revolutionary Government of the Armed Forces . . . it was the centrist military technocratic position that provided the elements of unity. Their goals may be summarized as the achievement of basic welfare goals through the increased production made possible by a planned mixed economy with state and private capital cooperating harmoniously to advance the national interest. In short, theirs was a utopian development project, divorcing production from distribution, relying on "will" separated from social power, and positing an abstract national interest above class and sectoral conflicts. . . . It was the centrists who played the pivotal role in both the initial phase of radicalization and in determining the ultimately conservative outcome represented by the Morales Bermúdez presidency.[24]

BRAZIL

Since 1964, the Brazilian military have consolidated a fairly sophisticated ideology rationalizing the institutional and projected national objectives elaborated by the Superior War College (ESG) in the 1950s and early 1960s. There is a continuity in the evolution of this elaboration, from the nineteenth century positivism of military activists who founded the republic under the banner of "Order and Progress," through the intensification of economic nationalism in the 1930s and the *Estado Novo*, to the Kubitschek era, when autonomous development became a priority to assure national security. A military ideology based on "Security and Development" (S & D) was thus a natural consequence.[25] According to General Golbery, the international arena is a difficult and dangerous environment, and to make its way "Brazil at present has only one choice: to become great or perish."[26] The authoritarian 1969 constitution charged the National Security Council (CSN) with setting "permanent national objectives."

The permanent national objectives established by the CSN during the Geisel government included the following: to establish a national community, politically, socially, economically, and culturally integrated; to guarantee the exercise of complete national independence; to foster democratic representative government; to preserve social peace and national prosperity; and to project the national personality in the concert of nations.[27]

In practice, the priority given the "national community" in detriment of the individual meant that development strategies were based on "national aggregates," and basic human individual needs and rights were usually sacrificed. This was ironic because one objective of rapid national development was to reduce the population's dissatisfaction and social disharmony.[28]

The S & D doctrine emphasized "elite unity" as a necessary condition for secure development, and the failure of elite sectors to work together for the good of the nation in the pre-1964 period was seen as one of the main causes of poor growth rates. The armed forces were seen as the only national institution with enough internal unity and discipline to force unity upon "uncooperative" elite sectors. When the military abandoned their traditional role as the "moderating power" in Brazilian politics and assumed the role of making politics rather than remaining the reluctant object of politics, the post-1964 consequence of the S & D ideology was the construction of a strong central government organized along military lines and fully responsible to the armed forces.[29]

During the years of military rule, two things weakened the S & D doctrine: erosion of unity and discipline in the armed forces themselves, and questions about strategies of economic development. The specter of military disunity arose at critical junctures of presidential succession, in 1965–66, 1969, and 1978. In 1984, in addition to disunity caused by the problem of succession, the armed forces were divided on the doctrinaire question of the viability of current economic models of dependent development and the problem of how the rampant corruption affects S & D. The ideology of economic nationalism appears to have attracted many officers. In the May 16, 1984 elections, over 40% voted for the Military Club in favor of the "National Sovereignty" slate of candidates.

Since 1964, S & D doctrine delineating the roles of state, national, and transnational capital in Brazil's economic development has suffered fluctuations. During the 1964–67 period the role of transnational capital was stressed; many domestic enterprises were "transnationalized," while state enterprise was not promoted. During the "miracle" period from 1967 to 1974, some transnational corporations were given special incentives to locate in Brazil, where a development strategy integrated into the "new international division of labor" stressed Brazil's role as exporter of industrial manufactured goods and component parts. At the same time, state enterprise began to receive heavy public investments. As the international economy began to crumble after 1974, the development strategy centered heavily on state enterprise and deemphasized the role of multi-national capital, except when associated with state enterprise and, to a lesser degree, with national capitalists. The result has been a nearly complete alienation of national industrialists from the current economic model and the S & D doctrine behind it. Thus, the military lost one of the key elements supporting the coup in 1964, and the problem of elite disunity reappeared. Military disunity became public in the late 1970s with the formation of three distinct "movements": the Revolutionary Democratic Movement, the Movement for the Defense of the Revolution, and the Military Democratic Constitutionalist Movement.

Because of the severe pressures of negative growth rates, economic recession, and an unmanageable U.S. $100 billion foreign debt, state enterprise (with its huge investments in megalomanic projects, often with no tangible returns) and centralized government planning and regulation of the economy are held in low esteem by most sectors of society. There is a nonideological, pragmatic aspect contributing to military opinion regarding state enterprise and centralization—the fact that several thousand ex-comrades (now in the reserve) hold high staff positions in state enterprise and centralized agencies.

The basic doctrine of S & D as applied to national economic development has proved inadequate, in spite of the fact that military personnel have been directly involved in the implementation of such policies. A more basic doctrine of military unity and institutional preservation seems to be evolving, one which favors military disengagement from the governing process, with efforts at consensus building with other elite sectors toward a more viable economic model.

One result of the "Memorandum of Understanding" regarding U.S.-Brazilian military relations (signed by Secretary of State George Shultz in early February 1984) was a meeting of the joint study groups to discuss "exchange of military doctrine." The results of this meeting, which was chaired by Brigadier General John Greenway of the U.S. army and Brigadier General Hans Haltenberg of the operations section of the Brazilian Armed Forces General Staff (EMFA), were not made public.[30]

Recently, a senior officer with the army general staff enumerated five basic points of current doctrine:

1. Problems of war and peace for Brazil are intertwined with the East-West and North-South dimensions of international conflict.
2. East-West conflict is extremely detrimental to underdeveloped nations because resources of the superpowers, which could assist the developing nations, are immobilized, and the developing nations are induced by the superpowers to spend scarce resources in arms purchases as a condition for international aid.
3. There are significant differences regarding the role the United States would like Brazil to play in support of U.S. policies in Central America and the Caribbean and the formation of a South Atlantic security arrangement.
4. Brazil has been seduced in recent years by the geopolitical myth of becoming a "great power," with grave risks of overestimating capabilities and mortgaging the nation to unsuitable projects incompatible with its effective conditions.[31]

CHILE

The Chilean armed forces are proud of their long military tradition. In the nineteenth century, Chile was engaged in warfare not only against Spain but twice against Peru and Bolivia and nearly continuously against the Araucanian Indians in the south of the country. All of these conflicts ended in victory; they continue to be celebrated and studied in military schools and form an important part of the Chilean military's outlook on the world.

The War of the Pacific resulted in territorial gains that have created continuing tensions between Chile and its neighbors. Neither Peru nor Bolivia poses a serious military challenge, but numerous border conflicts with Argentina—the latest over the Beagle Channel was just settled in late 1984—have reminded the Chilean military that they must be in a state of readiness. Thus an important part of Chilean military doctrine is a militant nationalism that emphasizes the possibility of armed conflict with neighboring countries, the need for preparedness, and the use of both diplomatic and military means to prevent a hostile combination of neighboring countries.

In recent years this concern about borders has been translated into an interest in geopolitics. President Pinochet himself taught geopolitics at the *Escuela Militar* and has published a book on the subject—largely borrowed, say his critics, from an earlier book by a navy admiral. Geopolitical considerations also influenced the navy's opposition to a settlement of the Beagle Channel controversy with Argentina that would in any way prejudice Chile's claims to parts of the Antarctic and an outlet to the Atlantic. Similar geopolitical considerations lead the armed forces to favor closer relations with Brazil in order to counterbalance the Peruvian-Argentine relationship.

A second legacy of the nineteenth century to Chilean military thinking is the spirit of military professionalism. From the time of Emil Körner's efforts to modernize—and Prussianize—the Chilean army, the armed forces have been proud of the high level of their military training and education. The few cases of military intervention in Chilean politics resulted from the armed forces' belief that the civilian authorities were impeding the modernization and development of the country. Thus in the 1924–27 period, the army forced the adoption of a new constitution and modern social legislation. When military rule became unpopular and competent civilian leaders reemerged in 1932, the military were content to go back to the barracks, only to return to politics 40 years later when the government of Salvador Allende seemed to be destroying the economy, polarizing the society, and above all, threatening the monopoly of the armed forces over the instruments of coercion.

Thirdly, the members of the Chilean military, like the military in many other countries, are strongly opposed to communism. That opposition has been attributed by many writers to exposure to national security doctrines taught by the United States in various training programs involving Latin American participants.[32] Yet research done on military writing in the 1930s, long before the United States became a significant influence, indicates that the Chilean military has always been opposed to Marxism. That opposition may have been reinforced by U.S. influence but was not created by it.

The most important source of the anticommunism of the Chilean military today was their experience between 1970 and 1973. The traumatizing effect of the Allende period and the shared belief that the coup saved the country from an imminent Marxist takeover are central to contemporary Chilean military thinking. The fact that the Communist party has now identified itself with the doctrine of "armed struggle" à la Nicaragua, in effect abandoning its previous adherence to the *via pacífica,* only reinforces military attitudes; and the wave of bombings carried out by the left in recent years confirms the military's belief in the necessity of a continuing struggle against subversion. Public statements by military leaders after the coup referred to the necessity of extirpating "the cancer of Marxism," and the Pinochet government's actions against the left have included torture, imprisonment, and assassination. When the investigation of the 1976 Washington murder of Allende's ex-ambassador (Orlando Letelier) revealed links to the National Information Directorate (DINA), which coordinated the antisubversive effort, Pinochet dissolved DINA, but he replaced it with the National Intelligence Center (CNI), headed by an army general and staffed by military men. It has been less brutal but still effective against the Marxist Left.

A fourth characteristic of the Chilean armed forces is their constitutionalism and legalism. When Körner took the side of the Congress in the 1891 civil war, he did so on the grounds that President Balmaceda had violated the constitution. When the military repeatedly intervened in the 1920s, those interventions were legitimized by bringing back the elected president (Alessandri), governing from behind the facade of a civilian president, or legitimizing the rule of the *caudillo* (Carlos Ibáñez) by a plebiscitary election. Before the 1970 election General René Schneider announced that the armed forces would not intervene if the constitutional processes were observed, and Central Intelligence Agency (CIA) efforts in 1970 to provoke a coup to prevent Allende from taking power were not successful. The 1973 coup took place only after the armed forces became convinced, as a result of Supreme Court and congressional statements, that Allende had repeatedly violated the constitution.[33] Since the coup, General Pinochet has maintained the support of the armed forces by holding a referendum in 1978 and a plebiscite in 1980 on a constitution that keeps him in power until 1989 (and possibly until 1997) and outlines a timetable for a transition to civilian rule and congressional elections. He has even succeeded in maintaining the constitutional myth that the armed forces are apolitical (the word *no-deliberantes* is used in the constitutions of 1833, 1925, and 1980) by arguing that the junta, composed of the military commanders of the army, navy, air force, and national police, is the only place where national policy is discussed by the military and their corporate consent given. Thus in 1977 Pinochet praised "our armed forces and national police (*carabineros*) for not having become politicized, and leaving matters of state to the responsibility of their commanders." Military legalism as applied to their own services has meant strict respect for hierarchy and a strong internal *esprit* that is not inclined to confide in civilians about the internal dynamics of the services. Aware of this, Pinochet has retained the post of commander in chief of the army throughout his presidency and has given the position legislative functions. Pinochet appointed a close confidant as representative of the army on the junta, but he retained the office of army commander.

The attitudes of the Chilean armed forces toward democracy are ambiguous. On the one hand, they accept constitutionalism and representative government as part of the Chilean tradition. On the other, they are fearful that the "demagogy" of the politicians will lead to a Marxist takeover—hence the need for a democracy that is "protected" by such institutions as the military-dominated National Security Council, which under the 1980 constitution will have a virtual veto on the actions of future elected governments. In earlier periods, some military men were attracted by socialism (Marmaduke Grove in 1932), the Chilean version of Nazism (1938–39), or Peronism (1950s); but the predominant view accepted Chilean constitutionalism while criticizing the excesses of the *politiquería* of the civilian politicians. In the mid-1960s, a U.S. researchers found the Chilean military to be more favorable to reform than others in Latin America; and a few army and air force generals (including the army commander in chief, General Carlos Prats, who was later assassinated in exile) looked favorably upon the changes introduced by the Allende government. (Prats and several of his fellow generals had to be forced to resign before the other generals could stage the coup.) The bulk of the army generals—and even more the navy and air force—opposed the Allende government, especially its tolerance of armed leftist groups and its proposals for a National Unified School (ENU), which would have imposed a curriculum based on "humanist" (more likely Marxist) socialism on all Chilean schools.

The first loyalty of the armed forces is to the military institutions themselves, but since 1973 they have adopted positions to the right of center in domestic and international policy. President Pinochet has been able to exploit the military's nationalist sentiments by denouncing his critics as foreign-influenced and financed, attacking the United Nations because of its annual condemnation of Chile's human rights record, and portraying Chile as "standing alone" in its fight against statism and the worldwide Marxist conspiracy. He won 75% approval in a 1978 referendum that placed a Chilean flag over the positive answer and a black square over the negative answer to the following statement: "In the light of the aggression unloosed against the government of our country (*patria*), I support President Pinochet in his defense of the dignity of Chile and I reaffirm the legitimacy of the government of the Republic to lead sovereignly the process of institutionalization." In September 1980, after hastily rewriting a constitutional draft submitted by his advisory Council of State, he held a plebiscite on a new constitution that received a 67% favorable vote. While maintaining the support of the armed forces, he continues to stand by the timetable outlined in the 1980 constitution, resisting civilian pressures for a Constitutional Assembly and a more rapid return to democracy.

In economics the Pinochet government has adopted a free-market policy in reversal of the statism of the Allende years. There is tension, however, between those military men who favor a corporatist nationalism and those who espouse economic liberalism of the laissez-faire variety. The "Chicago boys" economic policy, propounded by former students of Milton Friedman and Arnold Harberger of the University of Chicago and now substantially modified, originally called for a drastic reduction in the economic role of government, an opening of the Chilean economy to international competition, the promotion of exports, and the privatization of the state economic sector. In accordance with this policy, health services, social security, and education have been partially privatized, and an attempt has been made to promote regionalization of a previously highly centralized governmental system. Civilian apologists for the regime argued that they were establishing the basis for a new form of libertarian democracy based on local self-government, indirect elections, and voluntary associations, which would avoid the vices of centralized multiparty democracy as practiced before 1973.[34]

Yet there was always some reluctance on the part of the military to accept the libertarian program. This was seen at the outset in 1974 when they vetoed a proposal by the "Chicago boys" to denationalize the copper mines, which had been taken over by Allende. Copper was seen as important to national security, not only because it was responsible for a large part of Chile's foreign exchange but also because 10% of its foreign exchange earnings were earmarked for military purchases. Later, when the Chicago economic policy failed in the early 1980s, there was military support for a greater degree of economic nationalism, for increasing tariffs, and for supporting domestic industries and banks by loans and bailouts that were anathema to the

Chicago economists. In 1983 the military supported Pinochet's moves against prominent representatives of the economic oligarchy, and in 1984 they endorsed the imposition of a state of siege and rigorous censorship against the protest movement seeking a more rapid return to democracy. Some military men are believed to favor the establishment of a corporatist state, but the large vote for the 1980 consitutttion, which contains a timetable calling for a return to parliamentary democracy at the end of the decade, makes such an event unlikely.

ARGENTINA

The Argentine military, intensely indoctrinated in training schools, has been equally intensely ideological; yet its ideology has been outstandingly confused. The only constant has been intense nationalism regarding Argentina as a potential power with major foreign concerns. This has meant strong rivalries with the hereditary antagonists, Chile and Brazil, and an assumption of influence over Paraguay, Bolivia, and Uruguay. In the past decade there has been considerable talk of possible war with Chile (over trivial territorial issues) and a little talk of war with Brazil (over hydroelectric projects). Argentina rivals Brazil for Latin American leadership in geopolitical theorizing. Until the decline in recent decades, the military had viewed Argentina as the natural leader of Latin America and champion of Hispanic civilization against the challenge of the United States. No other country of the hemisphere has seen itself as a rival of the United States; Brazil in particular has tended to regard itself as rather the South American version of the hemispheric power. The military's vision of Argentina's broader role has also been conditioned by cultural-racist attitudes, such as the conviction of the superiority of largely European Argentina to the more mixed mestizo-Indian populations of most Latin American countries.

In more specific attitudes, however, the armed forces have shown many frequently contradictory and changing tendencies. There have been liberal, corporatist-authoritarian, democratic-legalist, fascistic, traditionalist, anti-Semitic, Catholic-nationalist, and technocratic-industrial currents. The officers have always been strong for order of some kind, and they have never been inclined to egalitarianism, but otherwise they have been ready to support a variety of solutions for the big Argentine problem: how to restore national greatness after the long period of embittering decline from the 1920s on.

The conviction that Argentina had to be great was based on size (second largest in South America), natural wealth, European population, and the phenomenal economic progress that was notable by the 1870s and brought Argentina to the ranks of the world's wealthiest nations by the 1920s. The professionalization of the armed forces began about the same time, with the foundation of the *Colegio Militar* in 1870, and was promoted by the eminent fighter against or exterminator of the Indians, President Julio Roca (1880–86 and 1898–1904). The officer corps took on the values of a highly oligarchic, snobbish society dominated by plantation owners, values that were retained even when the officers were (after 1901) drawn mostly from the immigrant (largely Italian and Spanish) middle class. After military service was made obligatory in 1901, the army took on the task of Argentinizing the newcomers or their sons, correspondingly stressing patriotism and the sacred Argentine mission.

The German influence, advanced by a mission in place from 1901 to 1940 (except for the time of World War I), did much to shape Argentine military spirit. It inculcated the love of order, Prussian styles, and rigorous obedience in austere training. It implied distrust for democracy and reliance on authority. It cannot be said that it was responsible for the proclivity of the officers to intervene in 1930 and afterwards, but it certainly did not discourage the application of force to national affairs. In the 1920s, German-Prussian spirit was mixed with admiration for Benito Mussolini and Italian fascism, which appealed to the pride of the large Italian sector of the population. The German influence was also allied with longstanding Catholic authoritarianism (like that of conservatives in other Latin American countries), plus the dictatorial tradition of Juan Manuel Rosas, whose barbarities were forgotten in admiration for his power.

The 1930 coup, which removed the incompetent civilian President Hipólito Yrigoyen, was made by two groups with dissonant ideological tendencies. One, led by General Agustín Justo, saw the military as called upon to restore decent and effective constitutional government and to remove political corruption. The other, led by General José Uriburu, wanted to establish a properly controlled and ordered fascist state on the Italian plan. The latter took control at first but could not convert the Argentines; the former, representing a majority of the officer corps, came to power after less than two years and proceeded to set up a pseudodemocratic order of rulership by electoral fraud.

In the 1920s, rich and rising Argentina felt confident of its progress and destiny; after 1930, puzzled by political and economic failure, it felt hurt and bitter. The officer majority, influenced by Italian fascism, German Nazism, and Spanish Falangism, went over to more or less fascistic nationalism. Seeing the corruption of the political process and the abdication of civilian leadership, officers came to hate both the oligarchy and the mob. A secret lodge, the United Officers Group (GOU), was organized to make the army custodian of nationalism and to oppose General Justo and the conservatives. Especially from the beginning of World War II and under the impression of Nazi victories, the pro-Axis GOU gained strength over the pro–United Nations moderates; by 1943, they were drawing up blueprints for the repulsion of Britain and the United States and the conquest of South America in alliance with Nazi Germany. At a time when Hitler's fortunes were already obviously sinking, they proposed to regiment Argentina for war and empire.[35]

After the defeat of the Axis powers (1944–45), the army was prepared to accept Perón's populist-mobilizing nationalism, which seemed to solve the problem of legitimizing military rule by bringing the masses, especially the workers, to its support through controlled organizations. But the army was too tradition-minded to assimilate Perón's and Evita's political style; it never prostrated itself before the supreme leader but held its reservations. In 1953, as his dictatorship was decaying, Perón undertook a major campaign to indoctrinate the army with the truths of Peronism, or *Justicialismo*, making this the ideology of the Colegio Militar and other schools and having the officers teach it to the conscripts. Loyalty to Perón was to replace traditional loyalty to nation and service.

This campaign was not successful, and the officers turned against Perón because of the contradictions of his policies, his economic failures, and above all his foolish attack on the Catholic church. After the fall of Perón, there was a remarkable ideological turnaround. Perón was denounced as a bestial tyrant or a communist; the United States suddenly became popular as never before; and many, especially younger officers, became fervent democrats. Divisions continued, however, principally between those who wanted to compromise and try to reincorporate the Peronists into the national life and those who wanted to extirpate every branch of the Peronist evil and deny Peronists any share of power. The latter, mostly activist younger officers, were often called "gorillas" because of their intransigence.

After the overthrow of Arturo Frondizi in 1962 for mildness toward Peronists, the gorillas became divided into *colorados* (reds), who would use dictatorial means against any possible resurgence of Peronism, and *azules* (blues), who looked to legal and moderate procedures and a civilian regime. The division was bitter and at times came to blows, with fatalities. The azules, however, came into the ascendancy and, in 1966, under the leadership of the most eminent of the legalists (General Juan Carlos Onganía), established the most thorough dictatorship of Argentine history.

This contradiction is typical of the confusion of ideas in the Argentine military since 1930, and especially since the removal of Perón in 1955. There have been many currents and eddies (based on both philosophies and personalities), many bitter antagonisms, and little agreement except on the need to make Argentina great or at least to stem its decline. Opposition to Peronism was a leitmotif for 18 years after 1955, but it eventually became melded with generalized antisubversion and anticommunism in line with U.S. Cold War policy. The army compromised, allowing Perón to return in 1973 and become president. Then in 1976 it turned against secondhand Peronism and undertook to annihilate terrorists and subversives and put new order into Argentine society. The military wants industrialization and modernization but does not know how to bring them about or how to make them compatible with the traditional values it cherishes. It understands "national security" to be intertwined with development, encompassing all aspects of national life, the modernization of the economy, and social union; but it cannot achieve these goals with either freedom or compulsion.

The most recent chapter of the ideological history of the Argentine military includes its failure to manage the economy, massive abuses of human rights (that is, large-scale torture and murder beyond the needs of combatting subversion), growing corruption in what was the least corrupt sector of the nation, and the bungled war to recoup prestige by taking the Falkland/Malvinas Islands. The demoralized armed forces allowed a democratic election, which was won by the more antimilitary candidate, Raul Alfonsín, who has tried to civilianize the forces as they have not been for nearly a century. If this attempt succeeds, it will entail a deep change of ideology.

NOTES

1. Jesús de León Toral et al., *El ejercito Mexicano* (Mexico City: Secretaria de la Defensa Nacional, 1979), p. 519.

2. Samuel P. Huntington, *Political Order in Changing Societies* (New Haven: Yale University Press), 1968, p. 317.

3. León Toral, *El ejército Mexicano*, pp. 532-33.

4. León Toral, *El ejército Mexicano*, p. 533; Lyle N. McAlister, Anthony P. Maingot, and Robert A. Potash, eds., *The Military in Latin American Sociopolitical Evolution: Four Case Studies* (Washington, D.C.: Center for Research in Social Systems, 1970), p. 209.

5. Guillermo Boils, *Los militares y la política en México (1915-1974)* (Mexico City: Ediciones El Caballito, 1975), pp. 127-30; McAlister, Maingot, and Potash, *Sociopolitical Evolution*, pp. 209-10; Thomas E. Weil, ed., *Area Handbook for Mexico* (Washington, D.C.: U.S. Government Printing Office, 1975), p. 360.

6. McAlister, Maingot, and Potash, *Sociopolitical Evolution*, p. 230.

7. McAlister, Maingot, and Potash, *Sociopolitical Evolution*, pp. 207-12; Martin C. Needler, "Problems in the Evaluation of the Mexican Political System," in *Contemporary Mexico*, eds. James W. Wilkie, Michael C. Meyer, and Edna Monzon de Wilkie (Berkeley: University of California Press, 1976), p. 341.

8. Eugene E. Keefe, "National Security," in *Guatemala: A Country Study*, ed. Richard F. Nyrop (Washington, D.C.: U.S. Government Printing Office, 1984), p. 181.

9. Steve C. Ropp, *Panamanian Politics: From Guarded Nation to National Guard* (New York: Praeger, 1982), pp. 50-51.

10. Andrés Stambouli, *Crisis Política: Venezuela 1945-58* (Caracas: Editorial Ateneo de Caracas, 1980) and Freddy Rincón N., *El nuevo ideal nacional y los planes económico-militares de Pérez Jiménez, 1952-57* (Caracas: Ediciones Centauro, 1982).

11. Robert J. Alexander, *The Venezuelan Democratic Revolution: A Profile of the Regime of Rómulo Betancourt* (New Brunswick, N.J.: Rutgers University Press, 1964), 136-47.

12. Charles Ameringer, "The Foreign Policy of Venezuelan Democracy," in *Venezuela: The Democratic Experience*, eds. John D. Martz and David J. Myers (New York: Praeger, 1977), p. 335; John D. Martz, "Venezuelan Foreign Policy toward Latin America," in *Contemporary Venezuela and its Role in International Affairs*, ed. Robert Bond (New York: New York University Press, 1977), pp. 183-87.

13. John D. Martz, "Venezuelan Foreign Policy toward Latin America," in Bond, ed., *Contemporary Venezuela*, p. 159.

14. Carlos Celis Noguera, *Elementos de estrategia* (Caracas: Oficina Técnica, Ministerio de Defensa, 1974) and Alfonso Littuma, *Doctrina de seguridad y defensa* (Caracas: Ministerio de Defensa, 1967) are the seminal works.

15. A scandal arose in 1981 over a story in *El Diario de Caracas* which reported an IAEDN war game. Civil courts overruled the jurisdiction of a military

court over reporter María Eugenia Díaz, and the public found out that IAEDN was taking hard looks at some difficult scenarios: in the war game, Venezuela lost in a confrontation with Guyana because of a diplomatic maneuver by the latter country.

16. Richard Maullin, *Soldiers, Guerrillas, and Politics in Colombia* (Lexington, Mass.: Lexington Books, 1973), p. 59.

17. Gustavo Gallón Girardo, *La república de las armas* (Bogotá: Centro de Investigación y Educación Popular, 1981), p. 21.

18. Maullin, *Soldiers, Guerrillas, and Politics*, p. 68.

19. John Keegan, *World Armies*, 2d ed. (Detroit, Mich.: Gale Research Company, 1983), p. 471.

20. Liisa North, *Civil-Military Relations in Argentina, Chile, and Peru*, Politics of Modernization Series, no. 2 (Berkeley: Institute of International Studies, University of California, 1966), p. 52.

21. Alfred C. Stepan, *The State and Society: Peru in Comparative Perspective* (Princeton: Princeton University Press, 1978), pp. 130–33.

22. Victor Villanueva, *El militarismo en el Perú* (Lima: T. Scheuch, 1962), pp. 174–75.

23. Richard Patch, *The Peruvian Elections of 1963*, American Universities Field Staff Service Reports, West Coast South American Series, vol. 10, no. 1 (July 1963), pp. 5–6, 57.

24. North and Korovkin, *The Peruvian Revolution*, pp. 64–65.

25. Edmundo Campos Coelho, *Em busca de identidade: o exército e a política na sociedade Brasileira* (Rio de Janeiro: Forense-Universitaria, 1976), p. 165. See also Miriam Limoeiro Cardoso, *Ideologia do desenvolvimento—Brasil, JQ/JK* (Rio de Janeiro: Paz e Terra, 1978).

26. Golbery do Couto e Silva, *Geopolítica do Brasil.* (Rio de Janeiro: José Olimpio, 1967), pp. 22, 24, 64.

27. Walder de Goes, *O Brasil de General Geisel.* (Rio de Janeiro: Nova Fronteira, 1978), p. 34.

28. Coelho, *Em busca de identidade*, p. 173; *Doutrina Básica* (Rio de Janeiro: Escola Superior de Guerra, 1979), p. 217.

29. Robert Wesson and David V. Fleischer, *Brazil in Transition.* (New York: Praeger, 1983), p. 138.

30. *Jornal do Brasil*, February 19, 1984, p. 8.

31. Geraldo Lesbat Cavagnari Filho, "Estudo de uma potencia media," *Folha de São Paulo*, March 31, 1984, p. 49.

32. See Genaro Arriagada, *El pensamiento político de los militares en Chile* (Santiago: CISEC, 1981); Roberto Calvo, *La doctrina militar de la Seguridad Nacional* (Caracas: Universidad Católica Andrés Bello, 1979); Hugo Fruhling, Carlos Portales, and Augusto Varas, *Estado y fuerzas armadas* (Santiago: FLACSO, 1982), especially p. 40. For earlier examples of military anticommunism, see Frederick M. Nunn, *Yesterday's Soldiers* (Lincoln, Neb.: University of Nebraska Press, 1983), pp. 170, 254.

33. See Paul E. Sigmund, *The Overthrow of Allende and the Politics of Chile, 1964–76* (Pittsburgh: University of Pittsburgh Press, 1977) ch. 9–11; and

Liisa North, "The Military in Chilean Politics" in *Armies and Politics in Latin America*, ed. Abraham Lowenthal (New York: Holmes and Meier, 1976), pp. 165-96.

34. See Paul E. Sigmund, "Chile: Market Fascism or Utopian Libertarianism?" *Worldview* (October 1981): 4-6. For the combination of free-market economics with militant anticommunism, see Pinochet's speech on the second anniversary of the 1973 coup, translated in Brian Loveman and Thomas M. Davies, Jr., eds., *The Politics of Antipolitics* (Lincoln, Neb.: University of Nebraska Press, 1982), pp. 200-7.

35. Marvin Goldwert, *Democracy, Militarism and Nationalism in Argentina, 1930-1966* (Austin: University of Texas Press, 1972), p. 57.

7

Political Role

The question of questions about the Latin American military establishments concerns not their combative but their political capacities and role. These capacities are large, especially since the soldiers usually have little to do with defending the borders. Medieval kings organized campaigns to keep the restless barons from making trouble; in Latin America, however, there is not much external conflict to occupy the generals (although the vibrancy of various boundary disputes doubtless owes a good deal to the desire to give the officers something to busy themselves with). On the other hand, it is obvious that national strength and the nation's autonomy are endangered by many internal economic and social problems, above all by mismanagement and political disorder. Hence the soldiers' thoughts, whether constitutionally or patriotically oriented, turn easily toward saving the country by strengthening, improving, or purifying the state; imposing the discipline missing in the confused self-serving of ordinary politics; and putting power into trusted hands.

The lack of much of the conventional defensive purpose of the armed forces combines with the weakness of civilian institutions to encourage military intervention in domestic affairs. In the aftermath of independence in Spanish America, rulership by rather crude force was virtually inevitable, not only because of Spanish tradition but also because of the nearly total lack of authoritative indigenous political institutions. The subsequent growth of constitutionalism was seldom strong enough to bar military intervention during troubled times or when the civilian politicians seemed to have betrayed their mandate.

There are various other reasons for the Latin American proclivity toward military politics. One factor is the intensive training of officers, who are among the best educated of groups and who usually have much more systematic instruction than most civilian politicians. There being no likely prospective international battles, the higher officers cannot be expected to enjoy spending many years studying battle tactics; it is much more interesting and perhaps more appropriate to delve into the study of high-level administration, national problems, international relations, and the like. Once the officers have immersed themselves in these matters, it is not remarkable that they should look to applying their expertise; the wonder is perhaps that they do not do so more generally. Military education also tends to make the military a relatively encapsulated group, without strong identification with any social class; they are consequently more prepared to act on their own than, for example, an officer corps representing younger sons of the aristocracy, more aristocrats than officers. In addition, Latin America generally lacks strong, penetrating political parties capable of checking or guiding the armed forces. Only Mexico has such a party; and this is, of course, the basic reason that the Mexican armed forces have been politically inactive for over 50 years.

There has been a general acceptance in Latin America of the theory of constitutionalism and the supremacy of civilian authority, as commonly incorporated in constitutional provisions that the military should be nonpolitical. On the other hand, constitutions frequently lay on the military the responsibility for maintaining the constitutional order, which amounts to sanction for setting it aside if they view the president as subverting it, as in Brazil in 1964 or Chile in 1973. Moreover, the armed forces are frequently bound to obedience to the civilian authorities "within the limits of the law," a provision that invites them to determine the limits of obedience.

The political role of the military in Latin America is, in any event, very large. Most Latin American presidents of the last decade, not to speak of previous decades, have come to the top through military careers. The degree of military influence or intervention has varied widely, however, from Mexico to Chile—from the mere availability of officers for political jobs or a presence behind the scenes (as in Mexico), to a potential for intervention if things should sour or a sort of quiet sharing of power (as in Colombia or contemporary Peru), to powerholding with a technocracy (as in Brazil 1964–85 and Chile since 1973), to an effort to administer the country (as in Peru under Velasco Alvarado).

Military coups do not occur without civilian support and seldom without the urging of a civilian party; the amount of interventionism or shifting from civilian to military government is determined to a large extent by economic conditions and the apparent success or failure of regimes in dealing with those conditions. The officers do not take power from well-regarded civilian governments presiding over prosperous countries but from disorderly and visibly incapable governments unable to handle severe economic problems. On the other hand, military governments that have obviously failed in their mission of putting the economy in order are likely to decide to turn the mess back to civilians. Military organizations are basically less prepared to administer a country than civilians, whatever their educational qualifications, because they are not set up to deliberate, take conflicting interests into account, and reach acceptable decisions. Countries cannot be well-managed on the military principles of hierarchy and command. Consequently military government regularly sinks into incompetence, and the orderly corporatist rule with which it set out decays to personalism and dictatorship.

These tendencies have much to do with the pendular swings between civilian and military power in Latin America. The great depression of the 1930s came when Latin America was tending toward civilian rule, and it brought a wave of military takeovers. Similarly, the hard times striking nearly all countries after 1980 deserve much of the credit for the broad retreat of the military since then, along with the simple fact that the military regimes inaugurated after the early 1960s were worn out after 10 or 15 years in power. The proponents of democracy can congratulate themselves on the fact that this time the economic blight did not become political sickness for such newly democratic countries as Ecuador and Peru or for the longer-standing democracies of Costa Rica, Venezuela, and Colombia.

The military propensity to intervention also has much to do with the real or perceived threat of leftist revolution. The praetorian tide of the 1960s was related to the triumph of Castro in Cuba, his plan to overthrow the established order in Latin America, and the hope of Latin American radicals that he represented a new future. The military establishment is basically conservative, independently of the class origins of officers, partly because order and discipline are inherent in the military way, partly because officership represents a successful condition with no interest in basic change, and partly because many officers rise to social prestige, even perhaps to wealth. Hence when officers saw populist governments creating a social ferment, they recalled the dismal fate of Batista's officer corps and thought of assuming power. The discredit of Cuba as a political model and the recession of radicalism in most countries of Latin America has made it seem less necessary for the generals to protect themselves by taking charge.

Such factors, however, change; and history tells us that the democratic-constitutional tide will probably one day be reversed, to a degree and for a time that circumstances will determine. Meanwhile the military men retain the power, or at least the potential, to come to the political forefront when or if they see the need.

MEXICO

Unlike many of its regional counterparts, the Mexican military has been unable to significantly influence its development as an institution over the past 50 years. For the most part, its direction and influence have been dictated by Mexico's political elite. The reaction to the massive bloodletting of the Mexican Revolution of 1910 ultimately contributed to a tradition of relative political stability, which eventually led to the depoliticization of the Mexican military after the 1940 termination of its status as an official sector of the country's monolithic political party, the *Partido Revolucionario Institucional* (PRI).

Since 1946, Mexico has been ruled by civilian presidents who have been relatively successful in their attempts to curb military influence in politics. The military has been granted political influence only during major internal crises. Over the past 15 years, however, such political emergencies have been few and short-lived; consequently, only a series of modest pay raises and improved professional standards have been required to retain the military's loyalty to the political system, although extensive military participation in that system has been discouraged.

The constitution of 1917 assigned the armed forces the responsibility of defending the sovereignty and independence of the nation, maintaining its constitution and laws, and preserving internal order. The last has been the principal mission since World War II.[1] As one analyst stated as recently as 1976, "for Mexico a military defense against a U.S. invasion would scarcely be possible; against one from Guatemala it would be hardly necessary."[2] The preservation of internal order never required exorbitant military budgets, major equipment acquisitions, or substantive structural changes.

In the 1980s, events have reversed traditional trends in a military institution which had not undergone any significant modernization since the end of World War II. The discovery and subsequent exploitation of large petroleum reserves made Mexico the world's fourth largest oil producer. Simultaneously, revolution seethed in neighboring Central America. The responsibility for safeguarding the new oil fields and preventing the Central American revolution from spilling over into Mexico fell on the military. With these new responsibilities, the armed forces embarked on a large-scale modernization program. Their expenditures rose from $567 million in 1979 to $1,403 million in 1981. Moreover, the fact that the Mexican armed forces are scheduled to almost double in size (from 120,000 to 220,000)[3] before 1990 certainly affects their political potential.

For the past 60 years, however, the most remarkable fact about the Mexican military has been its diminished involvement in politics. Roderic Camp found that over the last 40 years, only 14% of Mexico's elites have had military careers.[4] This statistic expresses the situation in Mexico today and the current perception within the military that political ambitions and a military career are no longer compatible. Political attitudes within the Mexican military have undergone a complete evolution since the waning days of the Revolution. Then, the military was the only political actor; today, the typical Mexican military officer considers himself removed from political circles and a political career.

Huntington argued that the nature of modern warfare required a highly skilled military force and a high degree of specialization that would tend to differentiate military from political functions. Thus, many Latin American governments in the 1950s believed that professionalization would remove the military from politics. Unfortunately, this transition only took place in countries which exhibited both political and economic stability. Mexico was one of the few Latin American nations so qualified.[5]

In accordance with the constitution, the secretary of defense (SECDEF) controls the army and air force, while the secretary of the navy (SECNAV) has jurisdiction over all naval forces. These two officers exercise control at the national level, while the respective military and naval zone commanders manage military affairs at the state and local levels in close coordination with the SECDEF and the SECNAV. This is a political safeguard which prevents any one command outside the capital city from possibly becoming too powerful.[6] Rotation every three to four years for military zone commanders and other high-level military commanders was initiated by Cárdenas to preclude the commanders from creating a power base.[7] A strong political tradition has also gradually caused the military to lose interest in politics; since 1929, Mexico has experienced a peaceful transfer of power every six years through the institutionalized presidential succession.

The military has been reduced from the role of principal political actor during and immediately following the Revolution to that of an interest group working within the system to articulate its interests and compete with other interest groups. Within that system loyalty counts heavily, and subordination to a civilian political elite has continued to bring rewards and satisfaction to the military institution. A position of political neutrality and subordination to the civilian government is reinforced in the curricula of military schools, the journals published by the various services, and the speeches of military leaders. The vast majority of officers share this position.[8] For example, when queried about a possible successor in 1982, Secretary of Defense Galván López stated that he was prohibited by law from making any comment on political matters.[9]

The officer corps is also exposed to some political co-optation. At the Superior War College, the first day of class each school year is spent listening to the president's state of the union address in its entirety. The president usually heaps lavish praise on the military for its major contribution to the well-being of the nation and affirms the need for the continuation of this valuable contribution. At the same time, the president authorizes an increase in salary for the armed forces. The importance of the PRI to the stability of the nation is constantly emphasized throughout the Command and General Staff Course. Key political figures come to the Superior War College to commend the officers for contributing to the welfare of the populace and to praise the "Revolutionary system" of which the military is a key part.

In the early 1970s, Lyle McAlister characterized the Mexican officer corps as a conservative group.[10] This generally holds true today; military political and economic attitudes seem to be more conservative than those of most political leaders. More importantly, the military opposes radical changes in the current institutional structure. The military does not object to change but will support it only within the existing framework.

The military resists intervention in politics because it is aware of its limitations as an institution. The military would certainly acknowledge that the PRI-dominated system is not free of shortcomings, but it believes the present system is better than potential alternatives of the extreme Left or Right. Moreover, Mexican officers have not been trained to run the government, as is the case in Brazil and Peru;[11] if the military began to interfere in something it had little preparation for, this would almost certainly detract from its favorable image and status. Finally, the experience of military rule in other Latin American countries has not been encouraging.

Outside the military framework, rewards for officers are limited. They hold a few positions within the various state enterprises, but an officer, to accept a political office or a position within the bureaucracy, has to obtain a leave of absence. During service as an appointed official, he is not permitted to use his military rank or title. A number of military officers elected to political office (governor, senator, or deputy) are permitted to keep their rank, and they probably exert some influence on decision making at the state or local level. However, their influence at the national level is slight.

The Mexican military has, however, been heavily involved since the 1920s in a wide range of civic action activities, including disaster relief, construction of roads, schools, and irrigation projects, supplementary medical assistance in rural areas, improvement of the nation's communications systems, and reforestation. The armed forces are the only federal institution that has the resources to provide disaster relief on a large scale. Because of the military's extensive civic action role, it is generally considered the government's principal agent of economic development in the rural areas.

In recent years, the government has integrated military civic action programs into the national development plan in order to increase efficiency. Although this integration has broadened the responsibilities of the military in economic development, it has restricted the independence the military formerly had in its management of civic action. It is difficult to determine what portion of the army's budget is allocated for civic action; nonetheless, in the mid-1960s, one source estimated that 60% of the military budget was earmarked for it.[12] There has been nothing since then to suggest that the budgetary allocation for civic action has been much altered.

Whereas military industry plays a key role in the economy of a few Latin American nations, this is not the case in Mexico. Mexico has a Department of Military Industry within the Directorate of National Defense, which has responsibility for manufacturing military vehicles and small arms. However, production is on a modest scale. Equipment is produced for domestic use only, and the arms industry generates no export earnings. The naval secretariat, which manages facilities for building, maintaining, and repairing naval vessels, also works only to meet national requirements.

GUATEMALA

The Guatemalan army has dominated the political scene ever since 1954, when, with the support of the Central Intelligence Agency (CIA), it overthrew Jacobo Arbenz. There has been considerable division within the army, however. Right-wing domination of national politics, spreading corruption, and resentment over U.S. use of Guatemalan territory to train Cuban exiles for the Bay of Pigs invasion contributed to a 1961 revolt of junior officers against the incumbent government. This failed, but a few of the officers involved later formed Guatemala's first major Marxist-oriented guerrilla group, the Armed Forces Rebellion (FAR). The following year, the army ousted the elected president and installed a military government, which ruled until 1966. The lack of an elected government restricted U.S. assistance during this period, but training efforts were increased and emphasis was placed on counterinsurgency and the development of civic action programs.

Guerrilla actions continued at a rather low level until 1966. In that year, the military permitted the election and inauguration of a civilian president but insisted that the armed forces be given a free hand in dealing with the guerrillas. The result was a bloody two-year campaign, which reportedly took 15,000 lives in the Department of Zacapa alone, but which effectively destroyed the rural guerrilla movement. The guerrillas then turned to urban terrorism and kidnappings, producing several more years of turmoil before being largely defeated in the cities as well. The dominant figure in the anti-guerrilla campaign was Colonel Carlos Arana Osorio.[13]

Arana's tactics and growing power led to clashes with the civilian president, Julio César Méndez Montenegro. By forming an alliance with Arana's military rivals, the president was able to force him into diplomatic exile as ambassador to Nicaragua. But Colonel Arana continued to cultivate his own support within the army from Managua and later returned to win the presidential election of 1970. As president, Arana completed the defeat of the urban guerrilla forces, killing roughly another 15,000 people in the process.[14] Prominent in this activity were the right-wing paramilitary and terrorist groups such as *Mano Blanco* (white hand) and *Ojo por Ojo* (an eye for an eye). Increasingly the targets of such groups included all potential critics of the status quo: democratic-left and even centrist politicians, labor and peasant leaders, and intellectuals. There were also increasing allegations of links between such organizations and the regular military and police forces.

Arana won the 1970 elections in a relatively honest fashion, but massive fraud characterized the 1974 contest. All three principal candidates were career military officers, but two were supported by moderate civilian reformers who might threaten the status quo. When early returns seemed to indicate a victory for the Christian Democratic-supported candidate, General Efraín Ríos Montt, the government halted the count and declared General Kjell Laugerud the victor.

The latter years of the Laugerud administration were a time of increased corruption, revived guerrilla activity, and growing strains with the United States. In 1977 Guatemala terminated its military assistance agreement with the United States to protest the Carter administration's pressures for improvements in human rights.

The 1978 elections again featured a contest among three military candidates and again the victory of the choice of the army high command was tainted with charges of fraud. After General Romeo Lucas García was sworn in on July 1, 1978, the internal political and military situation deteriorated. Even before his inauguration, an army massacre of Indian protestors at the small town of Panzos had indicated the trend. Violence escalated steadily, with new guerrilla groups, notably the Guerrilla Army of the Poor (EGP) and the Organization of the People in Arms (ORPA), joining the surviving remnants of the FAR in attacks on the government. The security forces and right-wing death squads accelerated their activities, eliminating prominent moderate politicians and eventually forcing even the incumbent vice-president to flee into exile. In January 1980 a group of protestors occupying the Spanish Embassy were slaughtered, leading to a break in relations with Spain and signaling yet another escalation in the level of conflict. All this was accompanied by growing evidence of official corruption and by a steady deterioration in relations with the United States, leading to a Guatemalan refusal to accept a new U.S. ambassador in 1980.

Despite the hopes of the Guatemalan military, the inauguration of Ronald Reagan failed to heal the breach. The U.S. Congress blocked efforts to resume military assistance, while Lucas rebuffed quiet Reagan administration efforts to gain some amelioration of the human rights situation. Meanwhile, the guerrillas made continued progress, gaining control of large sections of the Departments of Quiche, Huehuetenango, and San Marcos. Indians began, for the first time, to give significant support to the guerrillas, and even the traditionally conservative Guatemalan church clashed with the government. The economy also went into a steep decline. By early 1982 Guatemala appeared on the verge of a national civil conflict similar to that engulfing El Salvador.

In the presidential elections of 1982 the Lucas regime tried to impose a hand-picked successor, but a group of younger officers staged a coup, ousting Lucas, annulling the elections, and installing a military triumvirate headed by retired General Efraín Ríos Montt, who had been fraudulently deprived of the presidency in 1974. In June, with the support of the junior officers, Ríos Montt dumped his two partners in the junta and proclaimed himself president.

The 1982 coup reflected a junior officer consensus that spreading corruption and international isolation not only had weakened the fight against the guerrillas but also had reached the point where the army's very survival was threatened. One lieutenant colonel observed, "The guerrillas would not be a serious military problem if not for the corruption, inability to govern, exploitation, and violence that provides the guerrillas recruits and legitimacy."[15]

There were constant reports of plots by the extreme right and of disaffection among senior officers over the influence retained by the advisory council of junior officers. In addition, Ríos Montt's evangelism antagonized the Roman Catholic church, and his reform proposals upset the established oligarchy. In August 1983 another coup ousted Ríos Montt and installed his defense minister, General Oscar Humberto Mejía Victores, as president. This reflected a resurgence of traditional military leadership and an end to the influence of the junior officers. Many of Ríos Montt's social and political experiments, such as his proposals for agrarian reform and his Council of State, which included a large number of Indian representatives, were discarded; but his counterinsurgency program was largely retained. The basic goals of the new administration seemed to be to restore army hierarchy and internal unity, continue the fight against the guerrillas, and hand over the government to acceptable civilians.

The new regime did succeed in making considerable progress against the guerrillas. The establishment of local civil defense units was accelerated, as was the forced resettlement of some indigenous communities. First begun in the early 1980s under the administration of General Romeo Lucas García, the civil patrol units were greatly expanded during the regime of General Efraín Rios Montt and formed a key element of his counterinsurgency strategy. These units continued to expand and were estimated to number as many as 700,000 by early 1984. Participation in these poorly armed and trained self-defense forces is supposedly voluntary, but refusal to cooperate can be taken as evidence of support for subversion.

There was also widespread indiscriminate violence against Indians to destroy the guerrillas' support base. The incidence of urban violence declined dramatically, but the reports from the countryside continued to make it difficult for the United States to provide aid and kept Guatemala internationally isolated. The Reagan administration tried to provide some military assistance to Guatemala, but it was blocked by the Congress.

Officially, the Guatemalan army is apolitical. This principle is enshrined in the constitution and the fundamental laws and statutes of the military. Even career officers serving as president take pains to emphasize this theoretical principle.[16] Yet from 1950 to 1985 all but one of the Guatemalan presidents have been career military officers, and in the 1974 and 1978 elections all three major candidates were officers.

For the military, politics means essentially the struggle among parties, usually headed by civilians, for political offices and power. By its very nature, politics is seen as posing at least a potential threat to the power, privileges, and honor of the military. The commitment to an apolitical military is largely a commitment to avoid total identification of the military institution with any single party. It reflects the army's view that it is separate from and superior to the civil sector. It also reflects the widely held perception that the military's institutional interests are best served by encouraging all other sectors of society to compete for and be dependent on military support. It is typical that, in the Spanish tradition, officers are immune to normal civilian jurisdiction under the *fuero militar.*

In the 1970s this view of politics contributed to the development of what César Sereseres has defined as the *esquema politico*, which was developed by President Arana and his supporters. According to Sereseres: "The political order that evolved depended on tacit understandings among the military institution, the private sector, and political parties to create a facade of democratic politics, marked by periodic elections. Each of the major actors wanted the political system 'managed' and political surprises avoided." Under this esquema the objective was to "depoliticize" such organizations as the labor movement, rural cooperatives, and the university, but this meant increasing coercion and violence directed against "real and suspected political opponents" and produced growing dissent within the officer corps.[17] This dissent contributed to the 1982 junior officer coup. While the 1983 coup represented a return to hierarchy, it does not appear to represent a return to the esquema político. In the June 1984 Constituent Assembly elections, the military allowed relatively free campaigning and voting, producing a victory for the Christian Democrats, a party traditionally viewed with grave suspicion by the officer corps. The military today seems to be striving to find a new political role that will protect institutional interests while avoiding the divisions, conflicts, and international isolation produced by direct involvement in the political process. Politics will remain subject to military supervision and ultimate control, but within that framework the latitude allowed to politicians and other sectors may be considerably expanded.

A critical issue is the ability of the military to prevent the extreme right from using violence to regain the power lost in the June 1984 elections. Efforts by centrist politicians to reduce military privileges or interfere in counterinsurgency operations would greatly increase the chances of a return to older models of political behavior. But failure to make some progress in these areas will undermine the power and credibility of any civilian government.

Recent concrete data on officers' political attitudes are lacking. It is clear that the majority are quite conservative, strongly anticommunist, and suspicious of civilians, especially politicians. They are also nationalist, and there is a strong streak of developmentalism, especially among junior officers who see overcoming underdevelopment and economic dependency as a prime national goal. They are hostile to Great Britain, a feeling generated by Belize and reinforced by the Falklands/Malvinas conflict. They are suspicious of the United States, even more suspicious of Mexico, and actively hostile to Cuba. They feel superior to other Central Americans and are not eager to be drawn into regional conflicts, especially if such involvement would give them the image of being instruments of U.S. policy.

A study of the Guatemalan military in the 1960s divided the officer corps into three groups: economic reformers, moderates, and hard-liners.[18] To some extent this characterization still holds true. There is a minority closely linked with the extreme right-wing ideology epitomized by the National Liberation Movement (MLN). Others would favor a much more moderate, reformist course, even challenging the privileges of traditional elites. But the bulk of the officer corps, strengthened by disillusionment over the Ríos Montt regime, prefers to concentrate on protecting the institution and seeking to restore order and stability to the system.

Another study during that same period sought to measure the political attitudes of individual officers. It found the majority to be against labor unions, political parties, and close ties with the United States. In addition, most were unwilling to treat the Indians as equals. Their views were more divided over the question of military versus civilian government and over the nature of the economic system best for Guatemala.[19] Again, there is little reason to believe that any basic change has taken place in these attitudes, although there may have been a slight moderation in some areas. The military remains suspicious of politics, conservative, elitist, and in many ways isolated from the rest of society.

PANAMA

The Panamanian Defense Forces have performed a variety of military/security functions since the foundation of the republic in 1903. While the military evolved through various stages in most Latin American countries, this evolution has been much more rapid in the case of the Defense Forces, which since the 1940s have changed from purely a police force into a paramilitary institution and most recently into a military institution with an explicit external mission. To borrow Charles Anderson's term, the Defense Forces are to some extent a "living museum," since each new institutional mission is superimposed on preexisting ones and their associated structures.

The three general phases of institutional development (police, paramilitary, and military) appear to be associated with three different patterns of military participation in politics. When the policing mission was paramount (1903–54), the institution served as an instrumental appendage of U.S. and/or Panamanian political interests. From 1903–31, police participation as enforcer of the rules of the political game was largely at the behest of U.S. administrators in the Canal Zone acting with local politicians. Following the U.S. decision in the 1930s to no longer intervene militarily to influence Panamanian politics, the national police obeyed the orders of ruling domestic political factions. The common ingredient during this period was police participation in politics as a subordinate and dependent actor.

The second phase of military participation in politics (1954–78) is associated with the adoption of a paramilitary mission. During the police phase, internal organizational developments had produced a new leadership that was searching for an entry point and rationale for participation in the political decision-making process. After 1954, growing institutional power was married to the doctrine of national security and development (encouraged by the Cold War) to produce a new military-political presence, first as arbiter of elite feuds (under José Antonio Remón and Bolívar Vallarino) and later as central decision maker (under Omar Torrijos).

The third phase of political participation (1978 to present) is associated with adoption of a conventional military mission related to defense of the canal after signing of the 1978 treaties and to the growing realization of the defense implications of the regional crisis. This phase has been of such short duration that it is impossible to tell whether the new mission will affect the character of military participation in politics. Certainly, it is clear from the constitutional changes made in 1983 (in anticipation of the direct presidential elections of 1984) that the Defense Forces had no intention of "returning to the barracks" in any meaningful sense. While these modifications recognized the ultimate authority of the "will of the people," this popular will was to be exercised by a government which continues to rely on military advice: "Power emanates from the people and is exercised by the Government through a distribution of functions between the Executive, Legislative, and Judicial branches acting in harmonic collaboration with the National Guard."[20]

The continuation of an important (perhaps central) role for the Panamanian Defense Forces in politics even after adoption of an external defense mission should not be surprising given the series of historical developments. Prior to 1954, the institution did not have enough social status or cohesion to play a major role in politics. Once internal changes (including mission redefinition) produced such status and cohesion, the military assumed its "rightful" place in the political arena, a place not unlike that historically occupied by the military in many other Latin American countries.

The Guard/Defense Forces' new political status also gave it a growing voice in overseeing the national economy. Guard officers came to power in 1968 in alliance with a small group of *técnicos* within the Liberal party that had been frustrated by opposition of more traditional Liberals and members of the economic elite to tax legislation and other reforms recommended by the Alliance for Progress, reforms deemed necessary by the Liberal técnicos to stem the tide of urban migration, increase agricultural production, and place the national government on a firmer financial footing. Rather than running the economy directly during the 1970s and early 1980s, the military did so by appointing these técnicos to such institutions as the Ministries of the Treasury, the National Bank, and Planning.

In general, it would be fair to say that the military has commanded the heights of the economy since 1968 through this understanding with the modernizing técnicos and has moved the economy beyond the phase of early import substitution toward the provision of services to multinational corporations through, for example, upgrading the national banking laws in 1970. In supporting the election of Nicolás Ardito Barletta to the presidency in 1984, the military once again demonstrated its support for técnico leadership. In removing him in 1985, it demonstrated even more emphatically who really ran the country.

VENEZUELA

Institutionally, the military was only marginally involved in politics during the *caudillo* period, but many military men occupied political roles. Both the institutional and personal involvement of military men declined from 1935–48. General López Contreras took off his uniform but did not leave the ranks when he assumed the presidency. He, General Medina, and the *Acción Democrática* (AD)

leadership successively reduced the number of minstries, governor-
ships, congressional seats, and various other posts held by officers.
By 1948 the military were effectively returned to the barracks, to
which they had never before been confined.

With the coup of November 1948, however, the military formally
assumed more institutional responsibility than ever before, although
fewer officers than during the late 1930s actually occupied governmental posts.[21] Similarly, the recentness of professionalization, the
relative youth of the officer corps after the purges of 1945 and 1948,
the newness of institutional doctrine, the principle of hierarchy, and
the increasing reliance of Pérez Jiménez on his civilian cronies prevented much real institutional involvement in politics. There were
no officer councils, military think tanks, or mobilization programs led
by the ranks. Yet there was a corporate sense of responsibility, and
this was nurtured by junta members through a quasi-consultational
style in institutional meetings.

The military might have become more institutionally involved in
politics after Pérez Jiménez fell if the officer corps had been able to
retain control of the new junta, but the overwhelming civilian rejection of such a role removed both the institution and officers from a
formal political position.[22] That state of affairs has continued to the
present. Consequently, the political role that remains for the military
in Venezuela outside of matters of national security and defense is
informal and indirect, although it is important because of the potential that their near monopoly of force creates.

The military are involved informally in the Venezuelan political
system in at least four important ways. First, there is the informal
side of the material, legal, and moral entitlements which they hold.
This has been discussed elsewhere in terms of the understandings of
the democratic game, especially the norm that military matters will
be treated with delicacy. Politicians are not to engage in scandal-
mongering at the expense of the armed forces; and the preeminence
of the institution in professional matters, promotions, arms acquisitions, tactics, and so on is respected.[23] The material privileges of the
armed forces serve national purposes, so when national necessity
requires, such privileges may also be curtailed, as when the military
took a 10% pay cut with the rest of the civil service in 1961 and
numerous cuts more recently.

Second, the armed forces constitute an informal constituency or
interest group. Their personnel do not have the right to vote, but

both the Christian Democratic party (COPE), and AD and probably other minor political parties have long listened carefully to what servicemen are saying. This practice clearly respects the delicacy rule, and it improves the acceptability and appropriateness of the material, legal, and moral entitlements that are granted when demands are made. For instance, access to housing has recently been more important to both noncommissioned and junior commissioned officers. The demand has been met mainly through semiautonomous public institutions rather than by direct housing allowances or by providing military housing.

Like other interest groups, the military provides both diffuse and specific support for the system. This is most apparent with respect to the display of patriotic values and symbols. A message directed at the military and dignified by a prominent military presence gains status with other groups. Not surprisingly, President Herrera Campíns seemed to be present for every military ceremony imaginable when public approval for his administration reached its nadir. Similarly, the involvement of officers, usually on an individual basis, and sometimes of military units may help increase public support for government activities. Such has clearly been the case in many civic action programs and was probably a factor in many appointments of military men to head quasi-public institutions.

Third, soldiers have values, opinions, and attachments related to policy and political matters that do not involve their immediate military interests. This means that some officers sympathize with ideologies, political parties and leaders, and particular administrations, and at times promotions and assignments at the highest levels may be influenced by the existence of such sympathies. Military rank and responsibilities also confer access to other elites, and military evaluations may enter nonmilitary arenas, such as sports and recreation, youth groups, civic associations, educational institutions, and so on. Such military influence has also been alleged in public decisions about universities, criminal law, immigration, industrial policy, and other matters; but more often the military is simply viewed as part of the power elite or oligarchy, or as defenders of unspecified middle-class interests.

Fourth, the military is politically important because of what it is perceived to achieve. The amount of security people feel from the threat of domestic subversion and from foreign attack provides at least diffuse support for the regime and may actually deter attacks by specific enemies. The dignity and competence with which the armed forces execute their formal functions give testimony to the quality of government performance as a whole. Vocational, civic, and technical education in the armed forces creates social mobility and fulfills needs for human resources. Civic action programs and national guard activities meet specific needs for development and general requirements for social order, protection, and regulation. Moreover, the degree to which the needs, aspirations, and values of active duty and retired personnel and their families—perhaps a million persons or 6% of the population—are fulfilled by the military institution will greatly determine the stakes they feel they have in maintaining the system.

The question of whether the military will in fact maintain the system or will utilize their overwhelming force to change it is commonly linked to the third factor mentioned: the nature of the political values held by the military, the degree to which they are satisfied by the current system, and what direction they would give the country if they were in power. Very little systematic research has been conducted on Venezuelan elites, and officers have been relatively unwilling participants in much of it.

A single study of the general policy preferences of a small sample (only 20) of carefully selected officers was conducted in 1973.[24] Only 14 of the officers, who had been chosen on the basis of high likelihood of holding significant command positions in the future (most of the officers were young lieutenant colonels or the equivalent at the time), actually collaborated in the research. Besides the small sample of officers, party leaders, intellectuals, labor and educational figures, prominent businessmen, and so on were selected for inclusion in the study through a system of elite selection and validation panels. All of the respondents were then questioned about a variety of developmental causes. It was found that only 6 of the 14 officers tended to agree with one another more than they did with one of the seven other empirical groupings of preferences that were discovered (the sample was originally based on 19 ideological, occupational, and economic group categories). This was less coherence than was found among some other elite groups, especially in contrast to several relatively cohesive party and intellectual groups. Furthermore, on at least one policy dimension, the military panel coincided in its preferences with a wider variety of other panels than almost any other panel in the study. It coincided on some issue with every panel except the far-left political group. The military panel it-self tended to be slightly to the right on social issues and fiscal policy but to the left and very nationalistic on economic (trade, investment, and state role) policy. The majority of the officers were actually scattered elsewhere across the spectrum (not with the military panel) on most issues. The greatest consistency and the most common poles of the largest groupings of elites (both individually and in panels) were in the center-left and center-right political panels. This finding is consistent with Venezuela's remarkable policy continuity and with the bipartisan polarity which has developed under the democratic political system.[25]

If this dispersion of policy preferences on nonmilitary matters is assumed to be representative of the officer corps, this and other hints of officer values suggest some tentative conclusions. First, it is highly unlikely that the military would become more politicized over a sin-gle or even a set of nonmilitary policy issues. Second, the greatest likelihood of political activation by the military would be over some matter that involves patriotism or professional/technocratic values, where much more uniformity of views probably exists in the armed forces. Third, there appear to be no very attractive political alliances for the armed forces, a situation which differs substantially from what the military seemed to perceive on the eve of each of the last three successful coups. Finally, given the lack of ideological con-sistency and the degree of dispersion in military policy preferences and the greater centrality of civilian elite positions, any military regime that might come to power in Venezuela would probably be quite centrist in policy orientations.

In contrast to their political roles, the involvement of the Vene-zuelan military in economic and industrial activities first became im-portant during the long Gómez dictatorship. General Juan Vincente Gómez used conscripts extensively to work his enormous agricultural operations, including dairies and slaughterhouses, and he originated new industrial activities in dry-dock ship repairs, gold and salt mines, and other areas directly under the military. Gómez rewarded active duty officers with the opportunity to represent his personal interests in other businesses, such as textile and cement factories, electric works, and sugar mills.

The industrial and agricultural holdings of the Gómez family were expropriated and sold off or put under the control of state enterprises soon after the dictator's death in 1935.[26] During the dictatorship of Pérez Jiménez, industrial development in petrochemicals, steel, and hydroelectricity was again placed under the direction of officers. In both steel and petrochemicals, the officers involved were implicated in the personal profiteering of the dictator.[27]

In contrast, a new standard of managerial quality and honesty in Venezuelan state enterprises was forged by a young captain, Rafael Alfonzo Ravard, who was placed in charge of the first hydroelectric project in the Guayana region in 1952. The remainder of Alfonzo Ravard's military career was spent in developing the region, including the Guayana Corporation (CVG) and its major state enterprises in hydroelectricity, steel, and aluminum.[28] Between 1975 and 1982, Alfonzo, now a general, also developed the new state holding company, The Venezuelan Petroleum Company (PDVSA) and its system of operating companies for the nationalized petroleum industry functions in the same competent, technocratic fashion.

With the example set by General Alfonzo, it is not surprising that the responsibility for the management of a number of other Venezuelan state enterprises and autonomous institutes has been entrusted to a few active duty and retired officers. The companies most commonly directed by officers have been CAVN, the state shipping firm, and *Aeropostal*, the domestic airline, but officers have also run other entities in sports, petrochemicals, electricity, health, consumer protection, and so on. It is, however, rare for officers to serve at subordinate management or technical levels except in military industries.

Service in public enterprises is viewed by some as a violation of the spirit of the constitution, since officers with military duties are prohibited by the constitution from holding political authority. Officers in public enterprise posts are relieved from military assignment to avoid this problem. Yet promotion does not seem to have been inhibited for either successful or unsuccessful officer managers, and such service does not prevent returning to key military posts.

During the 1950s and 1960s the military corporately exercised ownership of a few enterprises on behalf of the Venezuelan state. These included the Institute for the Social Welfare of the Armed Forces (IPSFA), with its system of wholesale stores, retirement services, and pension programs, and the *Círculo Militar* and its extensive recreational and military club facilities. IPSFA eventually also acquired ownership of *Horizonte de Seguros* (a major insurance firm) and some minor holdings. In the early 1970s IPSFA and other entities, in corporate representation of the armed forces and its branches and usually in conjunction with other public enterprises, also began to acquire other business interests in housing, construction, and real-estate management in order to supply low-cost housing to armed forces personnel.

With the petrodollar bonanza of the mid-1970s, President Carlos Andrés Pérez started a new complex of military enterprises. These were to include aircraft production, shipbuilding, and munitions manufacturing. VENEMAICA was established for aircraft construction. However, DIANCA and CAVIM were inaugurated to create a national monopoly for munitions. When the petrodollar bonanza dried up, the plans were scaled back, and Venezuela remains an insignificant military exporter. The new military leadership is placing emphasis on maintenance, repair, and modification activities.

Among Venezuela's 300 or so public enterprises and autonomous institutes, which contribute close to a third of gross national product and have over 600,000 employees, the half dozen military enterprises and half dozen other military-controlled entities are of fairly minor importance. The armed forces have a similarly minor role in public finance and employment. The Ministry of Defense budget, at about Bs. 4.9 billion (a little under U.S. $400 million at the current free rate of exchange) in 1984, was only about 6% of the total central government budget and less than 1.5% of GNP; in addition, it is exceeded by the budgets of several other ministries. Defense employment of about 100,000 (including civilian, national guard, and active duty military personnel) is also less than 1.5% of the national labor force. The military provides its most significant political-economic contributions to the nation through its more commonplace military responsibilities, such as frontier settlement, control of borders and drug trafficking, protection of the petroleum industry, civic projects, provision of basic and vocational education to recruits, and the array of duties carried out by the National Guard (FAC) in forestry, natural resource protection, highway development, industrial and customs control, and so on.

COLOMBIA

It is paradoxical that Colombia, although it has suffered perhaps more political violence than any other country of Latin America, has seen less military politics than almost any other Latin American country. After 1886, only three generals have been president, and only one, Gustavo Rojas Pinilla, came to power by coup (1953). Colombia has had very long periods of uninterrupted constitutional government. In the early 1930s in Latin America, only Uruguay, Costa Rica, and Colombia had continuous civilian government; in the mid-1970s in South America, only Venezuela and Colombia could be called democracies. It has been the general expectation that the Colombian armed forces should remain out of politics, and they take pride in aloofness. In the 1960s and 1970s, however, the military was brought to the forefront by its role in defending the National Front against insurgencies. During this period the military occupied a large place in the government and from time to time there were rumors of a possible military takeover.

In the nineteenth century, the military tradition so strong in most Latin American countries did not take hold in Colombia. During the wars for independence a large fraction of the soldiers (especially officers) of the Federation of Gran Colombia were from Venezuela. Many of these troops remained in Colombia with Simón Bolívar and were resented during the early days of independence. Being predominantly of lower-class background, they were regarded with scorn by Colombian aristocrats, who acquired an antimilitary outlook. Throughout the nineteenth century the Colombian army seldom exceeded 3,000 poorly paid and untrained men, lacked a professional officer corps, and was sometimes more or less disbanded. During this turbulent period the regular army was frequently used as a pawn, if not an irrelevant factor, in the Liberal versus Conservative struggles. The several civil wars, in fact, were largely waged by amateurs.

The prestige of the military reached a low point in the disastrous War of the Thousand Days (1899–1902), in which the incompetence of the armed forces was apparent. The military suffered a further blow to its prestige in its botched attempt to quell the Panamanian revolution of 1903 by an overland march. In order to improve military prestige, General Rafael Reyes (1904–09) made a concerted effort to instill professionalism in the Colombian military; but the forces were little developed, being only 1,500 strong as late as the 1920s.[29] The Colombian army was the smallest in Latin America in proportion to its population.

The Colombian army acted as a national force for the first time in the conflict with Peru over the Leticia area (1932–34). The military's relative success raised its prestige and gave the army, enlarged to 14,000, political weight, in a bureaucratic rather than partisan sense. The neutrality of the military was brought into question by the inauguration of a Liberal president in 1930. The reformist Liberal president, Alfonso López Pumarejo, disliked the military, whom he publicly referred to as parasites,[30] and feared that the mostly Conservative officers would oppose his proposals for social change. He hence tried to secure promotion of officers loyal to himself, built up a national police to offset the army, and occupied the army with colonization projects in Colombia's eastern regions. Some officers consequently conspired against him and essayed a coup in 1936, but the majority remained loyal to the civilianist tradition. After the coup attempt, numerous Conservative officers were removed, including some not involved in subversive actions. The following presidency of a moderate Liberal, Eduardo Santos (1938–42), saw cool but less strained relations with the military. Santos tried to conciliate the soldiers by improved training in cooperation with U.S. missions of hemispheric defense. The succeeding second presidency of López, however, saw a repetition of the first, and policies similar to those of the first term provoked a coup in 1944: a military group briefly held the president captive. Again, the coup failed because of the distaste of most officers for political involvement and fears of civilian support for a popular president. One result was a constitutional amendment (reinforcing previous legal provisions) that forbade political activity by armed forces personnel.

The period of political peace and order that had begun in 1902 came to an end in the late 1940s, as both traditional parties divided and tensions rose excessively. A Conservative, Mariano Ospina Pérez, won the presidency in 1946 by a plurality because of the split of the Liberals into moderate and radical wings; and the Conservatives began bringing the military into play to keep order and reinforce their minority position. Many officers were placed in charge of *municipios.*

After the assassination of a popular Liberal leader provoked tremendous riots (the Bogotazo of 1948), Colombia descended into the terrible *violencia* that took ultimately as many as 300,000 lives. This was practically a civil war in the countryside of Liberals, who were a majority of the population, against the Conservative government. The latter, of course, called on the army to protect it; and in this role the armed forces increased several times over and acquired importance. In 1949 a group of officers asked President Ospina Pérez to turn power over to them because of his inability to cope with the disturbances, but they were not backed by the majority.

When a radical Conservative, Laureano Gómez, who became president in 1950, tried to make the armed forces completely the tool of his arbitrary regime and keepers of order over or instead of the police, Liberal officers and men left the army (or were forced out), often to join the guerrillas. The military became discontented, however, with being used, often illegally and brutally, to support an increasingly repressive dictatorship. Gómez's naming of a civilian as minister of war was also regarded as provocative.

Consequently, it was with the support of Conservative officers (mostly affiliated with the Ospina faction), not Liberals, that the commander of the army forces, General Gustavo Rojas Pinilla, overthrew Gómez when the latter tried to dismiss him in 1953. The coup was broadly welcomed, and Rojas was hailed as savior and peacemaker. An effort was made to stop the guerrilla warfare by amnesty, and the level of violence was much reduced for a time. Although supported by the armed forces, Rojas was rather a personal ruler than a representative of the military. Many soldiers had high positions, but they were selected as cronies of the president rather than as representatives of the forces.

The semimilitary government rapidly decayed. Rojas tried to become a demagogic leader of the masses in Peronist style and, this failing, turned to pure coercive dictatorship, with increasing reliance on a political police corps, the Colombian Intelligence Service. He wished to make the military his following, in opposition to the traditional parties, and he helped it with public funds. But for the officers it was an unwished role. In a deteriorating situation, Rojas had himself reelected president, and the army joined the popular movement of protest to remove him.

The prestige of the military was injured by the corruption and arbitrary actions of the Rojas government. It was revived, however, by the behavior of the high officers who formed a junta to restore constitutional government. The junta encouraged the Liberal and Conservative leaderships to compromise their differences and agree to the formation of a National Front dividing offices on a basis of parity formally for 16 years (an arrangement continued partially to this day). The military thereupon, after less than a year in power, turned the presidency over to a civilian in 1958. Pro-Rojas officers tried to disrupt the 1958 National Front elections, but they were repudiated by the large majority of the corps.[31]

The National Front enabled the armed forces to return to non-partisanship, with a military minister of war; and the smooth functioning of the Front made it possible for the forces to play a major part in the national life while remaining on the margin of the political contest. The Front also ended the Liberal versus Conservative aspect of guerrilla warfare, which became in part banditry, in part attempted revolution, to a considerable degree inspired and to some degree supported by Castro and Cuba. But the continuing guerrilla conflict gave the military an important role in support of the National Front and the established order.

In its antisubversive role, the army worked closely with the police in both cities and countryside and came largely to control the police organization.[32] Under the state of siege prevailing throughout this entire period, the army had powers of search, seizure, and investigation; officers held many local executive offices; and the army acted in a judicial capacity, trying and punishing crimes against the state, including not only guerrilla activity but such crimes as bank robbery, kidnapping, and land seizures.

Under the direction of army commander General Alberto Ruiz Novoa, the army undertook in 1962 a program of civic action (Plan Lazo) to reduce support for the guerrillas by teaching literacy, establishing clinics, bringing electricity to villages, digging wells, repairing roads and bridges, helping agriculture, and even to some extent distributing land. Plan Lazo plus aggressive campaigning eliminated many guerrilla areas and groups during the period of most activity, 1962–65. However, many officers came to feel that the army was out of place doing the work of the ministries of education, health, and public works. General Ruiz, on the contrary, wanted to do much more for social justice, seeing it as the better answer to the guerrilla threat; and he alarmed the elite by making his sentiments public. He also began talking and behaving slightly like one who has a coup in mind. In 1965, leading officers supported his removal, despite his great popularity,[33] and the principle of nonpoliticization was thereby affirmed. The next year Ruiz ran for president with poor results.

After the mid-1960s, the guerrillas seemed more clearly under communist leadership and foreign-influenced, and the conservative tendencies of the army were consequently strengthened. Following the departure of Ruiz, the civic action program was deemphasized, and relations with the government were smoothed. The submissiveness of the military was demonstrated in 1969 when President Carlos Lleras Restrepo discharged the popular commander of the army, General Jaime Pinzón Caicedo, because of his effort to secure more budgetary independence for the military; no audible protest was given by the general's fellow officers. In 1970 there were rumors that the army would intervene if Rojas Pinilla, who had returned to Colombia to run for president as a populist, should be victorious; however, the army proclaimed neutrality.

Coup rumors circulated again in 1975, when President Alfonso López Michelsen maneuvered the army commander Alvaro Valencia Tovar into retirement by moving one of Valencia's subordinates without consulting Valencia. As did Ruiz Novoa, Valencia wished the armed forces to mix more social improvement with military action against the perennial guerrillas. Again, there were coup rumors, but a majority of the officers apparently approved the ouster. Civic action was left behind by military action as guerrilla movements resurged somewhat in the mid-1970s.

In 1976 the armed forces were hurt by reports of corruption. In 1977, however, 33 generals and admirals, headed by the commander of the armed forces, publicly petitioned the president to protect the military reputation—a joint demand that was legally prohibited but politically accepted, demonstrating the strength of the military position. The following year a new National Security Statute increased the role of the military in the maintenance of law and order, including control of strikes and combatting of urban terrorism (led by the M–19 movement, a violent descendant of the Rojas Pinilla party). The military undertook mass arrests, and there were alleged abuses of political and civil rights, including the use of torture. Around this time in subsequent years there was also a rise of right-wing death squads, such as Death to Kidnappers (MAS), which eliminated supposed supporters of the guerrillas. The squads seem to have been made up largely of active duty or retired military personnel.

In 1978 President Julio César Turbay charged the army with suppression of the narcotics traffic. Despite the reluctance of leading officers, the army undertook this task. The job led, however, to demoralization and corruption; and after three years the army was relieved of the uncongenial assignment, although it has remained indirectly involved.

The officers preferred fighting communists, and the leadership of the 1980s increasingly emphasized the Cuban connections of the most important guerrilla bands. In 1981 Turbay tried to bring about an amnesty, but military hard-liners opposed it—as did the guerrillas—and launched a major offensive. Under pressure from the armed forces, Colombia broke diplomatic relations with Cuba in 1981, on grounds that the latter was infiltrating guerrilla trainers. On the other hand, General Fernando Landazábal Reyes, in the tradition of Ruiz Novoa and Valencia Tovar, warned of the need to change social conditions in order to combat the guerrillas; and the fact that he was not reprimanded was seen as derogatory to civilian authority.

The guerrillas, in any case, were a waning force; in May 1981 General Luis Carlos Camacho Leyva, commander of the armed forces, proclaimed victory over them. This was optimistic, but in mid-1982 the special powers of 1978 were largely (but not fully) revoked, and the long-time state of siege was lifted. In 1982 the new president, Belisario Betancur, proposed a general amnesty to bring the decades of bloodshed to an end. Top military men, including Landazabal Reyes, were wary of the idea, but they were induced to go along because the president gave them both a hardsome package of arms modernization and an informal veto over negotiations. After arduous bargaining, in August 1984 a truce was agreed between the government and the three chief guerrilla organizations, and the violence that had been sputtering or flaring since 1948 came more or less to a standstill until the truce came apart in 1985.

The winding down of the chief business of the military could not fail to change its political role. There was some suspicion in the 1970s that the army did not pursue the guerrillas as diligently as it might because of their utility for keeping up the status of the military. Indeed, it appeared that the threat of bands, numbering ordinarily under 2,000, hardly justified the broad powers assumed to fight them. In any case, the armed forces have acquired a strong position in the political system, even if they no longer have assignments outside the usual franchise of the military. They are close to the president, forming his *Casa Militar* (military household) and participating in both high-level councils and the budget process.

Officers have only moderate prestige, and the proportion of the nation's youth and material resources going to the armed forces is small. The military stake in the economy is small in comparison with such countries as Chile and Argentina. The traditional repugnance of the homogeneous elite for military government, dating from the experience of the war for independence and its aftermath, is a major characteristic of Colombian democracy. Yet the military, basically conservative and supportive of the status quo even though some of its members perceive a need for change, is an essential pillar of the oligarchic-democratic polity. The soldiers seem satisfied and have little or no inclination to take the reins of government; the civilians, on the other hand, are not likely to undertake anything very distasteful to the forces backing them.

PERU

The Peruvian military has shown no reluctance to become involved in politics whenever it is deemed necessary. Between 1914 and 1968 they carried out a *golpe* eight times, and a majority of Peru's presidents since independence have been military officers.

In addition, the constitution of 1933 gave the military a political role to play. Under Article 213, "The purpose of the armed forces is to assure the rights of the Republic, the fulfillment of the Constitution and the laws, and the preservation of public order." The constitution also allows members of the armed forces to participate legally in politics without having to retire from active service.

The military's political orientation since the early 1930s has been shaped by two forces: the platform of the progressive middle-class party, the American Popular Revolutionary Alliance (APRA), and the military's implacable opposition to that platform. On the one side, the party offered from the 1930s onward a nationalistic and progressive platform which became part of the national consciousness; on the other, the military opposed the tactics by which APRA tried to obtain power, thereby remaining through the 1950s the instrument by which the oligarchy and the elites maintained the status quo. The military developed no reformist orientation based on an identification with middle-class interests because APRA had already occupied that ground. During this period, military interventions took on a personalist and a populist cast, serving to support the status quo but at the same time trying to carry out measures which would gain widespread support, in part to wean the people from APRA.

A series of developments in the 1950s and 1960s served to change the way in which the Peruvian military conceived its political role. The new professionalism shifted emphasis from external security to internal security; from highly specialized skills incompatible with political skills to highly interrelated political and military skills; from a restricted to an unrestricted scope of military professional action; from professional socialization rendering the military politically neutral to socialization politicizing the military; from an old professionalism contributing to an apolitical military and civilian control to a new professionalism contributing to military political-managerialism and role expansion.[34] This change derived primarily from internal training and secondarily from external events, including a new wave of mass protests and mobilizations, the guerrilla actions of 1965, land invasions, repressions, the new militancy of the urban labor movement, the Cuban Revolution, and the new social philosophy of the Catholic church after Vatican II.[35] At the same time the Peruvian military met increasing difficulty in the 1960s in getting arms from the United States on their own terms.

Although the new reformist attitudes were influenced by external events, they were crystallized by study and reflection of the institutions themselves. The military had no class allies beyond a few individual progressive civilians and church people and no experimental laboratories or sounding boards outside itself when it took over in 1968 and began an activist reformist top-down political, social, and economic experiment of a nature and scope unprecedented in Peruvian—indeed in Latin American—history.

In view of substantial political-ideological diversity within the military, the results of the coup exceeded the boundaries of the consensus within the military and led to general alienation from those outside the military. "The military reformers discovered that an abstract national interest defined from above could not be superimposed on the specific interests of contending classes and class fractions. Internally divided and incapable of making a definitive choice of class allies, the regime alienated all classes."[36]

The 1979 constitution no longer gives the military the same political prerogatives as that of 1933, nor does it allow military personnel on active duty to hold elective political office. But complementary legislation, especially the Mobilization Law of 1980, gives the military the political prerogative, once a state of emergency has been declared by the president, to take over governing responsibilities in a disturbed area and to place that area under military control. This is a partial solution to the perennial Peruvian problem of a politically active military, enabling the military to play its role without having to take over the entire political system. Furthermore, in 16 articles of the constitution of 1979, the powers, duties, and responsibilities of the military and police are spelled out explicitly in an apparent effort to enable the elected civilian government to rule without constant fear of a military coup.

However, legal instruments have not prevented the Peruvian military from intervening in the past when it felt driven to do so and are unlikely to prevent it from doing so in the future. What keeps the military from political intervention in the mid-1980s is the sober realization from their 12-year experience that governing is much more difficult than planning for governing. In addition, there is a new flexibility on the part of civilian politicians, who are more prepared to compromise than to push for confrontation because they now know that they might be removed from politics for 10 or 15 years should a confrontation occur. With the erosion of the historic enmity between the army and APRA, the continuation and strengthening of the tenuous strands of civilian rule seem possible. It was truly a landmark when the military subordinated itself to an elected APRA president, Alán García, in 1985.

BRAZIL

In Brazil, military involvement in politics began shortly after the Paraguayan War, in the waning years of the empire. Conscious of their new power and important role in this conflict, irritated by efforts of civilian politicians to "put the military back in its place," and unhappy with the inglorious task of capturing runaway slaves, the military establishment began pressing its institutional demands on successive cabinets. Resentment grew because of the last cabinet's dispersal of "activist" officers to the hinterlands and its intentions to strengthen rival state militias.[37]

A forum for expressing institutional opinion was created in 1887 when the Military Club was established in Rio de Janeiro. Six days before the empire was toppled in a bloodless coup, Benjamin Constant, speaking at the Military Club, demanded "full powers to free the military from a state of affairs incompatible with its honor and its dignity."[38] On October 22, 1889 the same exponent of "Republican Positivism" claimed in a speech at the Military College "the undeni-

able right of the armed forces to depose the legitimate powers constituted by the nation when the military understands that its honor
requires that this be done, or judges it necessary and convenient for
the good of the country." Thus, the basis for the "moderating pattern" of civil-military relations in Brazil was established.[39]

Stepan summarizes the "moderating pattern" as follows:

1. All major political actors attempt to co-opt the military. A politicized military is the norm.
2. The military is politically heterogenous but also seeks to maintain a degree of institutional unity.
3. The relevant political actors grant legitimacy to the military
   under certain circumstances to act as moderators of the political
   process and to check or overthrow the executive, especially one
   involving massive mobilization of new groups previously excluded from political participation.
4. Approval given by civilian elites to the politically heterogenous
   military to overthrow the executive greatly facilitates the construction of a winning coup coalition. Denial by civilians that the
   overthrow of the executive by the military is a legitimate act
   conversely hinders the formation of such a coalition.
5. While it is generally held legitimate for the military to exercise
   temporary political power, it is not considered legitimate for the
   military to assume the direction of the government for long
   periods.
6. A rough value congruence is the result of civilian and military
   socialization via schools and literature. The military doctrine of
   development is also roughly congruent with that of parliamentary
   groups. The military officers' social and intellectual deference
   facilitates military co-optation and continued civilian leadership.

During the First Republic (1889–1930) the military was frequently used by civilian central governments to intervene in recal-
citrant states, replacing one land-based oligarchical clique with another favored by the government in Rio. The military intervened
directly in national politics only three times during this period, all
when there were deep divisions among civilian politicians. In 1910,
Army Minister Hermes da Fonseca was co-opted as presidential candidate, under the tutelage of Senator Pinheiro Machado, and served a
four-year term. In 1922, the military were again drawn into a presi-

dential campaign with a divided civilian oligarchy. Resentment against the latter exploded in the "lieutenants' (*tenentes*) revolt," but this was isolated from civilian groups. In 1930, a civil war broke out after a disputed presidential election. The military intervened to depose the ruling faction and immediately turned power over to the Liberal Alliance rebels led by Getúlio Vargas.

After 1930, military support for the new (and provisional) president was based on a doctrine that had its origins in the tenentes movement. The new doctrine, focusing on "preemptive modernization" of the state, was intended to head off a massive social revolution from below. In 1937, military support for the *Estado Noro* was based on institutional modernization interests and the desire to forestall mass mobilization of new political groups.

From 1945–64 the success of military intervention in politics was correlated with the degree of legitimacy that important civilian groups ascribed (before coup attempts) to the president or president-elect. Thus, in 1950, when President-elect Vargas's legitimacy was challenged on the grounds that he lacked an absolute majority of the popular vote (he had 48%), the military failed to act. In 1954, however, Vargas's legitimacy had been severely eroded by scandal and confrontation with the air force; and a military ultimatum provoked his suicide. In 1955, President-elect Juscelino Kubitschek was challenged for lacking an absolute majority (he had 36%), being part of the Vargas group, and having received votes from communists; this time the military intervened in a preventative coup to guarantee Kubitschek's inauguration. In 1961, Vice-President João Goulart's legitimacy was challenged (following Jânio Quadros's resignation), because Goulart was perceived to be a Vargas heir and to have links with communists. The coup attempt failed because important civilian sectors and part of the military supported Goulart and the constitutional succession.

All three republican constitutions (1891, 1934, and 1946) described the political role of the military in two key articles. One stated that the military was a permanent national institution specifically charged with the task of maintaining law and order in the country and guaranteeing the continued normal functioning of the three constitutional powers, the executive, the legislature, and the judiciary. The other made the military obedient to the executive, but only "within the limits of the law." Brazil's two authoritarian constitutions, however, drafted without a constituent assembly (1824 and 1937), gave the military no such missions. In the context of political debate regarding the election of a Constituent Assembly in November 1986, and its task of devising a new constitution in 1987, in late 1985 the military made strong public statements to the effect that "their traditional constitutional role should be preserved in the new document."

After 1930, Vargas gave the army a new political role as an agency of national reconstruction and development. Construction battalions built roads and railways in the vast interior, and officers were placed in high administrative posts and associated with industrialization projects such as the Volta Redonda steel plant and the Petrobras petroleum monopoly. This new mission reinforced the doctrine of industrial development as a basis for national strength and security and the positivist ideology of a technocratic scientific approach to national problems.

This "moderating pattern" of military involvement in politics changed abruptly in 1964. At first, the rhetoric and rationale of the conspirators were similar to previous interventions, that is, portraying the army as moderator. The government threatened to subvert the Congress through a popular assembly to execute basic reforms and unleash agitation by the illegal labor organization, the CGT. The threat to military discipline and hierarchy became real in late March, when amnesty was granted to mutinous enlisted men.

Once the 1964 coup had been successful, however, the military assumed power directly instead of installing an alternative civilian political elite in government. Because the nation's security and development had been damaged by a weakening of political institutions, it was felt that the firm hand of a military president backed by unity of the armed forces was needed. Most political and economic leaders supporting the coup against Goulart, including the several potential civilian candidates for president, agreed; and the Congress elected Marshal Humberto Castelo Branco to fill out the remainder of the presidential term through January 1966, when the new president, directly elected in October 1965, would take office.

Within the new military governing circle there were, however, divergent opinions regarding whether cosmetic or major surgery was needed on the body politic. The new president was granted special emergency powers for 60 days, and the liberal 1946 constitution was retained. The minor surgery strategy won out, although certain politicians, public employees, and military personnel (allegedly communist, radical, subversive, and/or corrupt) lost their jobs/mandates and political rights for ten years, and series of police/military investigations (IPMs) were installed.

The descent into full military dictatorship occurred in two stages. First, in 1965–66, when the hard-line faction became convinced that continued direct elections for governors and the next president would merely return the same Vargas/Kubitschek/Goulart coalition to power, Castelo Branco was forced to reshape the party system, make the election for the president indirect, extend his own term by 14 months, and renew the special extraconstitutional powers. During this crisis, Castelo Branco lost control of his succession; and his army minister, General Artur Costa e Silva, became the high command's choice. The 1946 constitution had been mangled and rendered inadequate, so the outgoing president forced a new constitution through the lame-duck Congress as an "inauguration gift" for the new president in March 1967.

The second stage of transition to military dictatorship evolved in two acts: the decreeing of the Fifth Institutional Act (AI-5) in December 1968, which gave the president complete dictatorial powers and adjourned Congress; and the August-September 1969 alterations of the 1967 constitution by the military junta, which took power from an incapacitated Costa e Silva. Brazil had arrived at the depths of military dictatorship as the "economic miracle" surged.

When the "economic miracle" began to sour from 1974 on, with increasing opposition from the business sector and middle classes, the Geisel and subsequent Figueiredo governments began a policy of military disengagement from politics and a "political opening" (abertura), aimed at the eventual return of full political power to civilian politicians.

This long task was not easy, however, because military penetration of civilian political decision making and public administration had been and still is quite deep. The military is involved in the security apparatus of the National Information Services (SNI), the Division of Security and Information (DSI), and the Offices of Security and Information (ASI), in addition to being involved in "extracurricular activities," from gold mining to land reform and financial scandals. Terrorist bombings and physical eliminations were in the hands of active duty and retired military personnel.[40] In 1983, a rough count totalled no less than 8,000 retired officers in administrative positions in the federal government or its state and autonomous agencies.[41]

In 1984, civilian politicians with apprehensions regarding the final stage of the abertura in the current succession were again trying to co-opt the military with the specter of an "Argentinization" of Brazil should populist politicians come to power and mass mobilization begin anew. The military understood that popular and elite alienation from the current government was widespread and that the current government's candidate would have no chance in a direct election. Because of a lack of unity among government-party politicians, would-be presidential candidates, and other elite groups (a disunity reminiscent of 1963–64), the three military ministers issued a stern note condemning politicians' abuse of the president, the armed forces, and government institutions.[42]

In early 1984, when massive demonstrations for direct presidential elections were held and polls showed nearly 90% of the population in favor of such a change, army commanders were very sensitive about using troops for crowd control/repression and thrust this burden on police troops under state governments. The government invoked a state of siege in Brasília to secure the defeat of an amendment for direct elections and federalized local police for this occasion. It was evidently feared that any attempt to turn back the abertura process would be resisted at the garrison level. In September 1984, however, following the formation of the Democratic Alliance coalition between the PMDB and PSD Liberal Front dissidents, the army high command summoned all 400 officers posted in Brasília to a session with slides and other documentation linking politicians in this opposition coalition to the Communist party and its splinter groups. The withdrawal of the military from the government, however, could not be halted.

In late 1984, the Army High Command checkmated Figueiredo's "continuist" strategies by stating that it would accept the outcome of the January 1985 electoral college election and that the Constitution and "rules of the game" would be maintained. As a sign of good faith to the Democratic Alliance led by Governor Tancredo Neves, the Commander of the Planalto Military Region, General Newton Cruz (who had commanded the state of siege in Brasília), was sacked by the High Command on November 20. The two key generals in this decision, Leonidas Pires Gonçalves and Iván de Souza Mendes, were named Army Minister and SNI Director, respectively, by President-elect Neves in early March 1985. In any case, the record of human rights violations by the Brazilian military was not comparable to the Argentine, and José Sarney, who became president because of the death of Neves, showed no inclination to add prosecution of the military for old infractions to his many troubles.

Although faced with increased economic and political dependence internationally and a severe economic crisis due to a bankrupt "model" (both of which contribute to new problems of internal security), the armed forces seem to retain reasonable unity and may perhaps continue their political role, or at least their tutelage of politics, for many years. One reason that the military is not likely to fully disengage from politics is the large number of retired or on-leave officers ensconced in the state enterprises, which comprise approximately a quarter of Brazil's economy.

The role of the Brazilian army in economic planning within the doctrine of national security began after the 1930 revolution, when the Vargas government embarked on a program for the autonomous development of heavy industry. During the period of economic nationalism in the 1950s and early 1960s, individual military officers held key positions, such as the presidency of the newly created state oil monopoly, Petrobras. It was only after 1964, however, that the military assumed a major role in the direction and administration of the nation's economy. Plans for reorienting the economy toward "Security and Development" (S & D) had been worked out prior to 1964 by the army's Superior War College; many of these plans were immediately put into effect when the military took charge.

The military has had a role in various sectors: the heading and critical staffing of many economic ministries; strategic planning within the National Security Council and interministerial councils, such as the Council for Industrial Development (CDI); the creation and administration of the vast complex of state enterprises, especially those created after 1967; and full control of the burgeoning Brazilian arms industry.

To keep foreign investment out of key areas, state enterprise was expanded, a growth stimulated by nationalist military officers and nourished by resources generated by the post-1967 economic miracle period and easy international credit. The directors, top administrators, and much of the staff of these enterprises were drawn from the military; most of those attracted by this new role left active duty. The Ministries of Mines and Energy, Communications, Transportation, and Interior have commonly been headed by military officers. After 1964, on occasion the portfolios of the Ministries of Education, Labor, Social Welfare, Justice, and Agriculture have been entrusted to ex-military officers. In the 1985 Sarney government, however, there was only one military minister of a civilian department.

The details of economic planning in the Ministries of Economic Planning and Finance have always been left to civilian technicians, although their performance has been criticized by military officers, especially during the hard times since 1974. Over past years, however, more and more key economic decisions were submitted to the National Security Council. When land tenure problems reached explosive proportions in 1982, General Danilo Venturini left his position as chief of Military Household (*Vila Militar*) to take charge of the newly created Extraordinary Ministry (without portfolio) for Land Affairs, while retaining the position of secretary general of the National Security Council.

The armed forces also dominate the arms industry, coordinating many civilian–run and owned corporations as well as managing state enterprises in this sector. The Brazilian arms industry not only supplies most of the needs of the Brazilian forces but has become a major rapid-growth high-technology earner of foreign exchange, recently bringing in about $3 billion annually.

The decision to establish a heavy arms industry in Brazil was a pragmatic derivative of the military's ideology of "Security and Development." By the late 1960s, Brazil had achieved an advanced level of industrial technology in the production of heavy capital goods, motorized vehicles, and light aircraft. Domestic supply of basic armaments, which would be immune to changing priorities of international politics, was a national security priority. By the late 1970s, Brazil's arms industry was a major foreign-exchange earner, thoroughly integrated with foreign and commercial policies vis-à-vis the Third World. The advent of the Brazilian arms industry furnished the armed forces with a new legitimate role in the nation's political economy, thus reinforcing the doctrine of Security and Development and at the same time providing the military with a legitimate nationalist function during the difficult transition to civilian rule.

CHILE

Except for a period of military and *caudillo* rule between 1924 and 1932, Chile had been under civilian rule from the time of the adoption of the 1833 constitution until the overthrow of Salvador Allende on September 11, 1973. Since that time it has been governed by General Augusto Pinochet and the junta of the armed forces. Military men are in many key positions in government, and the military institutions as such are represented formally in government through the four representatives of the army, navy, air force, and national police (*carabineros*) on the junta. Pinochet's position as president of the Republic originally was derived from his status as commander in chief of the army at the time of the coup and his assertion of predominance in the junta during the first few months thereafter, but it has since been legitimized by his election for an eight-year term. He was the only candidate in the constitutional plebiscite of September 1980. The junta can also propose a presidential candidate for another plebiscite in 1989, but given the pressures in Chile for return to elections and civilian rule, it seems unlikely that this will occur.[43]

While military men served as presidents of Chile from 1831 to 1851, they effectively subordinated the Chilean armed forces to the constitutional authorities and used the National Guard as a counterbalance to the small full-time military force. The Prussian tradition imparted to the Chilean army by Emil Körner not only emphasized strict discipline and a hierarchic conception of authority but also introduced a professionalism that became increasingly dissatisfied with the corruption and inefficiency of the parliamentary republic established after the 1891 civil war. In the 1920s the military became involved directly in politics, staging military interventions in 1924, 1925, and 1927. Four years of plebiscitary rule by the military strong man, Carlos Ibáñez, ended in 1931, and constitutional democracy was restored in 1932. Thereafter the armed forces joined other corporate interest groups whose main concern was protecting their salaries and privileges from the ravages of inflation. Direct political activity was rare, and when it occurred it was mainly to protect the eroding military standard of living.

By the 1960s Chileans could boast that they, in contrast to countries around them, had developed a nonpolitical and constitutionalist military. The test of that constitutionalism came with the 1970 election campaign. Early in the campaign, when it appeared that the

Marxist candidate, Salvador Allende, might be victorious, General René Schneider, the commander in chief of the army, announced that the armed forces would support whoever was elected through the constitutional processes; and during the period between the popular election and the congressional decision, the Chilean armed forces rejected covert U.S. efforts to encourage a coup. In the course of the Allende presidency, however, the military became increasingly politicized, a process which culminated in the September 11, 1973 coup that brought Pinochet to power.

Since 1973 nearly all important decisions have been made by Pinochet and a few close advisors, rather than in a corporate institutional way. Pinochet meets regularly with the generals and admirals to explain and defend his policies, but there is little evidence that they act collectively to limit or direct him. The Chilean constitutions of 1833, 1925, and 1980 describe the military as nonpolitical (*no deliberantes*), and Pinochet seems to have succeeded in maintaining this tradition, even in what is officially the Government of the Armed Forces.

Important decisions of Pinochet and his advisors are ratified by the four members of the junta (under the 1980 constitution there is a quasi-separation of powers, since the army is represented in the junta by General Oscar Benavides, rather than Pinochet himself), who represent the armed forces. Over the years there has not been much evidence of substantive discussion within the junta except when the direct interests of the armed forces are affected, as in relation to retirement benefits or the new mining law. In 1984, however, the representative of the navy, Admiral José Toribio Merino, vetoed or buried some Pinochet proposals (a tax increase and authorization to call plebiscites), and the air force representative, General Fernando Matthei, spoke out in favor of accelerating the political opening. Despite these exceptions, after a dozen years of military rule one can still describe the Chilean military as hierarchic, vertical, hermetic, and suspicious of civilians.

A careful examination of the 1980 constitution, however, reveals that it may be difficult to maintain this nonpolitical posture after Pinochet leaves the presidency. One of the constitution's most important institutions is the National Security Council, with two civilians, four military men, and the president as voting members. The Council not only names four *ex officio* members of the Senate from the four branches of the armed forces; it also chooses two of the seven members of the constitutional court and is empowered to express its formal opinion to any part of the government concerning actions or policies that may adversely affect Chilean institutions or national security. The term "national security" appears repeatedly in the 1980 constitution. It is specifically mentioned as a limit in constitutional clauses dealing with education, freedom of association, labor, the right to strike, freedom of economic activity, property rights, and mineral concessions—thus leaving open a wide area of activity for the National Security Council.[44] Since the constitution can only be amended by a three-fifths vote in both houses and a joint three-fifths vote of both houses 60 days later, it seems that the constitution has institutionalized a strong military role in Chilean government for the foreseeable future.

Apart from the specific mandates given the armed forces by the constitution, it is also likely to be difficult to persuade the military to withdraw from other important areas of national life where they now have significant influence, including education (military rectors have run the universities and important secondary schools), foreign policy (the deputy foreign minister is always a military man), the judicial system (the jurisdiction of military courts in cases of subversion), and the defense budget (which was increased substantially in 1974 and again in 1979 at the time of the crisis with Argentina).[45]

In 1983 the Chilean system began to loosen. A broad-based centrist coalition ranging from socialists on the left to former liberals and conservatives on the right formed the Democratic Alliance, which demanded the resignation of Pinochet and the election of a constituent assembly to write a new constitution. To the left of the Alliance, the Communist party and a faction of the socialists established the Popular Democratic Movement (MDP), which called for all types of action against the government, including a general strike. Finally the right wing began to organize a number of groups (including an attempted reestablishment of the former National party, which had dissolved itself after the 1973 coup) and to press Pinochet to allow the election of a congress before the constitutionally prescribed date of 1990. In August 1983 Pinochet appointed Sergio Oriofre Jarpa, the former leader of the National party, as minister of interior and spoke of the possibility of such an election, all the while insisting that his constitutional term until 1989 was nonnegotiable. After several meetings between Jarpa and the leaders of the Democratic Alliance and escalating monthly protest demonstrations and violence, Pinochet—with army support—imposed censorship and martial law (state of siege) in November 1984.

The imponderable for the future was the attitude of the armed forces. Were they beginning to think of their own roles after Pinochet left power? Would they be as intransigent in holding power as Pinochet had been? It was difficult to perceive any signs of military discontent, even as the Chilean economy continued in a state of deep depression and the political leadership continued to call for a political opening. Even after a transition to civilian rule, it seemed unlikely that the military would go back to the barracks as completely as they had in Argentina, if only because they had never left them to dominate the government in a formal institutional way, as had taken place in that country. There was a historical precedent of military government: in 1931 the military commanders forced Carlos Ibáñez out of the presidency after four years of plebiscitary dictatorship. That action initiated a period of instability and coups and countercoups that only ended in 1932 with the election of the civilian populist leader who had resigned the presidency in 1925, Arturo Alessandri. Would the military, fearing the possibility of instability and political radicalization, maintain Pinochet in power until 1989 (or 1997), or would they decide to return power to the civilian leaders as had been done in 1932? And in the latter case, what kind of veto powers would they retain, particularly in the newly broadened area of national security?

ARGENTINA

Of all nations of Latin America, Argentina has long been considered the most modernized, economically and socially. In wealth, it was roughly at the Western European level and not far from that of the United States in the first decades of this century. Its population was highly literate by virtue of a school system among the best in the world. The population is relatively homogeneous and urbanized. Yet Argentina has seen an exceptional number of military interventions; the soldiers meddled chronically in politics, overturned the government six times from 1930 to 1973, and themselves governed for long periods. Even more surprising is the fact that there has been little antimilitarism. Conservatives and radicals alike have freely called upon the soldiers to help them. For nearly a century opposition parties have regularly appealed to the armed forces or factions within them to remove their enemies. The ballot box has never been accepted as the sole means to power.

Why the military looms so large in Argentine politics has never been clearly explained. It seems, however, that the problem is broader than civil-military relations. Argentine society is divided, riven by rivalries, distrust, and hatreds, and no group or party has been able to impose itself for long—the military being the most stable and coherent, the guarantor of continuity. The failure of the great promise of the good decades and the nation's disappointment in itself doubtless have much to do with this condition, but there is no adequate explanatory theory.

The military role goes far back, to the glorious traditions of the war of independence, when the national hero, José de San Martín, marched his troops (1812 to 1822) from Argentina to Ecuador to make possible the liberation of the continent. The Argentine nation was subsequently shaped by several wars, the most recent being the Paraguayan War (1865–70) and campaigns against the Indians of the south (into the 1880s). The army could thus regard itself as maker of the nation, and the development of the modern army was part of the phenomenal expansion of Argentina, in wealth, population, and international standing—an expansion in which the army took pride. Moreover, the professionalization of the military progressed steadily after the 1870s. After 1901 the officer corps became largely middle class, and the army gained control over its promotions.[46] The army to a considerable degree escaped control of the ruling landowner oligarchy and became the only independent sector in a political system based on presidential power and fraudulent elections.

Since the electoral road was closed by fraud, the principal opposition party, the middle-class Radical Union, sought power in the 1890s and 1900s by appealing to the discontents of the army, especially junior officers. However, the Conservatives in 1916 permitted an honest election, and Hipólito Yrigoyen, the longtime Radical leader, became president. He proceeded to seek control of the army through patronage and used it to reward party faithful. He was not able to have his way fully, however. A lodge founded in 1921 became strong enough to impose its choice of General Agustín Justo as minister of war in the following presidency of Marcelo de Alvear.

In an atmosphere of hatred between the Radicals and the Conservatives, who were unreconciled to loss of control of the state to the immigrant middle-class politicians, Yrigoyen was reelected in 1928. Justo contemplated moving against Yrigoyen then, but nothing was done until 1930, when the country was reeling under the collapse of agricultural prices and Yrigoyen was showing himself prematurely senile and unable to attend properly to the business of government, while continuing to meddle in the army. Moreover, the Conservatives, still influential in the military, were alarmed by the drift of the Radicals to leftism.

It consequently seemed imperative to many that the army should force the resignation of Yrigoyen and transfer the presidency legally to the vice-president. It might have done so, but the moderate Justo left leadership of the coup to General José Uriburu, an admirer of Mussolini and dictatorship. The coup was eagerly welcomed by most of the public as well as the armed forces, but Uriburu's effort to establish a near-fascist state was not. He imposed, with partial success, censorship, dictatorial controls of politics, policies of economic nationalism, and so forth. But he was too far from Argentine tradition, and he failed to obtain the support of a majority in the military, much less in the general public.

In a year and a half, Uriburu was pressured out of office by the moderates or Conservatives, and Justo took his place. Justo released political prisoners and restored freedoms. It was his desire to return the army to nonpolitical professionalism. However, as it appeared that the Radicals would win honest elections, dishonest ones were held, first to elevate Justo to the presidency, then for other offices. The Conservatives would not repeat the mistake of 1916. The Radicals meanwhile went back to their old policy of insurrection, although an attempt in 1932 was severely repressed.

From 1930 to 1983 the army remained politically engaged. During the period of fraud, 1932–43, it was the instrument through which the Conservatives, lacking electoral legitimacy, held onto office. Officers at the same time became and remained heavily involved in both political and economic administration,[47] as the state took over a growing sector of industry.

During this period the army was much agitated by factionalism. Yet the officers, who had considerable faith in their own ability to manage affairs, lost whatever faith they may have had in the political class, so they were to feel no qualms about crushing a civilian government.

Military opposition was organized by a lodge, the United Officers Group (GOU), founded in 1942 on the model of a Japanese secret society. Led by four ambitious young colonels, including Juan Domingo Perón, an admirer of Italian fascism, the GOU gained strength in an army seething with intrigue and factionalism as the prestige of the government declined. Under the presidency of Ramón Castillo, who as vice-president succeeded the ailing Roberto Ortiz in 1940, the army became increasingly influential in the administration. Castillo had no popular basis, and no effort was required to displace him in 1943 when he seemed to favor those opposed to the Axis powers.

The coup was a purely military affair, with no important civilian support; the army, however, moved into something of a vacuum of fractured and ineffective political parties, weak unions, a discredited oligarchy, and an apathetic public. The jingoistic, profascist officers who formed a governing junta tried, as their hero Uriburu had done in 1930, to set up a fascist state: the press was put under censorship, unions were repressed, women were removed from public office, puritan laws were passed, industry was supposed to be geared entirely for war purposes, and the military budget was much increased. The officers, however, were at odds, as usual, and not much was really done.

The situation began to change by the middle of 1944. Perón emerged as the real leader of the military government, although he did not occupy the presidency. He did take the position (along with the positions of vice-president and minister of war) of chief of the Department of Labor and Social Security, and he used this office to bring about a new style of military-civilian relations. In this capacity he showed the existent unions that he could help them if they cooperated and hurt them if they did not; and he organized new unions under the patronage of his office as seemed useful. He raised wages, gave unions advantages in collective bargaining, increased benefits, and enforced old laws or decreed new ones for the protection of the workers; and he built up a following such as no soldier in Argentina had had before.

This made Conservative officers unhappy, but others were pleased at the new alliance of the army with labor in controlled organizations. Those who were distrustful of the approach or of the growing power of Perón prevailed in October 1945 (with the support of the navy and what there was of a democratic movement) and had him stripped of his offices and arrested; but the unions, with the help of the police, raised a monster demonstration in Perón's favor, the Conservatives caved in, and Perón was returned as acknowledged chief of the government.

Perón was thereupon able to organize a political party and win an honest election against all other parties combined, from Communist to Conservative, to emerge in February 1946 as legitimate president. Perón, assisted by the able Eva Duarte, exercised a personal more than a military government; but the army was one of its main pillars, along with the tamed unions, the Catholic church, many nationalists, and industrialists—industrialization being one of the priorities of the regime. The government was graced by a synthetic ideology of social justice, *Justicialismo*, which was claimed to be the true Third Way between capitalism and communism. It was an antirationalist popularization of hypernationalism, an appeal (backed by force) to the neglected of society, somewhat in the tradition of the crude semipopulist nineteenth century dictator Juan Manuel Rosas, whom Perón admired.

The principal supporters of Perón were the workers, whom he flattered, raising their self-image as Argentine politicians had not been disposed to do and to whom, more importantly, he gave material benefits, such as a substantial increase in the percentage of the national income going to wages.[48]

The army was more crucial to Perón, however. He tried to make it his instrument, providing new arms, fulfilling its military-industrialization program, and raising pay over the levels of comparable personnel of the U.S. army.[49] There were medals and sinecures, which helped to keep part of the army faithful (the navy was always hostile) to the end. But the officers were not very docile. In 1949 they forced Perón to give up some of his leftist-reformist policies, and in 1951 they vetoed the vice-presidency proposed for Evita, whom they despised both as a former entertainer and as an unwomanly intruder.

From 1951 on, the Peronist machine lost ground in the army. There was an attempted coup, which Perón punished with untraditional severity, leaving a number of officers deeply embittered. The economy was deteriorating; Perón did not have the resources to please both military and workers (having exhausted the large balances accumulated by Argentina during the world war) and was led to greater reliance on coercion, censorship, and violence against opponents and the merely noncooperative. Evita, whose political abilities were superior to those of her husband, died in 1952 and left him morally adrift. Perón turned to economic conservatism and made peace with the U.S. interests that he had denounced violently, thereby disconcerting and alienating many followers. He tried rather crudely and unsuccessfully to indoctrinate the army with Justicialismo, an insult to the intellectual independence of well-schooled officers and an injury to military professionalism. He moved, albeit indecisively, to form armed workers' militias, thereby threatening the army with a rival to its existence and alienating even pro-Peronists. Most importantly and most foolishly, he began a broadside attack on the Catholic church in 1954, thereby offending many officers.

The navy tried in June 1955 to remove Perón, but it had not assured itself of adequate army support and failed. Three months later, the anti-Peronists of the army were prepared to follow the navy's lead. It was a rather chancy engagement, because of the strength of Perón's following in the army and the police, which was much greater in number. But the insurgents were able to establish themselves in some important centers, the navy threatened to bombard Buenos Aires, and Perón had no stomach for a fight. Again the army had power in its hands with no clear idea of what to do with it.

For the 20 years after 1955, the big question dividing the military internally and dominating its relations with the nation was what to do about Peronism and the Peronists, how to handle Peronist workers, and most of all how to have legitimate constitutional government, that is, elected government, if people persisted in voting for Peronist parties. The divisions were bitter, the more so because the dictatorship had introduced a new truculence into Argentine political life and set class against class as never before.

At first the government attempted to compromise. General Eduardo Lonardi, who came into the leadership of the coup when the stronger leader, General Pedro Aramburu, held back, was inclined to leave most Peronists in place and avoid punishments. There was too much bitterness in the army, however, for such mildness. This was shown by the 1956 uprising in the army of Peronists unreconciled to defeat. They were repressed with executions, from which Perón himself had refrained and which deepened the gulf between parties. After less than a year, Lonardi was replaced by Aramburu, who undertook a campaign of repression beyond precedent in Argentine history.[50] Resolved to impose democracy by force, Aramburu undertook generally conservative policies, including a more open foreign investment policy, free enterprise economics, privatization of some state industry, control of unions, and reduction of wages.

Aramburu proposed, however, to return Argentina to democracy, and elections were duly held in 1958. The Peronists, of course, were officially banned; but any democratic party might well seek Peronist votes. Arturo Frondizi, the leader of the less anti-Peronist part of the divided Radical party, made a more or less explicit deal with Perón, promising toleration in return for votes; and he won by a large majority. The price was military distrust; Frondizi was fortunate to be allowed to take office and thereafter was barely tolerated. The military chipped away at his authority, conspiracies were continual, and the army constituted itself as supervisor of the government. Finally, in 1962, because Frondizi permitted the Peronists to win some provincial elections, he was dismissed.

The military tried elections again, and the victor in a much-divided field was Arturo Illía, who won a quarter of the votes. Or it might be said that the victor was Perón, whose followers cast more blank ballots than Illía received. Illía's anti-Peronist sector of the Radical party wanted to govern but lacked the power to do so, and the next years were politically futile. The armed forces were drastically divided (no one had been fully master since Perón), the government was impotent, and the state seemed headed for bankruptcy. Within a year there were expectations of a coup, and Conservatives and Peronists alike did their best to undermine the well-meaning president. There were many complaints, but the chief reason for the coup of 1966 (which the Peronists applauded) was that Illía seemed to be opening the way for Peronists to win elections.

Most Argentines seemed to agree that there must be a new beginning to end anarchy and put the country on its feet. The way chosen by the armed forces was to give full dictatorial power to the most eminent Argentine soldier, retired General Juan Carlos Onganía, who ironically had been the leader of the constitutionalist faction and chief proponent of legality. The result was rather an autocracy than a corporate military regime; Onganía assumed responsibility on condition that he have full power. He became not provisional but full president, charged with remaking the nation. He was to carry out the "Argentine Revolution," to abolish politics for ten years, during which he would remake the economy and the nation, and to bring modernization through order and discipline.

Projecting military values on society, for the sake of unity, solidarity, and national greatness, Onganía imposed the strictest dictatorship Argentina had yet known. He held executive, legislative, and judicial power. Elected officials at all levels were removed, parties and unions were dissolved, the universities were drastically purged, and the media were censored. All were to work together for the common good. In a logical contradiction, however, Onganía favored economic liberalism and free enterprise.

The program was not a total failure; at least, the economy responded with exceptionally good growth rates. But the lack of outlets for expansion and the total closure of the political process led to an accumulation of resentment against the tactless and uninspiring government. Terrorism sprang up, and discontents without legitimate channels turned to subversion. The crucial event was the Cordobazo of 1969, when a student demonstration turned into general riots that gripped the city for days. Thereafter the atmosphere of violence and guerrilla war worsened. The military chiefs became unwilling to support the government, in which they had little input—the cabinet was entirely civilian—and invited Onganía to retire again.

The military had no new recipe for governing the country but began to move toward conciliating public opinion. It seemed that the only way to cope with disorder was to permit political activity. Peronism was still a major force—by now consisting mostly of generalized more or less violent protest against military rule and the status quo rather than loyalty to the aging Juan Perón in Spain—and the military felt the need to deal with the Peronists. In 1971 President Alejandro Lanusse legalized parties and announced his intention to have elections. The military still hoped to get an acceptable president, and Perón was barred from running by a residence requirement. But the election of March 1973 showed only 3% of the votes for the candidate favored by the military regime and 82% for parties hostile to it. Héctor Cámpora, running as stand-in for Perón, was elected with half the votes.

Under Cámpora, the Peronist Left, chiefly the Montoneros, came to power. They seemed to want a regime like Castro's, but their day in power was brief. In June Perón returned. Cámpora resigned, and Perón received 62% of the vote in a new election. Still there was no harmony. The division of the Peronists came to the fore when leftists and rightists battled at the airport where Perón was to land, with many fatalities. Perón, no longer revolutionary in temper, made peace with the army and was restored to his old rank of general. He had no means of getting control of the military, however. Perón scolded his radical young followers and turned to generally moderate policies. Ailing when he came from Spain, he died July 1, 1974.

Under the presidency of his widow and vice-president, María Estela, commonly called Isabelita, who had no obvious political abilities, the government fell into the hands of mischievous hangers-on. The economy skidded and inflation jumped to make the peso nearly worthless. The violence that the military hoped to check by going back to elected government only kept mounting, between radical Peronists, Trotskyites, sundry revolutionaries, and anticommunist death groups, led by the Argentine Anticommunist Alliance (AAA).

In the political and economic disaster, everyone expected the military to resume power, and there were many calls for action. The soldiers might have acted at any time after the death of Juan Domingo Perón, and the officers began asserting more and more authority. But they did not wish to be blamed for greed and so waited until March 1976, when Isabelita was placed under house arrest to the applause of the nation. Ten years after the Argentine Revolution, a junta headed by General Juan Videla undertook the "Process of National Regeneration."

The reluctant coup was thorough. The military took over not only the central government but provincial and local governments, the courts, unions, and so forth. Parties were dissolved and strikes were outlawed. As in 1966, the new regime promised a fundamental restructuring of the nation's economic, social, and political systems.[51] Also as in 1966, the government turned back to liberal economics, much like the Pinochet government in Chile, and privatized some state firms (although too many officers had a stake in the state sector to allow as much return to private enterprise as occurred in Chile).

The strongest policy of the Videla government, however, was the counterrevolutionary "dirty war," the use of rightist terrorism to combat leftist terrorism. Thousands of radicals were arrested, other thousands fled, and approximately 10,000 "disappeared." By 1978 antistate terrorism had been largely eliminated, but disappearances and torture were only gradually brought to an end; and Argentines who had at first applauded the repression of disorder and political violence were aggrieved when officers went on—each military region having its own repressive apparatus—to arbitrarily kill or imprison persons only remotely or not at all connected to subversion.

The military government also failed economically. For a few years it had good results, but it failed to make significant reforms, spent its reserves, and after some reduction of inflation began paying its bills by printing pesos until inflation eventually became even worse than what was considered intolerable in the days of Isabel Perón. Finally, in 1982, partly to distract attention from economic problems and partly in hopes of restoring unity in the armed forces, the government launched a poorly considered attack to seize or recover the Falklands/Malvinas, which had been British-ruled since 1833.

The military seemed to have decayed from guarantors of order to a society for the usufruct of national wealth and liberties. Military government again proved a failure, perhaps even more so than civilian regimes. This was more clearly a failure of the armed forces rather than any individual because full powers had not been transferred to an individual, as in 1966, but had been kept with a junta of the three service chiefs. General Juan Videla, the president in 1976–80, had considerable authority as leader of the coup, but his successor, General Roberto Viola, had much less; and Viola was removed by the junta when it became dissatisfied.

Consequently, when Argentines, called to the polls in November 1983, elected the Radical candidate, Raul Alfonsín, it was hoped that the era of military politics begun in 1930 had been brought to an end. Alfonsín, who had made it his business to campaign against human rights violations, was the most antimilitary of the leading candidates. In office he named a civilian minister of defense, cashiered the top echelon of officers, remodeled the command structure, and initiated investigations and prosecutions for the abuses of years past, even putting former junta members on trial by civilian courts after military tribunals failed to act against them. He radically reduced the military budget and cut salaries severely as well as suspended re-equipment programs.

But Alfonsín, too, had his troubles, as the economy floundered out of control, inflation rose to ridiculous heights, and the officers resisted trial and punishment of those who claimed to have done only their antisubversive duty. Argentines were patient in hardships, and hardly anyone wanted the discredited military back, but no one could feel certain of the future.

The chief condition for the continued exclusion of the military from politics was obviously the agreement of the principal parties. In the past, parties that felt cheated of power were always ready to call on the soldiers to help them, usually with the result that all parties suffered. If the parties could agree on the priority of civilian institutions, as in Venezuela and Colombia, it seemed likely that the military would stick to military affairs. But this would require a revolution in Argentine political mores.

Moreover, it was difficult to expect the military to stay out of politics when it was so deeply immersed in the economy. Argentina is outstanding in Latin America not only for the military role in politics but for the number of officers in business.[52] From the interventions of the 1930s through the establishment of military industry during World War II, the state sector has tended to grow; and it encompasses not only an impressive munitions industry but also a large share of basic production, machinery, mining, fuels, the state petroleum monopoly (YPF), atomic energy, steel, and other branches generally controlled, implicitly or explicitly, by the military. State enterprise provides a haven for officers idled by the early retirement rules. Retirees have also gone in large numbers into mixed and private corporations, Argentine and foreign. They resist denationalization and the cutting of budgets, a resistance that is a major reason for deficit financing (losses of some state enterprises are larger than their total operating revenues) and irresistible inflation. The way to economic rationality and a competitive economy is not visible; yet it is difficult to see how the military is to be divorced from politics unless it is divorced from the economy.

The other crux of Argentine civil-military relations is the fact that the officers, ever since their Prussianization at the beginning of this century, have felt themselves superior to the society around them. They have regarded civilian presidents with scorn, when these headed corrupt administrations based on electoral fraud, or with distrust, when they represented mass parties not friendly to the military interest. From Yrigoyen in 1916 onward, elected presidents have been viewed as hostile to the armed forces, to be tolerated so far as necessary and removed if they became intolerable. The Argentine military, unlike those of Colombia and Venezuela, has never changed the government for the benefit of civilians. These attitudes are reciprocally reinforcing; in view of the record, a civilian president can hardly fail to seek to reduce the ability of the armed forces to act against him and so to become an adversary in the eyes of the military.

Only in the light of this superiority and antagonism does it become comprehensible that the officers of an advanced and cultured country would engage in such cruelty toward their fellow citizens as they showed in 1976–79. Unless these attitudes change, Argentina has not seen the end of military government. Unfortunately, Alfonsín seems likely to be viewed by the military not as a partner in improving the nation but as a rival and threat to military autonomy.

Poor civilian-military relations must bear considerable responsibility for the great Argentine shortfall. The major fact of Argentine history for the past century has been the change from rapid growth to decay. The nation came from backwardness and poverty in the 1860s to near the forefront of modern nations in the 1920s; from about 1930 onward it has almost continually lost ground, becoming a not very dynamic Third World nation. There is no good explanation for this turnaround, which came when economists would have said a "take-off" was in order, and causation is doubtless multiple and complex. But the military domination of politics from 1930 on must be a partial and may be a chief cause.

NOTES

1. For Mexico, national security is defined as the maintenance of the nation's economic, political, and social equilibrium by following the letter of the constitution of 1917. As such, national security corresponds more to ensuring class mobility and social reforms than to defending the country against a hostile force. Cf. Roberto Vizcaino, "La seguridad del país, fin primordial del estado," *Proceso*, September 22, 1980, p. 6.

2. Martin C. Needler, "Problems in the Evaluation of the Mexican Political System," in *Contemporary Mexico*, eds. James W. Wilkie, Michael C. Meyer, and Edna Monzon de Wilkie (Berkeley: University of California Press, 1976), p. 341.

3. "Military Eye on Central America," *Financial Times*, March 22, 1982, ISLA 1060.

4. Roderic A. Camp, *Mexico's Leaders, Their Education and Recruitment*, (Tucson: University of Arizona Press, 1980), p. 57.

5. Guillermo Boils, *Los militares y la política en México (1915-1974)* (Mexico City: Ediciones El Caballito, 1975), pp. 98–99; Samual P. Huntington, *Political Order in Changing Societies* (New Haven: Yale University Press), 1968, p. 317.

6. Thomas E. Weil, ed., *Area Handbook for Mexico* (Washington, D.C.: U.S. Government Printing Office, 1975), pp. 351–56.

7. Jorge Alberto Lozoya, *El ejército Mexicano (1911-1965)* (Mexico City: El Colegio de México, 1970), p. 89; Boils, *Los militares*, p. 112; Weil, *Area Handbook for Mexico*, p. 362.

8. Lyle N. McAlister, Anthony P. Maingot, and Robert A. Potash, eds., *The Military in Latin American Sociopolitical Evolution: Four Case Studies* (Washington, D.C.: Center for Research in Social Systems, 1970), pp. 235–37.

9. Christopher Dickey, "Modernization Could Lead Mexican Military into Politics," *The Washington Post*, September 23, 1982.

10. McAlister, Maingot, and Potash, *Sociopolitical Evolution*, p. 235.

11. For general background on the "new professionalism," see Alfred C. Stepan, *Authoritarian Brazil* (New Haven: Yale University Press, 1973) and Luigi Einaudi and Alfred C. Stepan, *Latin American Institutional Development: Changing Perspectives in Peru and Brazil* (Santa Monica: Rand Corporation, 1971).

12. McAlister, Maingot, and Potash, *Sociopolitical Evolution*, p. 210.

13. Thomas P. Anderson, *Politics in Central America* (New York: Praeger, 1981), pp. 26–27.

14. Daniel L. Premo, "Political Assassination in Guatemala," *Journal of Inter-American Studies and World Affairs* 23 (November 1981): 437.

15. U.S., Congress, House, *U.S. Policy Toward Guatemala* (Hearing before a Subcommittee of the Committee on Foreign Affairs, 98th Cong., 1st sess., March 1983), pp. 43–44.

16. Gabriel Aguilera Peralta, "The Militarization of the Guatemalan State," in *Guatemala in Rebellion*, eds. Johnathan L. Fried, Marvin E. Gettlemen, Deborah Levenson, and Nancy Peckenham (New York: Grove Press, 1983), pp. 124–25.

17. U.S., Congress, House, *U.S. Policy Toward Guatemala*, pp. 33–34.

18. Jerry L. Weaver, "Political Style of the Guatemalan Military Elite," in *Militarism in Developing Countries*, ed. Kenneth Fidel (New Brunswick, N.J.: Transaction Books, 1975), pp. 64–69.

19. Richard N. Adams, *Crucifixion by Power* (Austin: University of Texas Press, 1970), pp. 255–56.

20. *La Nación Internacional* (Costa Rica), December 29–January 4, 1984.

21. The military high command, Minister of Defense Colonel Delgado Chalbaud and Chief of Staff Lieutenant Colonel Pérez Jiménez, seized power and forced President Gallegos to resign. Their announcement of the coup to the nation came in the form of an "Exposition of the Armed Forces to the Nation," and it was announced that their act was "absolutely apolitical"; so they formed a *junta militar* to govern.

22. The overthrow of Pérez Jiménez on January 23, 1958 is generally regarded as a revolution rather than a coup, although elements of both were present. The most detailed and accurate account is J. J. Doyle, "Venezuela 1958: Transition from Dictatorship to Democracy" (Ph.D. dissertation, George Washington University, 1967).

23. Gene E. Bigler, "The Armed Forces and Patterns of Civil-Military Relations," in *Venezuela: The Democratic Experience*, eds. John D. Martz and David J. Myers (New York: Praeger, 1977). A corollary rule of equal importance is that the losers in politics will not appeal to the military for redress of grievances.

24. The elite subsamples were not explicitly named in Aníbal Fernández, Alejo Planchart and Gene E. Bigler, *Modelo demo-económico de Venezuela* (Caracas: Ediciones IESA, 1975). The military panel was identified only as a technocratic elite group.

25. See the articles by John D. Martz and David J. Myers in *Venezuela at the Polls*, ed. H. R. Penniman (Washington, D.C.: American Enterprise Institute, 1980) and Aristides Torres, "La experiencia política en una democracia partidista joven: el caso de Venezuela," *Politeia* 9 (1980).

26. See Gene E. Bigler, *La política y el capitalismo de estado en Venezuela* (Madrid: Editorial Tecnos, 1982), chapter IV; and Gene E. Bigler and Enrique Viloria, "The Political Economy of Public Enterprises and Autonomous Institutes," in *Venezuela: The Democratic Experience*, 2d ed., eds. John D. Martz and David J. Myers (New York: Praeger, 1985).

27. Freddy Rincón N., *El nuevo ideal nacional y los planes económico-militares de Pérez Jiménez, 1952-57* (Caracas: Ediciones Centauro, 1982).

28. The story of General Alfonzo Ravard and the CVG is told in John Randolph Dinkelspiel, "Administrative Style and Economic Development: The Organization and Management of the Guayana Region Development of Venezuela" (Ph.D. dissertation, Harvard University, 1967) and Enrique Viloria, *Petróleos de Venezuela: la culminación del proceso de nacionalización* (Caracas: Editorial Jurídica Venezolana, 1983).

29. J. Mark Ruhl, *Colombia: Armed Forces and Society* (Syracuse: Syracuse University, 1980), p. 19.

30. Ruhl, *Colombia*, p. 20; Edwin G. Corr, *The Political Process in Colombia* (Denver: University of Denver, 1972), p. 70.

31. Ruhl, *Colombia*, p. 25.

32. Gustavo Gallón Girardo, *La república de las armas* (Bogotá: Centro de Investigación y Educación Popular, 1981), p. 33.

33. Ruhl, Colombia, p. 27; Gallón, *La república*, p. 31.

34. Alfred C. Stepan, *The State and Society: Peru in Comparative Perspective* (Princeton: Princeton University Press, 1978), p. 130, Table 4.1.

35. Liisa North, *Civil-Military Relations in Argentina, Chile, and Peru*, Politics of Modernization Series, no. 2 (Berkeley: Institute of International Studies, University of California, 1966), pp. 40–41.

36. Liisa North and Tanya Korovkin, *The Peruvian Revolution and the Officers in Power, 1967-1976*, Occasional Monograph Series, no. 15 (Montreal: Centre for Developing-Area Studies, McGill University, 1981), p. 34.

37. Peter Flynn, *Brazil: A Political Analysis* (Boulder, Colo.: Westview Press, 1979), pp. 19-20.

38. June E. Hahner, *Civilian-Military Relations in Brazil, 1889-1898* (New York: Columbia University Press, 1969), p. 28.

39. Alfred C. Stepan, *The Military in Politics: Changing Patterns in Brazil* (Princeton: Princeton University Press, 1971), pp. 57-66.

40. Robert Wesson and David V. Fleischer, *Brazil in Transition* (New York: Praeger, 1983), pp. 127-28. The DSIs and ASIs are units within ministries and federal agencies.

41. Walder de Goes, "O novo papel das forças armadas do Brasil" (Paper presented at the Seventh Annual Meeting of ANPOCS, Aguas de São Pedro, SP, October 26-28, 1983).

42. Fernando Lemos, "Militares a políticos: tenham cuidado," *Correio Brasiliense*, February 29, 1984, p. 3.

43. See Paul E. Sigmund, *The Overthrow of Allende and the Politics of Chile, 1964-76* (Pittsburgh: University of Pittsburgh Press, 1977), pp. 273-74. For a criticism of the view that in the earlier period the military were apolitical, see Alain Joxe, *Las fuerzas armadas en el sistema político de Chile* (Santiago: Editorial Universitaria, 1970). On military-civilian relations in Chilean history, see Frederick M. Nunn, *The Military in Chilean History* (Alburquerque: University of New Mexico Press, 1976).

44. Hugo Fruhling, Carlos Portales, and Augusto Varas, *Estado y fuerzas armadas* (Santiago: FLACSO, 1982), pp. 32-33, gives eight constitutional clauses that mention *seguridad nacional*.

45. Figures for the defense budget are classified, but the U.S. Arms Control and Disarmament Agency, the International Institute for Strategic Studies (London), and the Stockholm Peace Research Institute (SPRI), while producing different estimates, agree that substantial increases took place in the years mentioned above.

46. Marvin Goldwert, *Democracy, Militarism and Nationalism in Argentina, 1930-1966* (Austin: University of Texas Press, 1972), p. 9.

47. Alain Rouquié, *Pouvoir militaire et société politique en République Argentine* (Paris: Fondation Nationale des Sciences Politiques, 1978), p. 627.

48. Donald C. Hodges, *Argentina 1943-1976: The National Revolution and Resistance* (Albuquerque: University of New Mexico Press, 1976), p. 13.

49. Goldwert, *Democracy, Militarism, and Nationalism*, p. 103.

50. Hodges, *Argentina 1943-1976*, p. 24.

51. Peter G. Snow, "Military Government in Argentina," in *New Military Politics in Latin America*, ed. Robert Wesson (New York: Praeger, 1982), p. 36.

52. Rouquié, *Pouvoir militaire*, pp. 634-39.

CONCLUSION

The foregoing sketches seem to indicate that there is something of a Latin American military institution, despite large variations between quite different countries. Moreover, those military organizations that have been most distinctive in the past (the Mexican coming out of revolutionary bands and the Panamanian evolving from a police force) are tending toward the more general Latin American pattern.

It is not surprising that the military establishments in the several countries should bear considerable resemblance. National authorities seeking to improve armies and navies have looked to the same advanced and powerful nations: Germany, France, and Britain in the earliest times of modernization and the United States more recently. These authorities have also taken lessons from other Latin American nations, especially leading South American powers. Further, there is something of a shared tradition from the Iberian background and a community of basic values.

There is some similarity of conditions, too. Latin American armed forces exist within the framework of more or less elitist societies and reflect their attitudes; their nations are peripheral to the centers of world political and economic power; and they suffer poverty and backwardness to some degree, although they are generally well off compared to Africa and South Asia. Latin American armed forces also lack a major mission of defense against possible invasion; so far as they have to meet a threat from abroad, it is of subversion encouraged and supported by anticapitalist states, which merges with the discontents of poorly structured and relatively unaffluent societies. The mission of the military is thus primarily the defense not of the nation as an entity but of its institutions and society, not to speak of the interests of the armed forces themselves. This mission implies a political role, which is probably justified by more or less of a security doctrine.

It seems possible, then, to make some generalizations of fairly broad validity. The ranks of the armies are made up of youths from the poorer strata, serving as conscripts or volunteers, perhaps under threat of conscription, perhaps drawn by possibilities of getting a little training and the start of a career. They serve for terms of per- haps a year or two. Nowhere are better-placed men required to serve in the ranks. Navies and air forces rely mostly or entirely on volun- teers. In countries such as Guatemala and Peru, where there is a sharp racial or socioeconomic division between ruling Hispanics (or His- panicized classes) and Indian masses, recruitment of enlisted person- nel and their subsequent treatment reflect this division. Formerly, the forces relied heavily on country youths, but the field for recruitment has shifted, perhaps in all countries considered here, toward urban areas. One reason has been rural-urban migration; another has been the growing need for literate and at least partially educated soldiers. An important function of the military, however, is to teach literacy and impart technical skills, patriotism, and respect for national values.

Noncommissioned officers (NCOs) are, of course, volunteers, commonly recruits who decide to stay on for a military career. An important development for the NCOs has been expansion and im- provement of their training in recent years. Commissioned officers, however, commonly do tasks that would be assigned to NCOs in the U.S. army. The NCOs, in contrast to the rather inchoate recruit ranks, often have some political awareness and consequently politi- cal importance. The troops have usually been disposed to obey orders of their superiors and to put down popular demonstrations or overturn governments, but the class origins of the majority of them have somewhat limited their political use. In times of political ferment, on various occasions in such countries as Chile, Brazil, and Argentina, the officers have had to take seriously into account the attitudes of their men, which means mostly the attitudes of the sergeants and subalterns.

In only a few countries (particularly Mexico and Panama and to some extent Chile) can an enlisted man reasonably aspire to become an officer; and if he does, he is probably barred from the higher ranks. The social distance between ranks and officers is great, and there is no bridge across it. Entry to the officer corps is restricted, with mostly unimportant exceptions, to graduates of the regular service academies. Cadets normally enter directly from secondary school, frequently a military school. This, plus the facts that the mili- tary career is rigorous (at least at the lower levels) and there is gen- erally equality among classmates, has caused the bulk of officers to be drawn from the middle or even lower-middle classes. It is not attractive for sons of the elite to go through the mill for many years along with social inferiors, while poor boys can seldom receive the secondary education necessary for applying to an academy. But the significance of the class origins of officers is limited by the fact that in Latin America the middle class is not a bourgeoisie in the European sense; on the contrary, it is composed mostly of aspirants to upper-class status.

Because the decision for an officer's career is made quite young, it is taken much more easily in families with fathers or relatives in military service. Furthermore, military families commonly live in segregated quarters; hence it is natural for the children to think of a military career. There is therefore a strong tendency, usually difficult to document, for the military profession to be hereditary and the institution thus to become more ingrown and apart from civil society.

Above the service academy, which usually has a four-year course, many officer-training schools have been established, and promotion to higher grades requires passing through one or several of these. The series is capped by a war college, ordinarily called the Superior War College, or *Escuela Superior de Guerra.* Emphasis on schooling, which owes something to the need to occupy an officer's time, has large effects. Not only are professional capacities raised but the sense of belonging to the institution is increased by the years spent absorbing its messages. The much-schooled officers are also likely to feel qualified to administer national affairs at least as well as the amateur politicians. Moreover, long schooling makes officers less receptive to political influence in promotions and external meddling in their professional organization. Officers who spend a quarter or more of their careers improving their capacities will not welcome outsiders evaluating them. Generally, political selection is acceptable only for positions of political significance at the top level. It is characteristic that in Mexico, where there is less emphasis on academic qualifications, there is more presidential intervention and more careerism by clique.

There has been controversy as to whether the professionalization of the armed forces makes them more or less inclined to intervene in politics (in the extreme to take the government to themselves). The difference of opinion may indicate that professionalization is not a strong determinant of the degree of interventionism. It is evident, however, that training and professionalization increase the cohesion and institutional orientation of the armed forces; hence the tendency to look to their collective self-interest. Moreover, it is not very productive or interesting for officers to spend many years studying battle tactics, military history, and weapon characteristics when they have little expectation of ever fighting a real battle. At the top level there has consequently been an increasing emphasis on studying national problems, questions of economics, politics, and other matters that are more likely to affect the strength and security of the nation than anything related to field maneuvers. This focus is expressed in the widely propagated security doctrine that considers all aspects of national strength—economic, social, demographic, and so forth—as important for the defense of the nation from subversion and hence of concern to the military. The military thus inevitably has a very large political interest, whether or not it chooses to exercise a political role.

Formal training is also the biggest channel of foreign influence. In many countries, in the last years of the nineteenth century and the early years of this century, foreign missions—German, in the first instance—were invited to improve the armed forces, and their most important action was to establish schools to prepare professional officers. Ever since, the officers' academies and schools have served to assimilate military doctrines and knowledge developed in Europe and the United States. Study abroad has also served this purpose. Germany was the most important teacher of the armies, especially in the Southern Cone, from late nineteenth century until World War I. Britain was the power to which navies naturally looked for guidance and supply of ships.

Since World War II the United States has been the prevalent foreign influence almost everywhere, in terms of missions to Latin American countries, training in U.S. schools (in Panama more than in the United States), and the furnishing of arms. On the part of nearly all the countries considered here, however, there has been a definite tendency to reduce or turn away from dependence on the United States. This tendency began with restrictions on arms sales in the 1970s; it was accelerated by human rights policies that were offensive to military regimes (such as Brazil and Guatemala) and by the congressionally mandated cutoff of military cooperative programs with countries found guilty of human rights violations. Many countries looked to other arms suppliers, Peru even buying large quantities of materiel from the Soviet Union. Various other countries have done what they could to manufacture their own arms. Brazil has been the most successful, having become an important arms exporter on the world market. Others, such as Argentina, Chile, Mexico, and Venezuela, have sought increasingly to satisfy their own needs.

The significance of U.S. aid for the military of Latin America is controversial. Many have decried such aid as support for unrepresentative governments and narrow interests. It has certainly contributed to the antisubversive directions of Latin American armies; U.S. counterinsurgency doctrine was very influential, with the consequent politicization of Latin American forces. It would appear, however, that whatever impulse has come from the United States had only to give Latin American armies a little push in the directions they were prepared to go; more determinant in the 1960s was doubtless the Cuban Revolution and its example of the sad fate of an officer corps unable to cope with guerrillas.

It is also questionable what influence means. It seems intuitively obvious that the United States would do well to do more to facilitate acquaintance of Latin American officers with this country and its values. But if South American armies send officers to Fort Bragg and use translated U.S. manuals, it does not mean that they are going to follow U.S. policies to advance any interests except what they perceive to be those of their own countries and organizations. Influence resides only in the way they perceive their own interests.

Regardless of questions of influence, the attitudes and ideology of the Latin American military are in some ways favorable to the United States and in other ways unfavorable. The officers are naturally nationalistic, but not more violently so than civilian politicians. They also may be favorable to state economic enterprise. There are exceptions, most prominently the regime of General Augusto Pinochet; but it is in accord with the military mentality to see the benefits of planned and controlled, that is, statist production. Moreover, state enterprise offers excellent employment opportunities, the more valued in countries such as Argentina and Brazil where officers rise rapidly and retire early. The military leaders are not enthusiastically democratic, but they have long found democracy quite tolerable in Colombia and Venezuela and have reconciled themselves to it in Peru, Brazil, and elsewhere.

The chief constants of military attitudes, which have often been viewed as favorable to U.S. interests, are that they favor order and stability, are not tempted by demagoguery, and are seldom leftists. Even if the military men, like the Peruvian regime after 1968, want reform (perhaps of revolutionary character), they retain authority. The Peruvians claimed to be acting for the masses, but they did not put the masses in power. Latin American societies are socially elitist and economically unequal; and it is unlikely that armed forces, based on hierarchy and carrying a strong class division between officers and enlisted ranks, are going to really change that character. In particular, even though the armed forces may have leftist-reformist inclinations, they invariably find Marxism and communism repugnant. This antipathy is expressed in the national security doctrines taught in many military academies, whereby the forces accept responsibility for combatting subversion in all aspects.

With some qualifications one might say that the armed forces are guarantors of the basic status quo in Latin America. Indeed, they are a major reason why Latin America has seen so very little social revolution—it has succeeded only where armies quite fell apart. This means, of course, that armies have a political role, although the question of the nature of military intervention in politics is extremely complex. The basic fact is that the military constitutes a major power in the countries considered here (and all other Latin American countries except Costa Rica) and must be taken into account as such. Another fact is that the military moves mostly not for the interests of the aristocracy, nor for the interests of the middle classes from which the officers come, nor for bourgeois values (which are certainly not identical with military values), but for its own interests and to fulfill the role for which it has been trained—the role of keeping order. A landholding elite may be satisfied for the military to have a large share of real power for the sake of stability, as in Guatemala; and urban middle classes may be among the most vociferous in calling for a military takeover in the face of menacing disturbances; but the military seems most moved by threats to itself, such as the formation of workers' or peasants' armed militias, which have contributed to coups in Guatemala, Brazil, Chile, and Argentina.

The military is moved to intervene against conflict and party violence and to displace a regime that does not seem able to keep order, as in Brazil in 1964, Chile and Uruguay in 1973, and Argentina in 1976. The military may overthrow the constitution, but it may also undertake to maintain it. Violation of the constitution is the best excuse for intervention, and civilian presidents would be much freer to act unconstitutionally if the military were not watching. Of course, an army intervening to protect the constitutional order from radicals, as in Brazil or Chile, may well do away with the constitution or make a new one after taking power.

The forces, nearly always sensitive to public opinion, are much more likely to intervene if major parties want them to. If the parties agree on the value of constitutional institutions and prefer going into opposition rather than allowing the soldiers to take over, the latter will probably refrain. In Colombia and Venezuela, this seems to be the biggest factor causing the abstinence of the military from intervention. Similarly, the solidarity of the Mexican ruling party caused the military to give up its habits of government.

It is also evident that external factors help trigger or inhibit coups. If it is known that the United States would look with favor upon removal of a civilian regime, as has often been the case, it is easy for the officers to move. On the other hand, if it is clear that the United States (and other powers) would be displeased by military intervention or that intervention may be costly to foreign trade, a coup may be effectively discouraged (as in the Dominican Republic in 1978). Changes in the international environment are probably the basic reason for swings between democratization and militarization in Latin America.

Although the military carries weight everywhere in Latin America, its political activism covers a spectrum from relative passivity to full management of the state. At best, civilian presidents are likely to have less full control over the minister of defense, traditionally an active duty officer, than over civilian ministers. The army may be a power chiefly in the sense that the administration cannot well go sharply contrary to its wishes; or it may have large responsibilities for keeping order, as in Colombia when fighting insurgencies or in Peru during the difficulties of the Belaunde government; or it may put an individual in the presidency, as in Argentina in 1966, without itself taking the helm.

The needs of the military are likely to be cared for quite as well by a civilian as by a military government. The Peruvian civilian presidency of Belaunde (1981–85) treated the soldiers better than the preceding military regime. More populist governments seem inclined to be especially openhanded. Allende, for example, tried by generosity to avert the coup he feared. The progressive administration of Jorge Blanco in the Dominican Republic showed itself more forthcoming with the soldiers than its conservative predecessor, that of Joaquín Balaguer.

The military may also exercise a good deal of power indirectly, as through irregular "security" forces in Guatemala or El Salvador, or by the penetration of the state by the "intelligence" service, as in Brazil. It is an additional point of strength if the military controls growing arms industries. The military probably does not really want to have the responsibility of occupying the seats of government. It is less taxing and less unpopular to stand back, watch, and enjoy great power.

Military-staffed governments are uncommon; the only one in our survey and in Latin American history was in Peru, 1963–75. In this case, the officers learned that they were not really so capable of governing as they had believed. In fact, superior war colleges to the contrary, the military is not trained, structured, and equipped to govern the country and is usually not eager to do so. Armed forces in Latin America have held power much less than they could have. The generals usually prefer to enjoy some benefits of power without the responsibilities, as in Colombia and Peru. And they are not very greedy. Despite its abundance of military politics, Latin America spends a smaller fraction of its wealth on its defense forces than any other region of the world and puts a smaller fraction of its men into uniform than any other area except much more backward sub-Saharan Africa. Latin American militaries do not try to mobilize their societies nor even, when running the government, do they seek to enlist much mass support. The Peruvians of the radical period were the chief exception, but their efforts lacked conviction and were unsuccessful. The soldiers do like to have the symbols of modern power, however, such as advanced planes and tanks for which they can expect to have no use.

Dictators almost always cling to power stubbornly, however worn out they may be. Corporate military government does not; it may give up rather easily when it feels that it is no longer effective. The excuse for taking over was probably the ineffectiveness of the civilians; when the officers prove equally ineffective, they seem fairly willing to wash their hands of the administration and return to the barracks. Military governments have not been notably successful, despite their discipline, modernization, rationalistic outlook, presumed relative immunity to corruption, and extensive education. The military regime is especially ill-prepared to handle economic problems. The Brazilians did well from 1968–74, but when complications mounted after the latter date, they were disposed to think of pulling back in an orderly fashion. Many military regimes have come to grief in their handling of the economy, a job for which military methods are not helpful. Not least, from the soldiers' point of view, is that tasks of government and particularly economic issues tend to fracture the precious unity of the institution.

In the years since 1978, in nine Latin American countries the soldiers have more or less withdrawn, turning the government over to civilians with more or less enthusiasm. There are various reasons for this remarkable democratic tide, including U.S. influence, the normal swing of the political pendulum, loss of the allure of the Cuban or Marxist model, and the democratization of Iberia. Probably the greatest factor, however, has been the economic depression covering Latin America. The depression has hit democratic as well as military regimes, of course; but the former have not been overthrown. It appears that democratic governments, with their greater flexibility, are less vulnerable to hard times (unless these lead to disorders). The military governments, where outsiders have no regular input, are more maligned than democratic administrations, in which people share responsibility and which are subject to renovation by election.

It may be that Latin America will see less of outwardly military government in the future if the prestige of democratic forms remains high. But the military establishment is the most coherent sector with the most leadership potential in generally incoherent societies needing effective leadership. The military stands out for order and discipline where these qualities are often scarce. It is relatively modern in orientation. While it suffers from corruption, it is, like the clergy, less subject to this vice so far as indoctrination is effective. It represents social mobility in societies characterized by social immobility. It represents a principle of unity over the divisions of culture and socioeconomic status that reduce the capacities of Latin American societies.

The armed forces retain the ability to prevent others from governing, even if the generals do not care to take office themselves. In most countries of Latin America, a generation of officers has grown up accustomed to the idea of commanding the state; and military government prepares for democracy only negatively, by giving a distaste for authoritarian rule while promoting undemocratic habits and values. The rule of the armed forces also distorts the party system, as the military in effect preempts the conservative position and ruins conservative parties. The experience of the Southern Cone, especially Argentina, makes clear that relative wealth, homogeneity, education, a large middle class, and material modernization by no means preclude military dictatorship; and Chile and Uruguay show that 40 years or more of civilian government is no preventative of military coups.

It is, moreover, difficult or impossible for a civilian government to remake the military institution, which more than any other (except perhaps the clergy) controls its own training and socialization and which (even more than the clergy) exists apart from the society supporting it. Military ideology does not exist in a vacuum, but no civilian president can turn it around by decree.

Perhaps the civilian rulership does not even really desire to eliminate the political role of the military, because it may be in a way essential. It may be that the fact that the generals are watching upholds the constitutional order, as claimed; in the fullness of presidential power and the weakness of democratic controls, perhaps only military surveillance prevents the president from abusing his authority. Certainly, the awareness of the soldiers standing by and always capable of marching in sobers all but the most enthusiastic politicians.

More broadly, it is probably impossible for Latin American countries to be genuinely democratic (in the sense that politicians are raised to office because they answer the needs of the masses, and the popular will is decisive on major issues). Obviously, this cannot be the case without violent revolution (and probably not with revolution either) in such countries as Guatemala; it is probably impractical in much less skewed societies such as Chile or even Uruguay. The stabilizing effect of the armed forces makes possible a certain approximation to democratic politics (with civil liberties and free elections) in such countries as the Dominican Republic and Ecuador, where inequality limits democracy in practical affairs. Civilian governments that have come to power by revolution and have destroyed the old army have (except in Costa Rica) built up a new one to protect themselves. In Bolivia in 1953 the revolutionary government reestablished the army, partly to offset the armed peasants and miners who had brought it to power.[1]

Unhappily, this need for the military represents a trap, because the political role of the military is generally to increase or at least maintain social inequality. The armed forces epitomize hierarchical relations, based allegedly on qualification rather than birth, and they stress law and order along with the right of the few to command. Their mentality can hardly be called democratic, although they may, as in Venezuela, accept theoretical sovereignty of the people as long as it remains basically conservative.

In sum, the power of the military, which subverts or denatures the democratic order, makes limited democracy possible. This limited democracy is often unstable, however; and the military retains the capacity to intervene. Yet the soldiers are not able to govern competently for an extended period. The result is an irregular mixture of fixity and fluctuation, blended with frustration over modern conditions and more material than social progress. The soldiers are not likely to quit the stage—if indeed the civilian leaders want them gone—until Latin American society is profoundly changed.

NOTE

1. Robert J. Alexander, *Bolivia: Past, Present, and Future of Its Politics* (New York: Praeger, 1982), p. 94. The political leaders thought they could manage the new armed forces, but the military soon became a power to itself.

INDEX

academies (*See* training academies) and schools

Acción Democrática (AD) party, 29, 171-172

air force(s): recruit sources for, 10, 15, 16; sizes of, 12, 14, 105, 107, 112, 113, 114, 116; training of, 11, 29, 31, 33, 34-35, 39, 41, 43-44, 45, 53, 86-87, 108

Albuquerque Lima (General), 118

Aleixo, Pedro, 119

Alfonsín, Raul, 69, 100, 122, 153, 206, 208

Alfonzo Ravard, Rafael, 176

Allende, Salvador, 67, 105, 127, 146, 147, 195

Allessandri, Arturo, 147, 197

Alliance for Progress, 99, 131, 171

Alvear, Marcelo de, 198

Amaro, Joaquin, 22, 23

American Popular Revolutionary Alliance party (APRA), 11, 37, 184, 186

Anaya, Jorge Isaac, 122

Andean hegemony, 29

Anderson, Charles, 169

Andreas Bello Plan, 32

Andrés Pérez, Carlos, 177

anticommunism, 105, 117, 126, 128, 130, 133, 139, 140, 146-147, 148, 153, 168, 183, 205

Aramburu, Pedro, 202-203

Arana Osorio, Carlos, 164-165, 168

Arbenz Guzman, Jacobo, 76, 164

Argentina: air force of, 97; arms industry of, 86, 99; arms supplies to, 96, 97, 99, 100; career patterns in, 68-69; command structure in, 121, 122-123; Cordobazo of

1969 in, 204; coups in, 151, 197, 199, 200, 201, 205; economic issues in, 199, 204; foreign policy in, 95-100, 122; ideology and doctrines of, 150-153; interservice relationships in, 121-123; junta in, 121; *Justicialismo*, 152, 201, 202; labor issues in, 200-201; military missions in, 96-97, 98; neutrality of, 97, 98; officer formation in, 44-45; politicization in, 122-123, 152-153, 197-208; Process of National Regeneration, 205; size of armed forces of, 121; training programs, 97-99; World War II and, 98

Argentine Anticommunist Alliance (AAA), 205

Argentine Revolution, 203

Armed Forces Rebellion (FAR), 164

armed struggle doctrine, 146

arms industries, 72, 95, 99, 164, 177, 193, 207

arms trade and supplies, 71; to Argentina, 96, 97, 99, 100; by Brazil, 75; to Brazil, 90, 91-92, 119; to Chile, 95; to Colombia, 86; to Guatemala, 76-78; to Mexico, 75; to Peru, 87-88, 114

army(ies): recruit sources for, 16; sizes of, 12, 14, 105, 107, 112, 113, 114, 116, 121; training schools for, 35, 37, 39, 42-43, 45

Austria: military supplies from, 76; training assistance by, 78

Balaguer, Joaquin, 219

Balmaceda, José Manuel, 94, 147

Banco del Ejercito (Guatemala), 55

Barletta, Nicolas Ardito, 171
Beagle Channel dispute, 122, 145, 146
Belaunde (president of Chile), 219
Belgium: arms supplies from, 78, 80; training assistance by, 87
Benavides, Oscar R., 87, 195
Betancourt, Romulo, 61, 134, 135
Betancur, Belisario, 183
Blanco, Jorge, 219
Bolivar, Simón, 178
Bolivar, Vallarino, 57
Bolivia, 93, 150
Brazil: Argentinization of, 191; arms industry of, 72, 75, 86, 92, 95; arms supplies to, 90, 91-92, 119; career patterns in, 40-41, 42, 64-66; civil war of 1930, 188; command structures in, 116; coups in, 14, 186, 188, 189; dictatorships in, 190; direct presidential elections in, 191; economic policies of, 190-193; First Republic, 187-188; foreign policy in, 89-93, 119; ideology and doctrines of, 126, 127, 142-145; interservice comparisons in, 116-120; Liberal Alliance, 188; lieutenants' revolt in, 188; military missions in, 74-75, 89-90; moderating pattern of civil-military relations in, 186-187; navy of, 92; nuclear strategy, 91, 93; officer formation in, 39-42, 64; politicization in, 14, 116-120, 186-193; ranks of, 12-14; revolution of 1930 in, 13; security and development doctrine, 189, 192, 193; size of armed forces, 116; training programs in, 12, 14, 39-42, 90-91, 92; World War II involvements of, 90
Britain (See Great Britain)
budgets, 106, 111-112, 113-115

Caldera, Rafael, 134
Calles, Plutarco Elias, 22
Camacho Leyva, Luis Carlos, 183
camarilla, 52
Camp, Roderic, 161
Cámpora, Héctor, 204
Canada, arms supplies by, 84
Canessa Robert, Julio, 66, 67
Caperton (Admiral), 97
carabineros, 14, 44
Cárdenas (president of Mexico), 162
career patterns, 49-71; in Argentina, 68-69; in Brazil, 40-41, 42, 64-66; in Chile, 43, 66-68; in Colombia, 33-34, 62; in Guatemala, 53-55; in Mexico, 24, 50-53; in Panama, 28, 55-58; in Peru, 37-38, 62-64; in Venezuela, 28, 58-62
career patterns, influences on: appointment structures, 67-68; assignments, 52-54, 55, 56-57, 59, 62, 64-68; class loyalty, 54; contacts, 52, 53, 54, 63, 65; merit, 60, 64, 68; political activity, 51, 52, 53, 57, 61, 62, 65, 67, 68; seniority, 54, 64, 67, 68; time-in-service, 50-51, 58-59, 64-65, 69; training and education, 51-52, 54-55, 57, 58, 62, 64, 66, 68
Carter administration, human rights policy of, 165
Carvajal, Patricio, 68
Castelo Branco, Humberto, 14, 64, 90, 118, 189, 190
Castillo, Ramón, 98, 200
Castro, Cipriano, 28, 29
Castro, Fidel, 134, 159, 181
Castro, José Ramos de, 65
Castro, León, 109
Catholic Church, 185, 201, 202
caudillo politics, 133, 171-172, 194
Chaves, Aureliano, 120

Chile: air force of, 93; appointment powers of president in, 67-68; arms industry in, 95; arms supplies to, 95; border disputes, 145-146; career patterns in, 43, 66-68; *caudillo* rule, 194; command structures in, 120-121; coups in, 68, 147, 197; Decree Law of 1974, 67; economic policies of, 149-150; foreign policy in, 93-95; ideology and doctrines of, 145-150; junta, 66, 120-121, 194-197; military missions of, 84, 93; navy of, 93; officer formation in, 42-44; Parliamentary Republic, 94; plebiscitary rule of, 194; politicization in, 94, 120, 147, 194-197; security and development doctrine, 196; size of armed forces of, 120; Statute of Democratic Guarantees, 67; training programs of, 94-95; World War II involvements, 94

civic action programs, 128, 140, 163-164, 174, 181-182, 189

civilian(s), suspicion of, 168, 207

civilian supremacy, 123, 127, 129, 134-137, 139, 153, 162, 178

Colombia: air force of, 85; arms supplies to, 86; Bogotazo of 1948 in, 179; boundary disputes of, 139; career patterns in, 33-34, 62; command structures in, 113, 114; coups in, 62, 178, 182; economic issues in, 183-184; foreign policy of, 84-86; ideology and doctrines of, 138-140; navy of, 85; officer formation in, 33-35; politicization in, 177-184; ranks in, 9-10; size of armed forces of, 113, 178; training programs in, 10, 86

command structures, 105-106, 107, 108-110, 115, 116, 120-121, 122-123

CONDECA (Central American Defense Council), 78, 132

conscription, 1, 3-4, 6, 7, 9, 10, 12, 16

conservatism, 125, 140, 148-150, 151, 162-163, 168, 184

Constant, Benjamin, 186

constitutionalism, 129, 135-136, 142, 147-148, 157, 160-161, 167, 184, 185-186, 188-189, 194-195

Contreras, Manuel, 121

corruption and fraud, 165, 166, 180, 182, 188, 190-191, 198, 199

Costa e Silva, Artur, 118, 119, 190

Costa Rica, 74, 178

counterinsurgency programs, 84, 86, 91, 134-135, 139, 140, 141, 153, 164-165, 167, 178, 180, 181-182

coups: in Argentina, 151, 197, 199, 200, 201, 205; in Brazil, 186, 188, 189; in Chile, 147, 197; in Colombia, 178, 182; in Guatemala, 166, 168; in Panama, 79; in Peru, 184, 185; in Venezuela, 172

Couto e Silva, Golbery do, 90

Cruz, Newton, 191

Cuba, 183; arms supplies by, 86; training assistance from, 73, 75, 86

Cuban Revolution, 185

Czechoslovakia, arms supply by, 76

Darío Paredes, Rubén, 132

death squads, 182, 205

decivilianization of army, 39-40

Declaration of Reciprocal Assistance and Cooperation for the Defense of the Americas, 98

defense assistance pacts, 74

Defense Forces of the Republic of Panama, 6, 28, 55, 57, 80, 108, 169-170

Delgado Chalbaud, Carlos, 82, 110
democracy, 127, 129, 134, 148, 151, 152, 191, 202-203
Democratic Alliance(s), 191, 196
depoliticization, 128, 138-139, 160, 167, 181, 194-195, 199, 206-207
developmentalism, 131-132, 140-141, 143-144, 149-150, 168, 189, 196
dictatorships, 190, 197, 203
draft registration, 11, 12, 16
Duarte, Eva, 201

economic policies, 149-150, 175-177, 183-184, 190-193, 199, 200-201, 204
Ecuador, 93
education (See training and education programs)
El Salvador, 93; military assistance to, 74; training assistance by, 28
enlisted personnel (See ranks)
esquema politico, 168
Estrada, Pedro, 111
exemptions from service, 9, 12, 14, 15, 16

Falklands/Malvinas War, 16, 92, 93, 100, 119, 122, 153
fascism, 151-152, 200
females in military (See women in military)
Figueiredo, João Batista, 65, 190
Fonseca, Hermes da, 89, 187
Fonseca, Maximiano da, 120
foreign military missions, 71; to Argentina, 96-97, 98, 151; to Brazil, 89-90; to Chile, 93; to Colombia, 84-85; to Mexico, 74-75; to Peru, 86-87
Foreign Military Sales (FMS) credit program, 74
foreign policy(ies), 71-103; of Argentina, 95-100; of Brazil, 89-93; of

Chile, 93-95; of Colombia, 84-86; of Guatemala, 75-78; of Mexico, 73-75; of Panama, 78-80; of Peru, 86-89; of Venezuela, 80-84
France: arms supplies from, 72, 73, 75, 78, 81, 84, 86, 87, 95, 99; missions of, 71, 84-85, 86, 87, 89; training assistance by, 27, 75, 78, 81, 82, 87, 89
Freire, Nelson, 118
Friedman, Milton, 149
Frondizi, Arturo, 153, 203
Fuerzas Armadas de Cooperación (FCA), 31

Galtieri, Leopoldo, 121
Gamelin, Maurice, 89
Geisel, Ernesto, 89, 142, 190
general staff schools, 26, 27, 41
geopolitics, 134-135, 145-146, 150
Germany: arms supplies by, 99; military missions of, 85, 87, 90, 93, 96, 97; training assistance by, 27, 93, 94
Goes, Walter de, 66
Gómez, Juan Vincente, 7, 28, 29, 80, 82, 110, 175
Gómez, Laureano, 62, 85, 138, 180
Gordon, Humberto, 67
Goulart, João, 12, 13, 65, 127, 188, 189
Great Britain: arms supply from, 75, 84, 87, 91, 95, 99, 119; military missions of, 71, 85, 96; training assistance by, 27, 75, 82, 87, 93
Greenway, John, 144
Guatemala: air force of, 4; Arbenz administration in, 76; Army Law of 1983 of, 55, 107, 130; career patterns in, 53-55; coups in, 166, 168; elections in, 165, 166; foreign policy of, 75-78; ideology

and doctrines of, 130-131, 168-169; interservice comparisons in, 107; navy of, 4; officer formation in, 25-27; political attitudes of officers in, 168-169; politicization in, 164-169; ranks of, 3-6; size of armed forces of, 107; training programs of, 4, 5-6, 25-27, 78

Guayana Corporation (CVG), 176

guerilla activity, 164-165, 180-183, 185

Guerrilla Army of the Poor (EGP), 165

Haiti, 74

Haltenberg, Hans, 144

Harberger, Arnold, 149

Havana conference, 98

Hay-Bunau-Varilla Treaty, 85

Herrera, Roberto Diaz, 131, 132, 137

Herrera Campins (president of Venezuela), 173

hierarchy principle, 125, 130-131, 151

human rights violations, 72, 91, 94, 95, 99, 148, 153, 165, 166, 202-203

Huntington, Samuel, 127, 161

Ibañez, Carlos, 94, 147, 194, 197

ideology: foreign influences on, 129-130, 131; inculcation of, 128-129; relevance of, 126

Illia, Arturo, 203

Institute for the Social Welfare of the Armed Forces (IPSFA), 176

intelligence activities, 37, 63, 65, 67, 92, 119, 121, 147, 180, 190

Inter-American Air Force Academy (IAFA), 53

Inter-American Defense System, 82-84, 98, 99

International Military Education and Training Program (IMET), 74

interservice relationships, aspects of, 104-124; budgets, 106, 111-112, 113, 114-115; command structures, 105-106, 107, 109-110, 113, 114, 115, 116, 120-121, 122-123; foreign policy issues, 119, 122; generational differences, 112; intraservice frictions, 106-107, 122; political power, 104, 109-111, 112, 115-116, 117-120, 122-123; professionalism, 112-113; salaries, 115-116; size of armed forces, 105, 107, 112, 113, 114, 116, 120, 121; social class backgrounds, 104-105, 115, 117, 122

interventionism, proclivity toward, 157-160

Israel: arms supplies from, 73, 75, 78, 80, 86, 95; training assistance by, 92

Italy: arms supplies from, 78, 84, 87, 99; military missions of, 86, 96, 97; training assistance by, 27, 75, 78, 82, 87, 94

Jardim de Mattos, Delio, 120

Jarpa, Sergio Onofre, 196

junta(s), 66, 120-121, 180, 194-197, 200, 205

Justicialismo, 201, 202

Justo, Agustin, 151, 152, 198

Körner, Emil, 93-94, 96, 146, 147, 194

Kubitschek, Juscelino, 117, 118, 142, 188

Lacerda, Carlos, 117

ladinos, 1, 4, 5

Landazabal Reyes, Fernando, 139, 183

Lanusse, Alejandro, 204

Larrazabal, Wolfgang, 109

Laugerud, Kjell, 53, 165
Leigh, Gustavo, 67, 120
Leoni, Raul, 134
Letelier, Orlando, 95, 147
Linares Alcantara, Francisco, 80
literacy training, 2, 4, 7, 10, 11
Lizardo Montero (Admiral), 115
Lleras Restrepo, Carlos, 182
Llovera Páez, Felipe, 81
Lobos Zamora (Mexican Army Chief of Staff), 54
Lonardi, Eduardo, 202
López, Galván, 162
López Contreras, Eleazar, 29, 81, 110, 171
López Pumarejo, Alfonso, 62, 138, 179
López Michelsen, Alfonso, 62, 182
Lott, Henrique T., 117-118
Lucas Garcia, Romeo, 26, 53, 54, 165, 166, 167
Ludwig, Ruben, 65
Luz, Carlos, 117
Lyra Tavares (Army Minister), 119

McAlister, Lyle, 129, 162
Machado, Pinheiro, 187
McGill, Samuel, 80
Márquez Anez, Martin, 81
marriage, among military families, 22
Massera, Eduardo, 122
Matthei, Fernando, 195
Medeiros (Brazilian General), 92
Médici, Emilio, 119
Medina Angarita, Isaias, 29, 81, 110, 171
Mejía Victores, Oscar Humberto, 54, 78, 166
Memorandum of Understanding, 92, 144
Mendes, Ivan de Souza, 191
Méndez Montenegro, Julio Cesar, 165
Merino (Admiral), 67

Mexican Revolution, 127-128
Mexico: career patterns in, 24, 50-53; command structure in, 161-162; foreign policy of, 73-75; ideology and doctrine of, 127-130; inter-service comparisons in, 105-107; military missions in, 74-75; NCOs in, 3; officer formation in, 21-25; politicization in, 160-164; ranks of, 2-3; size of armed forces of, 105; training and education in, 2-3, 21-25
Military Assistance Group (MAG), 77, 94
Military Assistance Program (MAP), 74, 76
Military Household(s), 183, 193
military missions (*See* foreign military missions)
Mobile Military Police (PMA), 4
Morales Bermudez, Francisco, 116
Motley, Langhorne, 91, 92
Maurão Filho (General), 14

National Front, 180-181
National Guard(s): training of, 31, 32, 83; women in, 9
nationalism, 134, 139-140, 143, 145, 149, 150-151, 152, 168, 175, 176, 192
National Liberation Movement (MLN), 169
navy(ies): recruit sources for, 9, 10, 12, 14, 15; sizes of, 14, 105, 107, 112, 113, 114, 116, 121; training of, 11, 29, 31, 33, 34, 39, 41, 43, 45, 85, 108; women in, 9
Nazism, 148
Neves, Tancredo, 191, 192
Nicaragua: armed struggle doctrine of, 146; military assistance by, 28, 73
Noguera, Carlos Celis, 136
noncommissioned officers (NCOs):

fraternization between and ranks, 3, 9, 13; functions of, 5, 8, 13-14; officers and, relations between, 15, 17-18; sources of, 10, 11; training of, 3, 4-5, 15, 16; women among, 9

Nordlinger, Eric, 74

Noriega, Manuel Antonio, 56, 57, 131, 132

nuclear arms, 91, 93

officer(s): business ventures of, 55, 66, 176-177, 190-191, 192-193; class loyalties among, 26; *disponible*, 54; illicit activities of, 56; immunity of, from civil authority, 168; political attitudes of, 20, 62, 65, 161-162, 168-169, 174-175, 184, 185, 197; post-retirement positions, 66, 68, 176-177, 190-191, 192-193; rank distribution of, 61, 64, 66, 67-68; recruitment of, from universities, 41-42; salaries of, 60-61, 65-67; self-interest of, 20; social background of, 21-22, 25, 28-29, 33, 35-37, 39-40, 42, 44, 115, 117, 122

officer formation, 19-48; in Argentina, 44-45; in Brazil, 39-42; in Chile, 42-44; in Colombia, 33-35; in Guatemala, 25-27; in Mexico, 21-25; in Panama, 27-28; in Peru, 35-39; in Venezuela, 28-33

oil production, 161, 176, 189, 192

Ongania, Juan Carlos, 153, 203-204

Organization of the People in Arms (ORPA), 165

Ortiz, Roberto, 200

Ospina Pérez, Mariano, 138, 179

Panama: air force of, 108; career patterns in, 28, 55-58; coups in, 79; economic issues in, 171; foreign policy of, 78-80, 132; general staff divisions in, 56; ideology and doctrines of, 131-132; interservice comparisons in, 108-109; Military Organic Law of 1983 of, 57; navy of, 108-109; officer formation in, 27-28; phases of institutional development in, 170; politicization in, 169-171; ranks of, 6-7; renationalization program in, 79; service branches in, 57-58; *tecnico* leadership in, 171; training programs in, 6, 27-28, 78-80, 108

Panama conference, 98

Paraguay, 93, 150

Paraguayan War, 116, 186, 198

paramilitary forces: demographics of, 1; functions of, 109, 110, 113, 169-170, sizes of, 105, 107, 116

Partido Revolucionario Institucional (PRI), 160

pensions, 66-67, 69 (*See also* retirement systems)

Pérez Jiménez, Marcos, 29, 60, 81, 109, 110, 133, 134, 172, 176

Perón, Evita, 201-202

Perón, Isabelita (Maria Estela), 205, 206

Perón, Juan Domingo, 17, 99, 105, 122, 152-153, 200-204

Peru: APRA-led rebellions in, 11; career patterns in, 37-38, 62-64; command structures in, 115; coups in, 116, 184, 185; foreign policy of, 86-89; ideology and doctrines of, 140-142; military missions to, 86-87, 88; Mobilization Law of 1980 of, 185; officer formation in, 35-39; politicization in, 88-89, 115-116, 184-186; ranks of, 10-11; revolution of 1968 in, 28; size of armed

forces of, 114; training programs
of, 11, 27, 35-39, 87-89; Velasco
cabinet makeup, 35, 37
Petrobras, 189, 192
Pierola, Nicolas de, 86
Pinochet Ugarte, Augusto, 66, 67, 120,
145, 147, 148, 149, 194, 195,
196, 197, 217
Pinzón Caicedo, Jaime, 182
Pires, Walter, 92
Pires Gonclaves, Leonidas, 191, 192
Plan Carabobo, 59, 136
Plan Enca, 63
Plan Lazo, 181
police forces, 4, 14, 28; functions of,
109, 110, 113, 133, 179; salary(ies)
of, 115-116; size of, 105, 107,
113; social background of, 44
politic(s), 157-211; in Argentina, 197-
208; in Brazil, 186-193; in Chile,
194-197; in Colombia, 177-184;
in Guatemala, 164-169; in Mexico,
160-164; in Panama, 169-171; in
Peru, 184-186; in Venezuela, 171-
177
politicization: in Argentina, 122-123,
152-153, 197-208, in Brazil, 14,
116-120; in Chile, 94, 120, 147,
194, 197; in Colombia, 177-184;
in Guatemala, 164-169; in Mexico,
160-164; in Peru, 35-36, 37, 38,
88-89, 115-116, 184-186; in
Venezuela, 109-111, 171-177
Popular Democratic Movement (MDP),
196
Prats, Carlos, 148
professionalism, 133, 134, 140, 141,
146, 151, 178, 185, 194, 198;
degradation of, 68-69; increased
political activity with, 88; origins
of, 20
promotion procedures, common effect
of, 50. (See also career patterns)

public enterprises, services in, 176-
177, 192-193

Quadros, Jânio, 12, 118, 188, 188

Rademaker Grunewald, Augusto, 116,
119
rank(s), 1-18; conscription of, 1, 3-4,
6, 7, 9, 10, 12, 16; demographics
of, 1; length of service by, 2, 4,
7-8, 9-10, 11, 14; literacy training of, 2, 4, 7, 9, 11; requirements
for, 2, 6-7, 9; salary of, 2-3, 9;
social class background of, 2, 4-5,
6-7, 10, 11, 12, 14, 15; stratifica-
tion among, 1-2; training and education of, 2, 4, 5-6, 8-9, 10, 11,
12, 13, 15; volunteer, 1, 2, 4, 7, 8,
9, 10, 11; women, 2, 9, 11
Reagan, Ronald, 166
Reagan administration, military
assistance programs of, 76-77,
100
recruitment (See conscription; volunteers)
reenlistments, 5
Remón, José Antonio, 27, 57, 131, 170
retirement systems, 15, 16, 55, 58-59,
63, 64-65, 66-67, 68, 69, 176-
177, 190-191, 192-193
Reyes, Rafael, 33, 84, 138, 178
Rio Conference of Latin American
Nations, 90
Ríos Montt, Efraín, 54, 130, 165, 166,
167, 169
Rio treaty, 94
Roca, Julio, 96, 151
Rojas Pineda, Gustavo, 33
Rojas Pinilla, Gustavo, 138, 139, 178,
180, 182
Rosas, Juan Manual, 151, 201
Rubens Vaz (Major), 117
Ruiz Novoa, Alberto, 139, 181, 182

salary(ies): determination of, 162; of officers, 52, 55, 60-61, 65-67; of police forces, 115-116; of ranks, 2-3, 9

San Martín, José de, 198

Santos, Eduardo, 178

Sarmiento, Domingo, 96

Sarney (president of Brazil), 193

Schneider, Rene, 147, 195

School of the Americas, 72, 86, 99

security and development doctrines, 126, 127-128, 131-132, 136-137, 139, 142-145, 170, 189, 192-193, 196

Security Support Assistance program, 74, 77, 86

Sereseres, Cesar, 168

service academies (*See* training academies) and schools

Shultz, George, 92, 144

sobresueldo, 55

social class backgrounds: of enlisted personnel, 2, 4-5, 6-7, 10, 11, 12, 14, 15; of officers, 19-20, 21-22, 28, 33, 35-37, 39-40, 42, 44, 115, 117, 122; of police forces, 44

social mobility, 22

South Africa, arms supplies by, 95

South Atlantic Treaty Organization, 91

Souza e Melo (Brigadier), 118, 119

Soviet Union: arms supplies from, 72, 73, 95, 114; military missions of, 87; training assistance by, 75, 87, 88-89

Spain, arms supply by, 75, 95

Stepan, Alfred C., 39, 40, 74, 90, 187

Superior War Colleges, 23-24, 34, 41, 45, 51, 63, 81, 90, 96, 142

Sweden, arms supplies from, 72

Switzerland: arms supplies from, 78; military missions of, 85

Taiwan, arms supplies and training assistance from, 78

terrorism, 205

Toribio Merino, Jose, 195

Torrijos, Omar, 6, 7, 27, 28, 56, 57, 79, 108, 131, 132

training academies and schools: in Argentina, 45, 97, 98, 151; in Brazil, 39, 41, 64, 89, 97; in Chile, 15, 43, 84, 93; in Colombia, 10, 33-35; entrance requirements for, 23, 29-30, 33, 39-40, 42, 43-45; in Guatemala, 5-6, 26-27, 75, 78; in Mexico, 2, 3, 21, 22-25; in Panama, 6, 8, 72; in Peru, 11, 37, 63; in United States, 72, 79, 87, 90; in Venezuela, 29, 31-33; women in, 32, 41

training and education programs: in Argentina, 44-45, 97-99; in Brazil, 39-42; in Chile, 42-44; in Colombia, 33-35; curricula in, 23-24, 30-31, 32, 37-38, 41, 45; degrees offered by, 32-33; foreign assistance with, 27, 28, 71-72, 73, 75-76, 78-79, 81, 82, 90-91, 92, 93, 94-95, 97-99; in Panama, 27-28, 78-80; in Peru, 35-39, 87-89; superior studies, 23-24, 26-27, 34, 41

transnationalism, 143-144

Turbay, Julio César, 182, 183

UNITAS exercises, 86, 99

United Officers Group (GOU), 200

United States of America: arms supplies from, 71, 75, 85, 95; declining influence of, 72-73, 166; Great White Fleet, 96; military assistance programs of, 74-75, 76-77, 86, 91-92, 94-95, 99-100, 165; military missions of, 85, 87, 88, 96, 99; overthrow of

Jacobo Arbenz and, 164; South
Atlantic Squadron, 95, 98; training assistance by, 27, 71-72, 75-
76, 79, 80, 81, 82-83, 86-87, 90-
91, 94
Uriburu, José, 151, 199, 200
Uruguay, 93, 150, 178

Valencia Tovar, Alvaro, 139, 182
Vallenilla Lanz, Laureano, 133
Vargas, Getulio, 117, 188, 189
Vargas, Julio César, 81
Velasco Alvarado, Juan, 36, 63-64,
105, 115, 132
Venezuela: *Acción Democrática* (AD)
party in, 29, 82, 133, 171-172;
air force of, 110; Andean hegemony in, 29; border disputes of,
137; career patterns in, 28, 58-62;
caudillo period, 171; CONASEDE,
136; coups in, 61, 111, 172; economic issues in, 175-177; foreign
policy of, 80-84; IAEDN, 136;
ideology and doctrines of, 133-
137; interservice comparisons in,
109-113; New National Ideal of,
133; paramilitary forces in, 110;
Patriotic Military Union in, 82,
112; Peruvian generation in, 81-

82, 133; politicization in, 109,
171-177; Prussianization of military in, 80-82; ranks of, 7-9; size
of armed forces of, 112; training
programs in, 8-9, 28-33, 82-84
Venezuelan Petroleum Company
(PDVSA), 176
Venturini, Danilo, 193
Videla, Juan, 121, 205, 206
Viola, Roberto, 121, 206
volunteers, 2, 4, 7, 8, 9, 10, 11, 16

Waldner, Teodoro, 122
Walters, Vernon, 91
War of the Pacific, 42, 81, 86, 145
War of the Thousand Days, 178
West Germany: arms supplies from,
72, 73, 87, 91, 95, 114; training
assistance by, 75, 78
women in military: career paths of,
32; in military schools, 32, 41; in
national guards, 9; in navy, 9;
among NCOs, 9; among ranks, 2,
11
World War II, 94, 98

Yrigoyen, Hipólito, 68, 97, 151, 198,
199, 207
Yugoslavia, arms supplies from, 78

ABOUT THE EDITORS AND CONTRIBUTORS

GENE E. BIGLER is a research analyst at the United States Information Agency (USIA) and a professional lecturer at the Johns Hopkins University School of Advanced International Studies in Washinton, D.C. He has previously taught at several U.S. and Latin American universities, including five years at the *Instituto de Estudios Superiores de Administración* in Caracas. He is the author or co-author of two books and many articles on Venezuelan politics and political economy. His latest book (with James L. Payne and others) is *The Motivation of Politicians.* The views he expresses in this book are personal and in no way reflect official views of the USIA or any other U.S. government agency.

DAVID V. FLEISCHER is professor of political science at the University of Brasilia. He received his B.A. from Antioch College and an M.A. and Ph.D. from the University of Florida. He worked in Brazil as a member of the Peace Corps and served with the Department of State on the Brazilian desk. He has been visiting professor at the Federal University of Minas Gerais in Belo Horizonte, the University of Florida, and SUNY-Albany. He has published numerous studies of Brazilian politics, especially about elites, electoral systems, parties, and legislatures. In 1982, he was named to the select Ministry of Justice Commission to draft legislation for a new electoral system.

ANTHONY W. GRAY, JR., is a retired U.S. navy commander with many years experience in Latin American affairs, including teaching at the National War College. He received an M.A. and a Ph.D. degree from the American University, the latter for work on U.S. naval policy in Latin America. His views are personal only and in no way reflect those of any official agency.

RICHARD L. MILLET received an A.B. from Harvard and a Ph.D. from the University of New Mexico. He is professor of history at Southern Illinois University at Edwardsville and adjunct professor of the Defense Institute of Security Assistance Management. He is author of *Guardians of the Dynasty: A History of the Guardia Nacional and the Somoza Family*, coeditor of *The Restless Caribbean*, and author of numerous chapters and articles on Central America.

DAVID SCOTT PALMER is chairman of Latin American and Caribbean Studies at the Foreign Service Institute of the Department of State and also lecturer at the Johns Hopkins University School of Advanced International Studies and at Georgetown University. Among his numerous writings on politics of the Andean countries is *Peru: the Authoritarian Tradition.*

STEVE C. ROPP holds a B.A. from Allegheny College, an M.A. from the University of Washington, and a Ph.D. from the University of California at Riverside. He is Milward Simpson Distinguished Professor of Political Science at the University of Wyoming. He previously taught at New Mexico State University. Dr. Ropp has published a number of articles and book chapters on various aspects of Central American politics and *Panamanian Politics: From Guarded Nation to National Guard.*

PAUL E. SIGMUND is professor of politics and chairman of the Latin American Studies Committee at Princeton University. He has written many books and articles on political theory and Latin American politics, including *The Overthrow of Allende and the Politics of Chile, 1964–1976*; *Multinationals in Latin America: The Politics of Nationalization*; and *The Political Economy of Income Distribution in Mexico* (coeditor and contributor).

STEPHEN J. WAGER is a U.S. army major and assistant professor in the history department at the U.S. Military Academy, West Point, N.Y. He received a B.A. from Fordham University (1970). Recently he was assigned to the U.S. Defense Attaché Office in Mexico City, where he also attended the Mexican Army Command and Staff College. He has traveled extensively throughout Mexico and Latin America. His views are personal only and in no way reflect those of any official agency.

ROBERT WESSON is senior research fellow at the Hoover Institution and professor emeritus of political science at the University of California at Santa Barbara. Among his recent books are *Democracy in Latin America*, *Brazil in Transition* (with David V. Fleischer), and *Politics, Policies and Economic Development in Latin America* (editor and contributor).

DATE DUE
